The Golden Girls

Fixodent
The Golden Girls
PRINCESS CRUISES
THE LOVE BOAT
THANK YOU
Depend
PROTECTION PLUS
TV GUIDE
RICE A RONI
Tide
nose
rubber hose
HOLY BIBLE
HUMAN
HAIR WIG
The Cheesecake Factory
WHERE'S THE BEEF?
WORLD'S GREATEST GRANDMA
I HAD TOO MUCH FUN IN CLEVELAND
Mr. Coffee
Cozy
FRESH
Foam Ear Plugs
VALUE PACK!
Turbie Twist
BRILLIANTLY WHITE
COLORFUL CLOTHING
Tostitos
Strap Perfect
FOOD GRINDER

The Golden Girls

Tales from the Lanai

Edited by
TAYLOR COLE MILLER *and*
ALFRED L. MARTIN JR.

RUTGERS UNIVERSITY PRESS
New Brunswick, Camden, and Newark, New Jersey
London and Oxford

Rutgers University Press is a department of Rutgers, The State University of New Jersey, one of the leading public research universities in the nation. By publishing worldwide, it furthers the University's mission of dedication to excellence in teaching, scholarship, research, and clinical care.

Frontispiece: *The Golden Girls* by Jason Mecier, trash and recycling on panel, 48" × 48", 2003. Photo © Jason Mecier and used with permission from the artist.

978-1-9788-3685-3 (cloth)
978-1-9788-3684-6 (paper)
978-1-9788-3686-0 (epub)
978-1-9788-3687-7 (web PDF)

Cataloging-in-publication data is available from the Library of Congress.
LCCN 2025005244

A British Cataloging-in-Publication record for this book is available from the British Library.

∞ The paper used in this publication meets the requirements of the American National Standard for Information Sciences—Permanence of Paper for Printed Library Materials, ANSI Z39.48-1992.

rutgersuniversitypress.org

To our four Golden Girls: Dorothy, Rose, Blanche, and Sophia
And our two Cocos: Mike and Tom

Contents

The Golden Girls

The Golden Girls. (Photo © Wayne Williams 1984–87. All rights reserved.)

INTRODUCTION

Thank You for Being a Fan

Forty Years of *The Golden Girls*

TAYLOR COLE MILLER AND
ALFRED L. MARTIN JR.

It was electric. The Golden-Con costume contest was under way; Glenna Beaver, dressed as "Walkathon Sophia" in a pink velour sweatsuit, a matching pink headband, and the number 151 taped to the iconic straw purse, began her shuffle down the catwalk. She was surrounded by a smorgasbord of Sophias, including "Classic Sophia," "Storybook Sophia," "Brooklyn Sophia," "Baby Sophia" (an actual infant), and two "Sonny Bono Sophias." Dozens of Dorothys, Roses, Blanches, and Stans, meanwhile, cheered these Sophias on from the wings, waiting for their own categories to be called. Glenna started off slow, cagey, like a panther. But when the time was right, she pounced! The crowd was on its feet: "Sophia! Sophia! Sophia!" As she neared the end of the runway, she unclasped the latch on her purse, scooped out a fistful of Pep-O-Mints—carefully avoiding the Feen-a-Mint and the rain bonnet—and tossed them into the audience to uproarious applause. This Sophia didn't hit a wall. She won.

Like trying to understand the preceding paragraph and its references to various episodes, the costume contest at the first-ever *Golden Girls* fan convention relied on an almost encyclopedic knowledge of the text. Attendees in the know found pleasure and joy in the costumes' deep cuts and references to jokes, story lines, and episodes. More casual viewers and plus-ones deepened their own engagement with the show by learning about ardent fans' most beloved moments, captured here in costume. Some forty years

Golden Girls fan Glenna Beaver competed as "Walk-a-thon Sophia" in the 2022 Golden-Con costume contest (*left*) and one of the Captain Jack Seafood Shanty Pirates in the 2023 Golden-Con costume contest (*right*). (Photo by Taylor Cole Miller)

after the show's premiere, maybe now more than ever, *The Golden Girls* is a cultural phenomenon.

Picture it: television, 2025—the proliferation of fan sites, social media groups, thousands of official and homemade merchandise items, specially themed Caribbean cruises, a half-million-dollar fan convention, live drag shows, equity tours, camp sleepaways, theatrical releases of episodes, and even a yearly presence at Comic Con all serve as testaments not just to the enduring power of *The Golden Girls* but to an explosive rise in its popularity within the past five years. *The Golden Girls* was one of Hulu's most watched shows during the first year of the COVID-19 outbreak, and the week after Betty White's death, it was in the Nielsen ratings' top ten acquired streaming shows.[1] We are living in the Golden Age—of *The Golden Girls.*

This collection is a decade in the making. As editors, both of us have long talked about, written about, and presented about *The Golden Girls* throughout our academic careers. We have included it in our syllabi, developed courses around it, and used it to demonstrate various media studies concepts. We continue to find *The Golden Girls* an extraordinarily rich resource for scholarly consideration in both our research and teaching, with new threads to tug, new audiences to discover, new insights on watching, and new ways to think about television's present as well as its past. It also became a personal connection between the two of us, offering a language of friendship as we would reach out to each other in moments of needed comfort that we could always find in a quoted line or a cherished scene. We inevitably come back to the same question in every conversation: In our field, why is there so little written about this show?

There are dozens of books on currently running "quality television" shows with a handful of episodes that, if we are being honest with ourselves, people will forget about in ten years. And maybe, to borrow from Sophia, jealousy is just "a very ugly color" on us, but reviewers rarely ask these authors to justify their objects of study as relevant—not their arguments but their entire objects of study. Relevancy, however, has become a common refrain in scholarly publishing in peer reviews of journal articles studying older shows. *The Golden Girls* premiered forty years ago and has never been out of syndication. A show about older women starring veteran actors whom TV execs once thought no one would ever want to watch again, a show that ended its original run three Bushes and two Clintons ago, continues to reach new, young audiences year after year, surging in popularity in the past five. And so, we wondered, What's all that about?

Although it is a seemingly simple question, What's all that about? has been a productive foundation on which to build *The Golden Girls: Tales from the Lanai.* The more both of us talked to other people about the potential of this collection, the more we realized how complex and multifaceted *The Golden Girls* is for many of its viewers in ways neither of us have read about. *The Golden Girls* is thus a model of a rich media studies text and a perfect object of study to demonstrate a wide variety of approaches to media studies. As we celebrate its fortieth anniversary, the cultural moment for an edited anthology about *The Golden Girls* has never seemed more urgent or ideal. About that beloved American sitcom, this book is a resource for scholars and students as well as dedicated fans and casual viewers fascinated by rich cultural television histories and portraits of audiences often unattended to by mainstream media outlets, large academic journals, or even fan communities. With twelve original chapters from scholars across the country and extensive original interviews with those who created the show, this book is a long day's journey into the marinara of *The Golden Girls*—an immersive, engaging opportunity for readers to learn more about the show without having to board the actual *Golden Girls* cruise liner and launch themselves into the Caribbean.

This book accomplishes four primary goals: First, it reclaims the production history and contextual development of an older text understood today as an important cultural touchstone. Second, it opens *new* conversations about an *old* show, giving us an opportunity to think less monolithically about network audiences of the 1980s by examining a variety of different kinds of viewers and audience cultures increasingly visible in the fragmented digital moment. Third, it offers a new model for a circuit of media culture approach to studying texts that considers the entire lifetime of a text a significant feature of its textuality.[2] And fourth, through its contributions, it models different methodologies that a student might take when researching any television text, not just *The Golden Girls*. Bringing together a diverse array of scholars, this collection does not speak with a singular voice but offers twelve different perspectives to render an extraordinary three-dimensional model of scholarly inquiry of an extraordinary American sitcom.

Divided into three parts, the chapters of this book collectively analyze *The Golden Girls*' production and context, audience appeal, and textuality so that together, this anthology provides an intimate portrait of the show's popularity and legacy and a model of a circuit of media culture approach to television research. The book also seriously investigates *The Golden Girls* as intersectional, considering how various aspects of its production and textuality made and continue to make it an important text for marginalized audiences, especially for Black, queer, and women viewers. Through a comprehensive survey of the show, its history, production, and allure with audiences, this collection reclaims and explores *The Golden Girls*, locating and analyzing its resurgent popularity in the present cultural moment.

The Relevancy Refrain: So, Why *The Golden Girls*?

Celebrating its fortieth anniversary this year, *The Golden Girls* was already an iconic American sitcom with longevity, and by this historical significance alone, it would be an intriguing case study worthy of attention and exploration. But its meteoric rise in popularity within the past five years has transcended the nostalgia and memory of its initial entertainment value, and that warrants a more in-depth investigation from a variety of different perspectives. Whereas most television studies work is either historical by design or tracking a series still in original production, in this book, we have the benefit of studying an older show in a newer context, demonstrating how the passage of time can become a meaningful feature of a text. The passage of time creates a text with newfound depth and invites critical analyses that unearth subtle nuance and thematic relevance that would have been overlooked in contemporary analyses, especially the show's wide-ranging appeal to diverse demographics that did not matter to network television executives in the 1980s but that matter to them now in the age of demographic targeting. To open a collection of essays about *The Golden Girls* as a model of a case study for our field, in this introduction, we begin by investigating how the show originally emerged as an innovative and challenging project for a changing industry, then discuss its development as a compelling text whose narrative complexities have enriched over time, and finally explore the uncharted territories of its diverse audience base, offering critical insights into overlooked communities.

INDUSTRY AND PRODUCTION HISTORICAL CONTEXT

In 1984, the veteran television actors Selma Diamond (then on *Night Court*) and Doris Roberts (then on *Remington Steele*) stepped out on the stage of NBC's *Fall Preview Special* and traded banter on one of the network's most promising new dramas, *Miami Vice*. "We're here to introduce a show that takes place in the most wonderful resort in the world, Miami," Diamond jokes as the two take the stage. "The Land of Coppertone and corned beef, mink coats, cha-cha lessons, *The Jackie Gleason Show*—" "It's been canceled," Roberts interjects, shrugging. "Better him than us." When Diamond continues describing a show about sitting on the beach, Roberts corrects her: "No, no, no, honey, this show is not called *Miami Nice*. This is called *Miami Vice*." Although the skit was merely meant for two of the network's veteran stars to introduce two of its up-and-comers ("the gorgeous Don Johnson and the gorgeous Philip Michael Thomas"), the chemistry between Diamond and Roberts was electric, and *Miami Nice* sparked an idea for a show that eventually became *The Golden Girls*.

With its four leads and their helpful gay houseboy, Coco, in place for its pilot, *The Golden Girls* "hit the ground running" in its original network run, blitzing into the Nielsen's top ten ratings for its premiere and staying there for six of its seven seasons.[3] An unexpected success, even in its freshman season, with a weekly estimated audience of nearly nineteen million, *Miami Nice* was doing better than its forerunner, *Miami Vice*. The 9:00 p.m. EST Saturday-night time slot allowed families of all ages to watch the show in leisure, at a time early enough for those who were early to bed and those who were late to leave for a night on the town. But despite its ratings successes, by 1992, NBC began to eye another kind of viewer: the young. As had happened with the "rural purge" of television at the end of the 1960s—canceling still-popular shows like *Green Acres*, *The Andy Griffith Show*, and *The Beverly Hillbillies* because of the older audiences they attracted—the promise of a new "quality" audience commodity in young viewers meant big changes in programming strategies as executives raced to create ever-edgier programming in the early 1990s, particularly at NBC.

NBC's "face lift" was coined "granny-dumping," an adopted phrase from a growing trend in the early 1990s of the literal abandonment of elderly relatives at Shady Pineses across the country.[4] Shows still popular for NBC's over-fifty crowd, like *Matlock*, *In the Heat of the Night*, and *The Golden Girls*, were dropped in favor of series targeting a younger demographic with more emphasis on "edgy" trends like nudity, violence, risqué language, and nonheterosexual characters. Then–NBC President Warren Littlefield vowed to "continue the successful transition from households to [a new] demographic focus" on young viewers.[5] Surprised by NBC's move, ABC and CBS picked up versions of all three of these shows through the mid-1990s. Even after *The Golden Girls* and its sequel were canceled, it went on to become one of the most successful series in broadcast syndication, as discussed in chapter 3. When Lifetime bought the exclusive rights to the show in 1997, the popularity of *The Golden Girls* picked up steam as the channel began airing dozens of episodes each week, more than it aired ever before. In 2004, when Walt Disney Studios Home Entertainment began releasing the episodes in complete seasons on DVD, the show found a third generation of fans, and with the advent of streaming, *The Golden Girls* found yet more viewers, many comfort-watching their way through the pandemic. As a production of an independent studio (the Walt Disney Company) for a major broadcast network (ABC) and with three and a half decades of top-rated syndication under its belt, *The Golden Girls* is an exemplary object for industry histories and investigations of production cultures. Its robust performance across multiple generations of the television business illustrates changing formations in the industrial landscape that have shaped and will continue to shape television programming and syndication for years to come. Part of its staying power is in the time-tested episodic sitcom structure, but it is also in the compelling narratives and rich characterizations that the show built despite a fairly rigid narrative formula.

THE TEXT

While the premise of the show itself is probably its most groundbreaking feature, episodes of *The Golden Girls* often tackled topics that most contemporaneous television shows had been afraid or incapable of addressing, such as disability, class, menopause, chronic disease, and the failures of the myriad American systems of governance for the elderly. Early on, the show's eagerness to engage topics that other shows would not dare helped it reach both a mass and niche audiences. Through its fluid presentation of a variety of femininities (and thus masculinities), the comedy of *The Golden Girls* runs on a combustion engine of gender upheaval and social taboo. First, and most centrally, it is a comedy featuring an ensemble of women that emerged during a political and televisual era that erased much of the liberal feminist programming of the 1970s, including Bea Arthur's own series, *Maude.* The kind of cultural specificity that *The Golden Girls* originally faced as the political pendulum swung to the right in the 1980s resonates as timely with its audiences again in the 2020s. The shoulder pads, chunky earrings, and hairstyles may date the series, but its comedies and comforts are timeless. The show also brings a critical, intersectional gender questioning to cultural power in a much more complex way than traditional television programs do. After all, *The Golden Girls* is not just a series about women; it is about *older* women and their subsequent reconstitutions of family. The show's interrogations of gender create nuanced representations of womanhood and women's bodies that appeal to women looking for more complexity in their characters in both mind and body.

Although the women of *The Golden Girls,* as an ensemble cast, were and are perhaps the most exemplary case study of older bodies on the small screen, a number of earlier programs often featured iconic transgressive older women characters. *I Love Lucy*'s crotchety Mrs. McGuillicuddy; a whole crew of angsty ladies on *Bewitched,* including and especially the flamboyant mom Endora, the absent-minded Aunt Clara, the gossamer Esmerelda, and the nosy neighbor Gladys Kravitz; *The Jeffersons*' Florence; *Roseanne*'s butch grandma Nana Mary and (sometimes) lesbian mother Bev; *All in the Family*'s zany Edith Bunker; and the no-nonsense Mama from *Mama's Family.* However, whereas these other sitcom characters relied on fairly stable identities and expressions of gender, *The Golden Girls* frequently reconfigured the gender phenotype of its characters through a more complex seriality. Betty White's Rose Nylund, the naïve Scandinavian-Minnesotan with a library of unusual St. Olaf stories, vacillated on a spectrum between the sturdy farm girl and the glamorous Miami dame. Blanche Devereaux always proffered the dainty persona of a southern belle but subverted the purity, innocence, and age of the belle through her constant references to her late-in-life promiscuity and menopause. Bea Arthur's towering Dorothy Zbornak exuded masculinity through her booming low voice and take-charge attitude as the first among equals. But she also sang and performed tender musical numbers while blushing and batting her eyes at a long line of suitors. Meanwhile, her "Ma," Sophia Petrillo, was the devil-may-care Sicilian New York unruly marm with no regard for self-editing within a culture in which women were expected to censor their speech (this is occasionally attributed to her having had a stroke).

Additionally, *The Golden Girls* was no stranger to explicitly LGBT material: Blanche's gay brother, Clayton, makes two appearances, coming out in one episode and introducing his fiancé in another; Dorothy's long-lost friend Jean falls in love with Rose; a slap-happy gay married caterer and his sensitive assistant plan Sophia's wedding; the lesbian lovers Pat and Kathy provide image consulting services; the gay artist Lazlo reveals the Girls' essence; Sophia thinks Dorothy's cross-dressing brother, Phil, might be queer; and a trans man named Gil Kessler runs for city council. Indeed, the original main cast of *The Golden Girls* featured a gay houseboy named Coco whom the network later dropped due, allegedly, to network concerns of homophobia. Much like the outcomes when film studios attempted to erase queerness and queer bodies from film in the era of the "Production Code," in NBC's attempt to erase gayness via Coco, *The Golden Girls* ultimately produced a much queerer space that offered more room at the table for a wide variety of sexualities and gender identities. What made the show itself especially queer was that each of these explicit characters and story lines represented moments of explicit representation walking onto and then right back off the set. They appeared just long enough to anchor conversations about other forms of sexualities and gender practices so the girls could voice their embrace, tolerance, and love, but they left quickly enough to return the series to a queerer sensibility and politics, where the queer familial bonds between the women superseded any relationship with other characters or male suitors. And this representation of same-sex love and friendship is part of what makes it so comforting and resonant, especially with marginalized viewers.

AUDIENCE

Many scholars have studied gender roles within domestic spheres and their mediation on television. We review issues of patriarchy, marriage, and childbirth that make demands on women's bodies and hail them into oppressed subject positions based on their gender. We discuss how women enter into and negotiate the expectations of heteronormativity as a time and a space—even how they might be complicit in their oppression. But what happens when they get chewed up by that very same system of power and spit out the other side? The Girls performed their expected gender roles in a white-hegemonic, heteronormative society correctly, but nevertheless

The Golden Girls. (Photo © Wayne Williams 1984–87. All rights reserved.)

they ended up outside of it just like so many of us. Their journey is our journey, and we have ultimately found comfort and identity in their exile. As some of the chapters in this collection detail, *The Golden Girls* deeply resonated—and continues to resonate—with Black audiences, queer audiences, and women audiences who similarly do not fit within all frames of power and are often searching for but not finding themselves on their television screens.

Fans, social media groups, and friends made during fan conventions sharing their viewing habits have become more visible than ever before, opening vast new sites of digital examination as social media departments scrutinize every this and that of their users. A growing trend of young users bingeing *The Golden Girls*, sharing the series, quoting it, and using it as a framework through which to do their own identity work continues to incentivize television platforms, merchandise manufacturers, and fan culture industries to use *The Golden Girls* to attract younger people to their platforms, which is a bit ironic given that *The Golden Girls* was "granny dumped" for young audiences, as discussed earlier. As these "tales from the lanai" attest, the secondary lives of *Golden Girls* episodes continue to find new and different and often underserved audiences who have coalesced with mainstream fans to make *The Golden Girls* a 2020s phenomenon.

Tales from the Lanai

Taken together, the chapters and original interview portions of this book create a sustained portrait of a cultural touchstone through a circuit of media culture that models a new format for media studies books reclaiming rich older media texts, making scholarship and scholarly voices accessible and engaging for multiple audiences while deeply exploring a singular show. Not simply attending to *The Golden Girls* textually, this collection is divided into three parts, with the chapters primarily addressing the show through the corresponding circuit of media culture framework and interviews providing rich primary source context about the show and its stars. Although each of the chapters is about *The Golden Girls*, this collection is scalable for media approaches to other texts. Each of the chapters provide different methods to approaching a single media text, all loosely categorized into three sections in a circuit of culture approach: industry histories, text, and audience. Also included are the editors' original interviews with behind-the-scenes figures, offering primary source examples for students and researchers.

PART 1: INDUSTRY AND CONTEXT

In part 1, authors Kate Fortmueller, Peter C. Kunze, Taylor Cole Miller, and Jessica Hoover discuss the television business, addressing the historical context of the show's original production and how it has navigated—and continues to overcome—industry challenges in the decades it has remained on television. We start by immediately addressing the exciting surge of popularity that *The Golden Girls* has experienced in the past five years before backing up to contextualize that phenomenon with deep investigations of the show's origins, technical approach, and marketability. In chapter 1, Fortmueller discusses the resurgent popularity of *The Golden Girls* during the pandemic, focusing on its Hulu success story as part of the "comfort TV" trend. Despite changes in the media landscape and influx of new shows, Fortmueller argues that classic sitcoms found renewed attention, illustrating their cultural relevance and the role of streamers in leveraging nostalgia to gain subscribers.

Backing up to the beginning of the show, in chapter 2, Kunze's historical investigation of Disney locates *The Golden Girls* as a significant property for the studio's renaissance of the 1980s and 1990s, often unevenly attributed to its animation work and the release of *The Little Mermaid* in 1989. Through a captivating portrait of creator Susan Harris, he argues that film and television comedies like *The Golden Girls* were central to Disney's revitalization.

Kunze's argument that the show was a key property for Disney is further elaborated in chapter 3, as Miller discusses the enduring popularity of *The Golden Girls* in syndication. Bringing attention to Disney's investment in the show for reruns, Miller details how gender played a role in its marketing and viewership while noting the polysemic ways the show has been rebranded to appeal to different audience segments. He investigates the cultural impact of the show in syndication, emphasizing its role in viewers' lives through the various marketing strategies used to sell it.

To round out the discussion of industry and context, in chapter 4, Hoover analyzes the flashback episode structure, using specific episodes like "The Way We Met" and "A Piece of Cake" to highlight how flashbacks deepen character connections and demonstrate how the show departs from conventional sitcom tropes that stereotype women characters. She explores the industrial benefits of flashback episodes for networks and producers while discussing how such structures deepen the narrative of sitcoms for audiences. Hoover's analysis of a television trend typical of 1980s TV considers how producers and writers negotiate the demands of the business with the artistry of screenwriting, offering a transition to a discussion of the text in part 2.

PART 2: TEXT

In part 2, authors Claire Sewell, Ashleé Clark, Andrew J. Owens, Jared Clayton Brown, and Beth L. Boser take a more traditional textual analysis approach to *The Golden Girls* but offer very different perspectives. Building on the context of part 1, we start by first contextualizing how the press and other media engaged with the show and its stars before shifting to chapters that offer a closer textual analysis of episodes. In chapter 5, Sewell explores the interplay between tabloid culture and the show, discussing how *The Golden*

Girls' characters, story lines, and actors were intertwined with tabloid headlines. She argues that tabloid journalism's intersection with the show's narrative sheds light on the cultural significance of both in the broader context of American society.

In chapter 6, Clark discusses how the show explores the characters' relationships with food and body image in the context of 1980s diet culture, mirroring social pressures on women's appearances across history. Utilizing episodes with weight-related story lines, Clark notes how the show challenged norms by relegating dieting narratives to secondary "B" plotlines and using characters like Dorothy to voice opposition to diet culture while emphasizing the significance of the Girls' comfort food, cheesecake.

The show finds numerous ways of addressing headline social issues without such episodes feeling like a departure from the feel of the series. In chapter 7, Owens discusses the series's portrayal of the HIV/AIDS crisis in media, focusing on how *The Golden Girls* tackled the issue in its episode "72 Hours." He explores the show's significance in challenging stereotypes and educating viewers while addressing how the episode broke norms in its representations of fear and prejudice among the leads, ultimately showcasing how television shapes perspectives of important cultural moments.

More directly discussing the Girls' sexual lives, in chapter 8, Brown examines how *The Golden Girls* challenges stereotypes about older women's sexuality and aging. He argues that the show's portrayal of sexually active and empowered older women confronts prevailing cultural norms, reshaping perceptions of female sexuality. Such representations of the Girls stand in contrast with earlier TV portrayals in which older women, though often fierce, were typically desexualized in favor of coding them as moms and grandmas, a helpful preface for the final chapter in this section.

In chapter 9, Boser shares a deeply personal story about caregiving and fertility struggles to contextualize how *The Golden Girls* became a kind of salve for her. She sought out the show by initially aiming to avoid overwrought media narratives about motherhood but instead found a surprisingly complex engagement with motherhood mediated through its characters. In her autoethnographic essay, Boser dissects the show's challenge to ideas about traditional motherhood by exploring how the characters navigate the tensions of postfeminism and intense maternal expectations. Boser's chapter provides deep textual analysis while considering how new kinds of audiences might find differing meaning in the show, contextualizing the final three chapters in part 3.

PART 3: AUDIENCE AND RECEPTION

In part 3, authors Alfred L. Martin Jr., Ken Feil, and Eleanor Patterson build on the earlier discussions of the industry and textual aspects of the show to discuss the significance of *The Golden Girls* with audiences. They investigate three different groups of marginalized viewers over the lifetime of the show and, in so doing, offer meaningful insight into how even studying an older show can still provide new insights into how people interact with their televisions. In chapter 10, Martin explores what he calls the show's implicit Blackness by delving into the experience of Black women as fans of *The Golden Girls*. Through a focus on the show's programming, its production practices, and how Black fans engage with the series, he highlights themes like alternative kinship and celebration of joy that Black fans find in a series even in the absence of explicit representations of Blackness.

In chapter 11, Feil examines how *The Golden Girls* fits into various forms of queer camp culture, highlighting the show's portrayal of aging divas engaging in bad manners comedy. He traces how the sitcom navigates camp tropes, humor, and sexuality while forging a camp community among its characters and (queer) viewers and argues that the show resists normative constructs, uses humor to challenge stereotypes about age, gender, and sexuality, and operates within the context of the 1980s in response to new social and political climates.

And finally, in chapter 12, Patterson charts the transformation of drag performance centered around *The Golden Girls* from a subcultural expression to mainstream entertainment. Featuring one of the last known interviews with the famed San Francisco drag queen Heklina, she discusses how the extensive planning, marketing, and staging work of Golden Girls shows highlight the business aspects of drag alongside the performances themselves. She explores how television shows help drag performances attract diverse audiences and generate social media buzz for subcultural fan communities, offering a blend of familiar TV humor with the excitement of queer drag while providing cover to face down homophobia and intolerance.

Ultimately, this book provides readers with a comprehensive exploration of a television show that transcends eras and offers a versatile blueprint for approaching other television touchstones. This anthology goes beyond nostalgia, exploring the intricate layers of industry dynamics, textual complexities, and audience relatability that have made *The Golden Girls* as culturally relevant and resonant today as it was during its original broadcast run. Through its diverse array of scholarly voices, this collection reclaims *The Golden Girls* as a model for media studies analysis by presenting its rich historical context, thematic depth, and intersectional relevance. Through its discussions of industry, text, and audience, this anthology not only commemorates the enduring legacy of *The Golden Girls* but also underscores its pivotal role in challenging norms, amplifying marginalized voices, and forming into a modern-day marvel. This book thus creates a testament to the enduring power of television as a cultural artifact and a catalyst for critical scholarly inquiry.

Beyond its scholarly dimensions, this collection also deeply explores a show about four women who, through the "miracle" of a room-available ad on a grocery store bulletin board started out as housemates and became a family. Remembering their time together, as Dorothy moves out in the final season, she says to the Girls, "It's been an experience that I'll always keep very close to my heart. And that these are memories that I'll wrap myself in when the world gets cold, and I forget that there are people who are warm and loving. . . . You're angels, all of you." And for so many, in the end, that story is the same, a beautiful portrait of how *The Golden Girls* changed our lives. Picture it: Four friends, once alone and misunderstood, now together and blessed, circling a table with a cheesecake and holding hands while smiling with tears in their eyes—lovingly singing, "Thank you for being a friend."

Notes

1. Tony Maglio, "'Golden Girls' Cracked Nielsen's Top 10 Acquired Streaming Shows in Week After Betty White's Death," *The Wrap* (blog), February 3, 2022, www.thewrap.com/golden-girls-ratings-betty-white-death-hulu-streaming/.

2. Since at least the 1970s, scholars have considered disparate spheres in studies of media and culture, including social relations, industry and production, text and distribution, and reception practices. Scholars like Richard Johnson and Julie D'Acci have been critical of a tendency in that work to focus on only one of the four spheres at a time, which risks depoliticizing the object of analysis from questions of power. As proposed by Paul du Gay et al., a circuit of culture approach provides a blueprint for analyzing cultural phenomena like products or practices that circulate through five interconnected nodes: representation, identity, production, consumption, and regulation. In this book, we utilize a simplified version of this approach for a media text specifically (a circuit of media culture), to demonstrate an accessible way for scholars, students, and everyday viewers to think more critically about media texts. Although each chapter of this book leans into one area, all focus on all the interconnected elements of a circuit of media culture approach—production and context, text, and reception—that together make for a rounder analysis. See Paul du Gay, Stuart Hall, Linda Janes, Hugh Mackay, and Keith Negus, *Doing Cultural Studies: The Story of the Sony Walkman* (Sage, 1997); Richard Johnson, "What Is Cultural Studies Anyway?," *Social Text* 16 (1986–87): 38–80; Julie

D'Acci, "Cultural Studies, Television Studies, and the Crisis in the Humanities," in *Television After TV*, ed. Lynn Spigel and Jan Olsson (Duke University Press, 2004).

3. Tim Brooks, *The Complete Directory to Prime Time Network and Cable TV Shows 1946–Present*, 9th ed. (Ballantine Books, 2007), 1691.

4. Stuart Elliott, "NBC Likes Young Viewers, Judging from Its Fall Plans," *New York Times*, May 13, 1992, sec. D, 18.

5. Daniel Cerone, "Television: The Fountain of Youth Equation," *Los Angeles Times*, June 7, 1992, www.latimes.com/archives/la-xpm-1992-06-07-ca-258-story.html.

PART I

Industry and Historical Context

CHAPTER 1

"Picture It, U.S. 2020 . . ."

Sitcom Nostalgia During the Pandemic

KATE FORTMUELLER

The Golden Girls arrived to streaming, perhaps appropriately on "Galentine's Day," a sitcom holiday invented by *Parks and Recreation* writers. The acquisition happened in early 2017, and in *Variety*, it was given equal weight with *Black-ish* in the headline: "Hulu Nabs Exclusive Streaming Rights to 'Black-ish,' 'Golden Girls.'"[1] Three years later, *The Golden Girls* streaming rights would turn out to be a boon for Hulu when COVID-19 swept across the world, shut down scripted media production, and sent millions of viewers to Hulu, where they found *The Golden Girls*.

Streaming services like to brag about breakout successes like *Stranger Things* or *The Handmaid's Tale*, but the successful journey of *The Golden Girls* on Hulu is far more common. Despite significant changes to the media industries and a seemingly constant flow of new shows, streaming services more closely resemble what Derek Kompare has said about television as a "machine of repetition."[2] Network stalwarts like *Friends*, *The Office*, and *Big Bang Theory* are consistently among the most watched programs on streaming. During the pandemic, a different set of vintage network sitcoms found renewed popularity with streaming audiences; however, many of these shows had been available on streaming services for several years when the pandemic disrupted our lives.

Audiences turned exclusively to their home screens for entertainment and distraction when live venues and movie theaters closed in 2020. *Tiger King*, which earned the crown of "Netflix's most popular U.S. original of

2020," may have garnered more attention in the popular press and social media memes; however, audiences flocked to classic sitcoms in droves.[3] With many shows on unplanned hiatus, streamers began licensing more programming, while networks looked to bygone programming strategies like the "movie of the week" to fill their schedules, further increasing their reliance on library content.[4] During this historical epoch, Nielsen reported some anomalies within its top watched shows. In April 2020, Hulu viewers watched eleven million hours of *The Golden Girls*, making it one of Hulu's top ten shows during the second month of lockdowns.[5]

To explain the reemergence of *The Golden Girls* on Nielsen lists, industry analysts and journalists attributed the popularity of classic sitcoms such as *The Golden Girls* to a need for "comfort" and "nostalgia" shows during troubled times.[6] What popular critics relied on to explain the allure of *The Golden Girls* is what Katharina Niemeyer explains as media nostalgia, or a "longing . . . expressed for specific media texts."[7] Of course, streaming services and their deep catalogues of readily accessible films and television shows are almost perfectly designed to fulfill those feelings of longing. Although streaming platforms can house seemingly endless numbers of classic and contemporary films and television shows, not every show satiates audience nostalgia. In this chapter, I take an industry studies approach to demonstrate how the decision to license *The Golden Girls* is typical of a streaming business that relies on historically successful and nostalgic offerings, while considering how U.S. audiences resonated with Dorothy, Blanche, Rose, and Sophia during the pandemic lockdowns.

To understand the particular comforts of *The Golden Girls* during the pandemic, I situate 2020 interpretations alongside Eleanor Patterson's 2016 analysis of the San Francisco drag show *The Golden Girls Live*. Writing about the famed SF Golden Girls drag performances, Patterson examines *The Golden Girls* as a "residual object," or one that is no longer a dominant program but, instead, is part of U.S. television heritage.[8] Building on this understanding of *The Golden Girls* as both a cultural and historical object, Patterson explains how contemporary queer viewers relate to the show as a cultural relic, specifically "as a site of collective memory for LGBTQ viewers who were able to feel connected to a larger community when they saw communal issues like the AIDS pandemic discussed."[9] Of course, the very nature of this argument hinges on industrial practices of recirculation so that shows like *The Golden Girls* can transcend their historical moment and connect to contemporary viewers. In 2020, absent shows that could address the contemporary sociocultural landscape of the pandemic, viewers used *The Golden Girls* to help them process the contemporary moment.

The *Golden Girls* living room. (Photo © Wayne Williams 1984–87. All rights reserved.)

Television networks have long relied on audience nostalgia to create demand for back catalogues of films and television shows, but during the pandemic, nostalgia took on greater importance for audiences who gravitated toward comfort TV on their streaming services. Against this broader industrial and cultural backdrop, the pandemic also created a new social context for understanding and rereading *The Golden Girls*. Viewers certainly watched *The Golden Girls* out of nostalgia, but they also memed the show to frame the historical significance of the pandemic. Drawing on 2020 reviews, blog posts, memes, and pandemic ephemera, I demonstrate how the show's appeal was not only in its familiarity but also in its skillful handling of contemporary social issues, something sorely lacking from pandemic-era television.

The Lure of Licensing

From the broadcast networks that replayed old westerns in the 1950s to cable networks and later streamers acquiring content libraries, media distribution relies on an interest in and nostalgia for old films and television shows. The function of classic sitcoms in streaming resembles their role in nascent cable networks. Existing series acquired by cable networks, like USA, helped cable networks build their financial coffers to later develop original series. The same applies to streaming services like Netflix, which made a deal with Starz for streaming rights to its one thousand films in the early days of streaming in 2008 and drew large numbers of subscribers to the nascent service.[10]

When Hulu licensed *The Golden Girls* in 2017, the culture of licensing and rebooting television shows for streaming was firmly established. Hulu announced that the long-running series *South Park* and *Law & Order: SVU* were their most watched shows of the year, also noting that viewers watched sixty-five million hours of *Seinfeld* in 2017.[11] As Taylor Cole Miller points out, "TV's economic logic has always been one of repeating its successes, the most profitable of which are reruns."[12] Like cable before it, the licensing of classic titles has continued to be an essential strategy for streaming services. Writing an end-of-year *Variety* roundup, Kevin Tran identified "bidding war for classic TV hits" as one of the top nineteen media trends that defined the business in 2019. As Tran points out, survey data have shown that audiences listed acquired rather than original titles as their favorite shows on both Netflix and Amazon, which has contributed to the competition for the rights to network television shows.[13] The result of this race for classics is that audiences now have access to a library of on-demand shows to choose from—in addition to the hundreds of new shows produced each year.

Many of the "new" shows produced for streaming services are tied to the classic acquisitions. In the context of Netflix in particular, scholars and critics have identified several types of nostalgic productions, from *Stranger Things*, which relies heavily on media and cultural references from the 1980s, to their network television reboots with shows like *Arrested Development*, *Gilmore Girls*, *One Day at a Time*, and *Fuller House* (just to name a few).[14] Rebooted network shows represent a different form of nostalgia that is not simply for media from a previous era; as Katharina Niemeyer explains, it also "concerns media institutions and industries that . . . yearn nostalgically for their own past productions, practices and archives."[15] Streaming services have radically disrupted television financing and distribution models, but when it comes to content strategy, they clearly long for shows that found success on network television.

From the show's premiere at the top of the Nielsen rankings in 1985 to its initial debut in the syndication market, *The Golden Girls* has been a hot commodity for networks.[16] When Buena Vista began selling the syndication rights to *The Golden Girls* in 1988, the trade publication *Broadcasting* predicted the that show would bolster lineups anchored by *The Cosby Show*, which had sold for record prices ranging from $180,000 to $350,000 per episode.[17] In the weeks and months following, Buena Vista consistently touted the show's ratings reputation with advertisements that refigured the ladies as the "heavies." In one *Broadcasting* advertisement from 1988, Blanche, Dorothy, Rose, and Sophia are costumed as armed gangsters and referred to as "the local muscle" who have "the firepower to blow away Superman and the World Series."[18] Although *The Golden Girls* had an industrial reputation for being tough on competition, as Taylor Cole Miller explains in this volume, their power and profit came from their comforting presence first in syndication and later on streaming services, trademark licensing, and branded goods.

Although the show continues to be beloved, its presence on Hulu did not make the news until the pandemic (which also coincided with the thirty-fifth anniversary of its premiere). Months after *The Golden Girls* topped the ratings charts in 2020, Regina King, Tracee Ellis Ross, Sanaa Lathan, and Alfre Woodard participated in a table read. However, as of 2025, *The Golden Girls*' creator, Susan Harris, has been true to her word that there would never be an official U.S. reboot of the show.[19] Harris's restriction has meant that the afterlives of *The Golden Girls* have followed a successful yet familiar trajectory of off-network syndication deals but will not be part of the streaming trend of reboots.

Streaming might be the future of distribution, but streamers have yet to prove that they are the future of production. The success of *The Golden Girls* during the pandemic (and following Betty White's death in 2021) was noteworthy in the history of the show, demonstrating its continued cultural relevance. However, the idea that a classic sitcom could attract millions of viewers was not new. While it is easy to point to the financial logic of acquiring a show with an existing audience rather than shouldering the risk of financing a new show, this model is only profitable if audiences find value in revisiting old shows.

The Nostalgic Audience

Much of the scholarship about nostalgia opens with its Greek origins (*nostos* = home, and *algos* = pain), explaining that at its core, nostalgia is homesickness. Svetlana Boym uses this etymology to identify two different types of nostalgia, restorative nostalgia, which emphasizes the rebuilding of the home to look back at the past, and reflective nostalgia, which is about remembrance.[20] Although Americans had been subjected to the nationalist mythmaking of restorative nostalgia throughout Donald Trump's presidency, the pandemic inspired a tremendous amount of reflection as people around the world longed for normal social interactions.

Media complicate nostalgia. As Andreas Huyssen explains, there is an essential temporal dimension to the word "nostalgia," explaining that it "has to do with the irreversibility of time: something in the past is no longer accessible."[21] Since syndication, VHS, DVDs, and streaming have made portions of our media history available for instant replay, nostalgia for media is not simply about inaccessibility of texts but more about an attempt to access collective memory or feelings associated with classic television shows.

Nostalgia and the desire to look to the past, as theorists of nostalgia have observed, are "protective reactions to crisis."[22] Thus, the nostalgic impulse often keeps people from moving forward. However, as Gary Cross has observed, nostalgia "can [also] become a playful reinterpretation of the past."[23] This playful understanding of nostalgia is one that best aligns with Eleanor Patterson's discussion of queer *Golden Girls* audiences and especially the drag shows. As Patterson and other scholars have noted, the homosocial environment of *The Golden Girls* has always left the show open to queer readings; however, the drag shows pull "queerness to the forefront of this show in a way that was not possible during the original production of *The Golden Girls*."[24] Although these reading practices and reinterpretations of shows might take a playful form, the impulse to revisit the show is, to some degree, born out of the necessity of creating a common queer media and cultural history.

The nostalgic impulse of the pandemic was a survival mechanism of a different sort, as viewers sought familiar twenty-two-minute sitcoms in which conflicts were resolved within a single episode (and the occasional multipart episode). *The Golden Girls* follows a typical network narrative structure that resolves narrative conflict within the episode and offers a model (the "very special episode") for addressing contemporary social issues, something sorely lacking during the pandemic. This form of nostalgia resembles the qualities that Charlotte Howell and Joyce Howell identify in *The Joy of Painting with Bob Ross* when they argue that the nostalgia for the classic PBS show is partially grounded in nostalgia for "a time when public media was able to deliver on its promises."[25] The desire to revisit a particular period of media represented by *The Golden Girls* and *The Joy of Painting with Bob Ross* does not undermine the unique qualities of the shows, but it does indicate the shortcomings of the contemporary television landscape.

During the pandemic, *The Golden Girls* offered an escape. Escapist media is often culturally maligned, but during the pandemic, when people were either confined to their homes or working as essential workers and living with the daily risk of catching COVID-19, almost all film and television became an escape from the visual culture of the pandemic. Media offered a world of crowded rooms and unmasked people, a world within a single frame rather than compartmentalized into a patchwork of boxes. In *The Golden Girls*, the fact that the show features a group of women harmoniously occupying the same home may have also offered a necessary fantasy for some viewers, whether this was a fantasy of living harmoniously with others or socializing with friends or a means to spend time with television grandparents while people were separated from elderly relatives. Or, as one creator of *Golden Girls*–inspired pandemic humor explained to me, "We weren't allowed to be around our friends and family so we had to have surrogate friends-who-are-like-family through our TVs."[26]

The Golden Girls as Comfort TV

As soon as COVID-19 restrictions loosened, actors and directors began making films and limited series about pandemic lockdown conditions. These shows were not well received by critics; as one reviewer said of Jenji Kohan's *Social Distance*, "if the series' goal is to provide some much-needed relief during these very uncertain times—while also capturing a glimpse of the zeitgeist—it's unfortunately just tedious."[27] It turns out that people weren't interested in watching actors working in quarantine conditions pretend to be regular people living in a pandemic.

Rather than watching films and television explicitly about the pandemic, audiences worked through their pandemic experience through various forms of comfort TV. What constitutes comfort TV for an individual? While streaming services might try to define it through examples, comfort is highly subjective. Throughout the pandemic, the term "comfort TV" peppered the critical landscape in publications from *Variety* to *The New York Times*. Industry professionals weighed in on the qualities of comfort, speculating that comfort came from a wide range of sources including self-contained episodic stories, familiar characters that audiences enjoy sharing time with, and life-affirming stories.[28] Despite the ubiquity of the term, as Charlotte Howell and Joyce Howell point out, comfort TV lacks an agreed-on definition in popular culture. However, they theorize this term as one that is culturally and industrially contingent. "Comfort TV," they write, "is not associated with low-brow, mass-appeal programming or viewers; in fact, it has very little presumed audience overlap with the television forms against which quality TV defines itself."[29] For Howell and Howell, comfort needs to be distinct from reality lowbrow offerings of contemporary television but also distinct from the serious, and often dark, television that is labeled as prestige.

As audiences sought out nostalgic offerings, streaming service interfaces leaned into the pandemic crisis by curating comforting shows, and Hulu, home of *The Golden Girls*, placed the show in its "Comfort TV" category for all to find.[30] Thus, during the pandemic, streaming services began to develop a definition of comfort TV. Although these shows don't share textual characteristics, comfort TV fits Jason Mittell's understanding of television genres. According to Mittell, genres should possess an "operative coherence," meaning shows that fit into the category of comfort TV might not share discernable visual or narrative characteristics, but it is a term that has meaning for audiences, journalists, and industry.

Media consumption has become increasingly individualized, and even amid a simultaneous global event, as Howell and Howell note, the temporality of streaming's on-demand viewing means that "there is no working through the trauma of the ongoing pandemic, only alleviating the stress."[31] And films and television shows became essential ways for people in quarantine to self-soothe, rather than reflect, during unprecedented times.

The term "comfort TV" can encompass a wide array of genres and is a term that is ideally suited to the algorithmic sorting of streaming services. Rather than sorting by genre or media type, streamers like industry-leader Netflix sort by verticals (hyper-specific genres) and taste clusters (shows that the service knows have been linked by viewers).[32] The taste cluster tends to offer more affective links between shows and offer suggestions of the kind of *feeling* ("comfort") a viewer might be looking for in future shows.

In some ways, the narrative qualities of *The Golden Girls* sit between comfort and prestige in this contemporary context. The show's success on prime time and in syndication means that it has decades of viewers who might turn to it as a nostalgic and familiar offering, as it reliably resolves narrative conflicts within a single episode. However, even though the show premiered thirty-five years prior to the pandemic, many of the social issues, such as Blanche's struggle to accept her gay brother's marriage, are relevant to a contemporary audience. In this way, the show might perhaps be the perfect classic show: familiar enough for a rewatch but socially relevant to keep viewers coming back. The combination of familiarity and social relevance not only was a source of comfort for viewers, but it would also be important for how audience members engaged with the show on social media.

The Golden Girls Live Through the Pandemic

The collective pandemic viewing experience seemed to largely transpire through think pieces and memes. In the earliest weeks of the pandemic, many people found their timelines full of the viral sensation of the pandemic: *Tiger King*. *Tiger King* memes, as Tanya Horek explains, were a way of "discharging public emotion at the annus horribilis that was 2020," often using "shocking" domestic scenes to contrast with the boredom of life in lockdown.[33] The humor of *Tiger King* memes mocked Joe Exotic (especially his fashion), the big cat community, and Exotic's sexuality.

In contrast, *The Golden Girls* received a loving memetic treatment. Writers and fans were interested in using characters and humor to work through their own pandemic experience by imagining how Dorothy, Blanche, Rose, and Sophia would navigate the same challenges. Writing about the thirty-fifth anniversary of the show in an LGBTQ magazine, Michele Yeo ended her piece as a fan by posing a series of questions about how the characters would have handled the pandemic. While some of her questions are lighthearted—"Would freshly baked banana bread have replaced store-bought cheesecake?"—other questions were more serious, such as "Would Sophia be coping with the loss of friends who succumbed to the virus while living in a nursing home?"[34] Yeo's potential plotlines indicate genuine affection for the show, both by her ability to incorporate running jokes and also by her thoughtful inclusion of many of the serious issues facing people during the pandemic.

One of the most common Golden Girls memes featured Sophia's oft-repeated phrase "Picture it . . ." mock-nostalgic rhetoric. While many of these memes have disappeared from social media sites, the merchandise remains; Etsy designers made Sophia "Quarantine 2020" stickers and Christmas ornaments, and the meme was popular enough to warrant screen printing on a T-shirt and, of course, a cloth mask.[35] As one Etsy seller remarked, they made cloth Golden Girls masks because they love the show and they also noticed their popularity "surging" online. They ceased production as customers prioritized medical-grade masks.[36] These memes take a couple of different forms: some simply provide commentary on a picture of Sophia, and others use "Picture it . . ." as a jumping-off point to write pandemic-inspired dialogue. In one particularly hopeful meme, the creator combines a photo of Sophia midsentence accompanied by the text, "When your future grandkids start complaining about their day and you hit them with another

2020 story."[37] The "Picture it . . ." memes express not only a longing for the past but also a longing for a time in which the present is past.

The memes were largely geared toward humorous punch lines and hopeful conclusions; in contrast, nine pandemic "episodes" of *The Golden Girls* written by Heidi Lux all culminate with the same dark ending of one or all the women catching COVID-19.[38] In each episode, Lux uses pandemic restrictions as a source of humor. In personal correspondence about this piece, Lux acknowledged her piece was dark, but because "the characters are so well written and specific, it's [so] easy to slide them into that [pandemic] scenario."[39] For example, in one she called "Bursting the Bubble," Blanche gets tired of spending her nights alone: "Horny as hell, Blanche decides it's probably okay to let a few gentlemen callers into her 'bubble.' When she gets a call from a contact tracer who says one of the men she's been sleeping with has the virus, Blanche realizes her bubble extends to half the men in Miami. Miami is an early hotspot. She gets COVID."[40]

In each pandemic-inspired episode, introducing conflict eventually means catching COVID-19. These pandemic plots connect clearly to the characters, their quirks, and the show's humor, but the bleak outcomes reflect the nature of the pandemic. Television requires characters to make active choices, but the pandemic required people to be actively inactive and remain in their homes. In the imagined episodes, the Girls are all faced with difficult pandemic-inspired decisions, but COVID-19 was the logical outcome of most social mixing in 2020.

Social media posts are only one metric for understanding viewing practices, but the loving engagement with *The Golden Girls* during the pandemic demonstrates how the show operated as a source of comfort for many people. The show wrapped original production long ago, but social media commenters used its running jokes as a language for framing pandemic hardships. Whereas the humor of *Tiger King* memes was often cruel and debasing, the *Golden Girls* memes were as kind as the characters themselves.

The Golden Girls in Pandemic History

Pandemic audience numbers and memes show the continued relevance of *The Golden Girls*. Eleanor Patterson demonstrates how *The Golden Girls* has long been a show that has brought together a multigenerational queer audience. However, during the pandemic, many people found comfort in the show's ability to address and resolve social tensions and frame hardship in comedic terms. The repeated use of "Picture it quarantine 2020 . . ." openly acknowledges the stress of the pandemic, but the joke portends a hopeful future in which the teller survives to later annoy future generations with stories of lockdown.

Media reflect production contexts, which includes the production culture that produced a media artifact as well as the social and political context in which it was made. Since there were very few live-action, scripted television shows and films made during the widespread lockdowns of 2020, we have fewer media artifacts to analyze as a reflection of this unusual period of history.[41] The absence of new programming, coupled with the uptick in "comfort viewing" means that audience responses to and viewing habits of shows like *The Golden Girls* will be essential objects of study to historicize the pandemic experience.

Notes

1. Oriana Schwindt, "Hulu Nabs Exclusive Streaming Rights to 'Black-ish,' 'Golden Girls'," *Variety*, January 7, 2017, https://variety.com/2017/tv/news/hulu-golden-girls-streaming-blackish-1201954868/.

2. Derek Kompare, *Rerun Nation: How Repeats Invented American Television* (Routledge, 2005), xi.

3. Gavin Bridge, "'Tiger King' Is Netflix's Most Popular U.S. Original of 2020," *Variety+*, December 28, 2020, https://variety.com/vip/tiger-king-is-netflixs-most-popular-u-s-original-of-2020-1234874574/.

4. Todd Spangler and Brent Lang, "Why 'Harry Potter,' Other Big Movies Have Become Hot Commodities During COVID Pandemic," *Variety*, August 18, 2020, https://variety.com/2020/digital/news/harry-potter-movies-hbo-max-peacock-covid-1234738031/.

5. John Koblin, "Lockdown TV: Netflix Dominates, News Surges and Bea Arthur Is Still Golden," *New York Times*, April 30, 2020, www.nytimes.com/2020/04/30/business/media/coronavirus-television-netflix-ratings.html; Chris Harnick, "What Do *Parasite* and *The Golden Girls* Have in Common?," *E! News*, April 14, 2020, www.eonline.com/news/1140661/what-do-parasite-and-the-golden-girls-have-in-common.

6. Nielsen, "LOL: Amid Uncertain Times, Consumers Take Comfort in Nostalgic Comedy Shows," March 2021, www.nielsen.com/insights/2021/lol-amid-uncertain-times-consumers-take-comfort-in-nostalgic-comedy-shows/.

7. Katharina Niemeyer, "Media Studies and Nostalgia: Media Philosophy and Nostalgizing in Times of Crisis," in *Imitations of Nostalgia: Multidisciplinary Explorations of an Enduring Emotion*, ed. Michael Hviid Jacobsen (Bristol University Press, 2022), 158.

8. Eleanor Patterson, "*The Golden Girls Live*: Residual Television Texts, Participatory Culture, and Queering TV Heritage Through Drag," *Feminist Media Studies* 15, no. 5 (2016): 839.

9. Patterson, "*Golden Girls Live*," 840.

10. John Dempsey, "Netflix, Starz Strike Streaming Deal," *Variety*, October 1, 2008, https://variety.com/2008/digital/news/netflix-starz-strike-streaming-deal-1117993139/.

11. Michael Schneider, "'South Park' and 'Law & Order: SVU' Were Hulu's Most-Watched Shows in 2017," *Indie Wire*, January 8, 2018, www.indiewire.com/features/general/hulu-most-watched-shows-2017-south-park-law-and-order-svu-1201915503/.

12. Taylor Cole Miller, "Rewitched: Retextuality and the Queering of *Bewitched*," *Camera Obscura* 36, no. 3 (108) (2021): 5.

13. Kevin Tran, "Top 19 Media Trends of 2019: Bidding War for Classic TV Hits," *Variety*, December 31, 2019, https://variety.com/2019/tv/news/top-19-media-trends-of-2019-bidding-war-for-classic-tv-hits-1203454261/.

14. Katherine Pallister, ed., *Netflix Nostalgia: Streaming the Past on Demand* (Lexington Books, 2019).

15. Katharina Niemeyer, "Media Studies and Nostalgia: Media Philosophy and Nostalgizing in Times of Crisis," in Jacobsen, *Imitations of Nostalgia*, 158.

16. Fred Rothenberg, "Ratings for 'Golden Girls' Sparkle in Debut," *AP News*, September 17, 1985, https://apnews.com/article/e3426c422a5c7afd9d0fd27a694b2269.

17. "Programming: 'Golden Girls' Gets Golden Price in Syndication," *Broadcasting*, June 6, 1988, 57.

18. "Meet the Local Muscle," *Broadcasting*, June 20, 1988, 1.

19. Amy Wilkinson, "Why You'll Never See a Golden Girls Reboot," *Entertainment Weekly*, February 17, 2017, https://ew.com/tv/2017/02/17/golden-girls-reboot/.

20. Svetlana Boym, *The Future of Nostalgia* (Basic Books, 2001), 41.

21. Andreas Huyssen, "Nostalgia for Ruins," *Grey Room* 23 (Spring 2006): 7.

22. Niemeyer, "Media Studies and Nostalgia," 151.

23. Gary Cross, *Consumed Nostalgia: Memory in the Age of Fast Capitalism* (Columbia University Press, 2015), 141.

24. Patterson, "*Golden Girls Live*," 841.

25. Charlotte E. Howell and Joyce B. Howell, "Happy Trees in a Black Box: Elevated Escapism as Comfort Television in *The Joy of Painting with Bob Ross*," *JCMS* 62, no.5 (2022–23): 61.

26. Heidi Lux, personal correspondence with author, May 15, 2024.

27. Tambay Obenson, "'Social Distance' Review: Netflix's Quarantine-Shot Series Is a Bore," *Indie Wire*, October 19, 2020, www.indiewire.com/criticism/shows/social-distance-review-1234589941/.

28. Danielle Turchiano, "Comfort TV in the Age of Coronavirus," *Variety*, April 8, 2020, https://variety.com/2020/tv/features/comfort-tv-coronavirus-friends-office-one-day-at-a-time-psychology-1203549216/.

29. Howell and Howell, "Happy Trees in a Black Box," 59.

30. Howell and Howell, "Happy Trees in a Black Box," 60.

31. Howell and Howell, "Happy Trees in a Black Box," 58.

32. Josef Adalian, "Inside the Netflix Binge Factory," *Vulture*, June 2018, www.vulture.com/2018/06/how-netflix-swallowed-tv-industry.html.

33. Tanya Horek, "#carolebaskinkilledherhusband: The Gender Politics of *Tiger King* Meme Culture," in *Tiger King: Murder, Mayhem and Madness—A Docalogue*, ed. Jaimie Baron and Kristen Fuhs (Routledge, 2022), 89.

34. Michele Yeo, "Still Golden: Why 35 Years Later, We're Still Thanking 'The Golden

Girls' for Being a Friend," *IN Magazine*, September 14, 2020, https://inmagazine.ca/2020/09/still-golden-why-35-years-later-were-still-thanking-the-golden-girls-for-being-a-friend/.

35. Nostalgia Designs SG, "Golden Girls Face Mask—Picture It Quarantine 2020," accessed June 10, 2023, https://nostalgiadesignssg.com/products/golden-girls-face-mask-picture-it-quarantine-2020.

36. Libby (from Libby's Designs), Etsy correspondence with author, May 14, 2024.

37. Ashley Tibollo, "When your future grandkids start complaining about their day and you hit them with another 2020 story," Facebook, December 12, 2020, *A Journal of the Plague Year*, accessed June 10, 2023, https://covid-19archive.org/s/archive/item/44891.

38. Heidi Lux, "Pandemic Episodes of The Golden Girls," *Medium*, February 15, 2021, https://medium.com/slackjaw/pandemic-episodes-of-the-golden-girls-ea176e08bafe.

39. Heidi Lux, personal correspondence with author, May 15, 2024.

40. Lux, "Pandemic Episodes."

41. Kate Fortmueller, *Hollywood Shutdown: Production, Distribution, and Exhibition in the Time of Covid* (University of Texas Press, 2021), 17–19.

INTERVIEW

Meet Our Special Guests and Their Little Slice of *The Golden Girls*

Isabel Omero, Production Associate/Script Supervisor, Writer

I was on the set with the director and the actors. I went by the name Robert Spina back then. [My job started] with the table read [and included] two rehearsal days and two on-camera days. Throughout, I kept notes on dialogue, movements, timing, and other areas relating to performance or [anything] needed by the editor and postproduction. I also was the liaison between the director and actors on set and the writers and producers in the office. If anything changed in the script or if a change was requested, it usually went through me, often resulting in revised pages or even a revised draft of the script. Also, I was—more than a little—the dialogue coach for the ladies. I'd run lines with them onstage. On show days, we'd spend ninety minutes to two hours rehearsing lines over lunch, just the five of us. (Not surprisingly, that was my favorite part of every week!)

I loved going to work. The people were great. I was good at my job, and folks told me so. What's not to love. But as far as challenges go, I'd say I pushed really hard to be given scripts to write. It was an uphill climb because *Golden Girls* writers were great writers. But I got to write three (which, of course, were rewritten by the staff). But three is pretty cool, and I get to be a small part of comedy history ("If at Last, You Do Succeed," S06E03; "Melodrama," S06E19; and "Rose: Portrait of a Woman," S07E20).

Marc Sotkin, Executive Producer

So, they started me as co-executive producer. Terry Hughes really didn't want me to have an executive producer credit right away, because they

The *Golden Girls* cast and crew. (Photo © Wayne Williams 1984–87. All rights reserved.)

didn't know what I was going to do. So, [on my] second season, . . . my credit is executive producer/showrunner. A showrunner is kind of like a head football coach in that you're responsible for every facet of the show. So, for instance, I don't design the costumes, . . . but Judy Evans shows me sketches of what she has planned. I don't build the outside sets, but I see plans for what Ed [Stephenson] is planning to do. I am responsible for casting outside characters, I go to casting, I see edits of the show, although on that show, Nina Feinberg and Tony Thomas were mostly doing the editing, but I would see cuts. My biggest responsibility though is head writer.

Marsha Posner Williams, Co-Producer

When you see a sitcom's credits, and you see twelve producers, eleven of them are writers with agents who make good deals. But there's one, the executive in charge of production, who oversees the money, the budget. [That's me, . . . the one] who is the liaison between the head writers, the stage, and the network, and mostly making sure that we don't go over budget. . . . I remember, one of the last things I did in the business was a pilot for CBS, and they said, "Here's a million dollars. Try not to spend it all." And so that was my job. I hire. I oversee the crew. All the department heads report to me. So, it was a job of a thousand decisions a day. They give me the script, and it's my job, along with the director and actors, to bring it to screen.

I was very good in postproduction. It was after editing was done, adding music, laughs, and effects, what's called "sweetening" the show. That was me. I did that for every show I did, and I learned it on *Soap*. I sat with the audio mixer and the laugh guy. There's two parts to audio at the end. There's prelay, which is the cheaper room, and then there's the big audio session in the giant room. Okay, prelay is actually where we add sound effects. I would sit with the composer, and we would put the music cues in. He'll lay in a music cue for a transition right from set, scene to scene, and I'll say, "pull it up ten frames," and there are thirty frames in a second, so I'm getting pretty particular. "Pull it up ten frames," and he'll say "five," and I'll say "seven." And we'll negotiate until we're both happy. And then if there's sound effects, whether it's a doorbell, a horn, hawk, a dog bark, whatever it is, that's all done in prelay. Then, when all that's done, now we're going to do the final mix to make sure everything's even, all the laughs, the dialogue, the effects. And I sit with two people in a giant room with a sound mixer and a laugh guy.

Wayne Williams, Photographer
There were a couple of times the production asked me to come on set when Mickey Rooney was there or Burt Reynolds or some of the other big famous people, and Witt/Thomas wanted to have control of a set of those images and not leave it to the network, where they would have to grovel to get some of those shots. So, I did a few of those type of production things, but for the most part, I was not shooting the on-set production that much. They asked me to shoot publicity for *The Golden Girls* because they thought the network was not doing enough of its own promotion and Bea did not want to do it.

Cindy Fee, Main Titles Performer
Cindy Fee is a performing artist who sang the show's theme song, a cover of Andrew Gold's "Thank You for Being a Friend."

CHAPTER 2

Disney's Renaissance Woman

Susan Harris, *The Golden Girls*, and Touchstone Television

PETER C. KUNZE

The standard narrative of Disney's impressive turnaround in the 1980s and 1990s from a struggling theme-park company to a global entertainment conglomerate often has been attributed to one thing: executive brilliance. This version of corporate transformation, unsurprisingly, was discursively crafted by Disney executives Michael Eisner and Jeffrey Katzenberg themselves and reinforced in publicity materials, stockholder reports, and press coverage.[1] Within a few years of their 1984 arrival, journalists and scholars alike were heralding a veritable renaissance at the company, led by this visionary regime.[2] But this narrative is ultimately an incomplete—and, at times, incorrect—one. Walt Disney Productions, the company's name prior to 1986, had long been associated with creativity, yet it has an equally long history of downplaying the creative contributions of its laborers.[3] Yet in neglecting the work of actors, animators, directors, producers, songwriters, and screenwriters, we fail to understand the essential role that women, LGBT people, and people of color—among them, Susan Harris—played in setting Disney on a new course.

While 1989's *The Little Mermaid*, an animated feature released five years into Eisner's tenure, is the film credited with starting the so-called Disney

This real Brentwood, Los Angeles, home was used as the exterior filming location for the Girls' house from the first through much of the third season and in select episodes of the fourth. Recognizing the show's growing popularity, Disney constructed an exact replica of the house façade on Residential Street at Disney-MGM Studios, both for continued filming and to attract tourists on its backlot tour. All sets on Residential Street were torn down in 2003. (Photo by Taylor Cole Miller)

Renaissance, a closer look at Disney in the 1980s reveals that animation was far from Eisner's top priority. In fact, it was live-action comedy, on both the big screen and the small screen, that he thought would save the lagging studio, struggling under the restrictions of its family-friendly brand and over-attention to the more profitable theme-park division.[4] Disney's 1985 annual report tells stockholders, "A network presence is crucial for the entire company. Television acts as a marketing and creative catalyst for all our interrelated businesses: each business area is made stronger because television supports and is, in turn, supported by other Disney enterprises."[5] Histories of Disney during this period generally overlook television's role in the Renaissance and its crucial role for the Walt Disney Company ever since. Many people would be surprised to learn that Disney's first television success under the Eisner regime was not a cartoon but a sitcom: *The Golden Girls.*

This chapter surveys Susan Harris's influential career as a television writer, with particular focus on how her work on *The Golden Girls,* to understand one creator's instrumental role in reorienting corporate strategy at Disney in the 1980s. I draw on popular and trade press coverage as well as archival research to make several interrelated points about the so-called Disney Renaissance. First, comedy—not animation—was the strategy the new executive team believed would reinvigorate Disney film and television. Second, rather than targeting the family audience that is essential to the Disney brand, the executives pursued sophisticated, adult-directed fare through the Touchstone banner established by their predecessors. Indeed, the initial successes of the Eisner years were made under Touchstone, not Disney proper. Third, and most importantly, creative laborers such as Susan Harris, the writer-producer behind *The Golden Girls*, were essential to the company's renewed vitality. Examining Harris's contributions to Touchstone Television cements the role of comedy in the Disney Renaissance, the renewed importance of television for Disney, and the crucial contributions of women in a narrative of creative revitalization that too often privileges the boardroom over than the writers' room.[6]

Disney Before the Renaissance

In the years following Walt Disney's 1966 death, the company struggled financially, due in no small part to the top-down organizational structure that positioned Walt as the top of the company. Although his brother, Roy, steered the company through the opening of Walt Disney World, his own death in 1971 sparked a showdown between Roy's and Walt's sides of the Disney family for corporate control, with Walt's son-in-law, Ron Miller, emerging as the new heir apparent, over Roy's son, Roy E. Disney. Although Miller's tenure was marked by a stream of box-office failures, his successes were by no means insignificant: the opening of EPCOT, the founding of the Disney Channel, and the establishment of a new production company for adult-directed fare, Touchstone Films (soon after renamed Touchstone Pictures). These milestones were not enough to save Miller, though his successors benefited considerably from them. An attempted hostile takeover by Saul Steinberg, complicated further by Roy E. Disney's resignation from the board and vocal criticism of the company, eventually led to Miller's ouster. With Roy's support, Michael Eisner was hired from Paramount and Frank Wells from Warner Bros. to serve, respectively, as the CEO and president. The installation of two seasoned professionals signaled not only a shake-up at the company but a hope that the company would reinvest in film and television production in the years ahead.

The animated features had long proven to be an annuity for the company via broadcasting (usually in condensed form) and, more often, theatrical rerelease. But feature animation was a costly pursuit, and the new executives, including Jeffrey Katzenberg, who was hired away from Paramount to oversee film and television production, were not keen on animation's ability to boost corporate profits. Reportedly, some higher-ups recommended outsourcing animation overseas or even shutting it down all together. Animation persevered in large part at the insistence of Roy Disney, who argued that animation was the lifeblood of the company that fed other divisions. The newly appointed executives, seeking to satisfy the board member who had helped to secure their hiring, acquiesced and placed Roy in charge of animation. But for Eisner and Katzenberg, comedy held the greatest potential for the company since it was noticeably missing in the market.[7] It also could help Disney's television efforts, which had diminished in recent years as the company focused on EPCOT. Eisner came up in television production: first in Saturday-morning television, then in prime-time comedies, overseeing *Laverne & Shirley* and *Happy Days*. Eisner knew that a syndicated series could generate hundreds of millions of dollars in revenue for years to come.[8] Unsurprisingly, he actively pursued producing Saturday-morning cartoons and prime-time sitcoms.

The Significance of Susan Harris

By this time, Susan Harris was perhaps the television industry's premier comedy writer. She had entered the business as a single mother hoping to support her child. Unimpressed with the quality of writing, she imagined she could do better and wrote a spec script for the NBC action series *Then Came Bronson*, which was purchased for $4,500. She then worked on *Love, American Style* under Garry Marshall, whom she credited with teaching her the craft of television writing.[9] But it was as a writer for Norman Lear shows—first *All in the Family* but, most famously, *Maude*—that she established her reputation in the industry. She scripted the controversial two-part episode "Maude's Dilemma," which aired two months before the 1973 *Roe v. Wade* decision. Harris's reputation as a socially conscious writer with a sharp wit led her to then create *Fay*, a sitcom about a divorcée (Lee Grant) that many observers believed was a victim of the short-lived Family Viewing Hour. An FCC policy in place from 1975 to 1977, it required broadcast television networks to use the 8:00 p.m. to 9:00 p.m. block for "family-friendly" shows. Several creative laborers and producers—most notably, Lear—felt that the regulation infringed on their First Amendment rights, and a 1976 court decision agreed. In the meantime, however, *Fay*'s contemporary treatment of marriage and divorce meant that it was a casualty of conflicting creative and social interests during this brief period.[10]

Long before Harris's "sophistication" piqued Michael Eisner's interest, it garnered attention from Fred Silverman. Years earlier at CBS, he had notoriously canceled popular sitcoms such as *The Beverly Hillbillies* and *Green Acres* during the so-called rural purge and replaced them with more "relevant" programming, including *All in the Family*, *M*A*S*H*, and *The Mary Tyler Moore Show*. In 1975, Silverman moved to ABC, where Harris created *Soap*, a serialized sitcom that elevated soap-opera scenarios to satirical farce. It became a cause célèbre even before its premiere because of a leaked censor memo in the *Los Angeles Times*, which noted, for instance, that an Oreo could not be substituted for the Eucharist.[11] A strong denunciation by Harry F. Waters in *Newsweek* accused the show of salaciousness. Despite protests from the left and the right, Silverman stood by the show: "It is an intelligent show written and produced by intelligent people, and in time it will be perceived as a moral show."[12] The show nevertheless struggled to find top-rate sponsors, even though it was a rating success that touched on adultery, queerness, and racial injustice. While most shows depend on a team of writers, Harris herself wrote or cowrote every episode of *Soap*, giving her a level of creative control—and burnout—rarely seen in television production. Ultimately, right-wing detractors prevailed. Harris noted, "they didn't like the way we portrayed nice gays, for instance, and they were horrified when we showed women having affairs."[13] *Soap* ran for four years and inspired a successful spin-off, *Benson*, but by that time, Harris had the clout and the money to take a more backseat approach. Preferring to write from home and communicate through her producing partners, Tony Thomas and her husband, Paul Junger Witt, Harris embraced the "creator-deserter" label her husband affectionately ascribed to her.[14] As she confided to the press soon after the 1988 premiere of *Empty Nest*, "Once we know what we have, and it's established, I'll be gone. I will never do again what I did on *Soap*."[15]

Despite her personal success, Harris was often compared with her male counterparts, especially her former boss, Norman Lear. In a pan of her 1982 series *It Takes Two*, the *Washington Post*'s Tom Shales remarked, "Harris' work is the bad result of the good breakthroughs made years ago by Norman Lear."[16] Furthermore, several critics took issue with what they perceived to be a vulgarity in her work. In reviewing *The Golden Girls* in 1985, Martha Bayles wrote, "Ms. Harris has definite flair for comedy, but unfortunately her range extends only from the mattress to the toilet."[17] Three years later, with the premiere of *Empty Nest*, Noel Holston of the *Star Tribune* deemed Harris "the Dr. Jekyll and Mr. Hyde of comedy. . . . A marvelous sense of the absurdities of modern life, but she also has a crass, insensitive streak that can give her shows a foul aftertaste."[18] Harris's alleged inability to produce respectable sitcoms reveals a strong double standard for women writer-producers at a time when women were rarely granted such power in the industry. As Harris explained in 1990, "I don't think I was taken seriously until they saw the writing. And then they began to treat me like a writer."[19]

Harris's success in television speaks not only to the need to satisfy standards and metrics imposed by a male-dominated industry but to the way she insisted on accommodations for herself as a mother and creative laborer that seemed unimaginable at the time. Both onscreen and behind the scenes, she brought a feminist consciousness to her work that distinguished her from most of her contemporaries. While she was far from the first woman writer-producer in television, she is an important generational link between Gertrude Berg, Agnes Nixon, and Irna Phillips in the early days and Amy Sherman-Palladino, Shonda Rhimes, and Jenji Kohan in the post-network era. Harris was the most successful writer-producer in sitcoms of the 1980s, paving the way for other women writer-producers in the genre, such as Linda Bloodworth-Thomason (*Designing Women*), Diane English (*Murphy Brown*), and Winifred Hervey (*Fresh Prince of Bel Air*; Hervey started out as a writer on *The Golden Girls*).

Yet, throughout the interviews Harris has given both then and now, she appears to be deeply ambivalent about writing for television. On the one hand, she asserts her own distinctive and original voice in her work. On the other hand, she seems keenly aware that such singularity and control are rare within television production. In 1977, for example, she told *The Los Angeles Times*, "Television is at best a compromise. I don't want to write for television forever. I'd like to do books or plays."[20] Whereas literature or the theater allegedly afford fuller artistic autonomy, Harris suggests that the collaborative, hierarchical, and commercial nature of television closes off such personal expression. "I'm not out to change the world," she notes in the same interview. "I want to entertain with [*Soap*], to make people laugh, to intrigue them, to make them cry occasionally. There's nothing I'm really saying. I didn't set out to write *Death of a Salesman*."[21] Harris downplays the significance of television writing in a way that diminishes the medium as both an artform and a social force. Just as John L. Sullivan in Preston Sturges's *Sullivan's Travels* (1941) disavows the crowd-pleasing comedies that made him famous, she articulates a desire to do more "meaningful" work. Also, like Sullivan, Harris seems to have had a change of heart about television's cultural significance and power. By the time of *The Golden Girls*, Harris told the press, "The least threatening way to have impact is through comedy."[22] While she observed in 1985 that television is "always several steps behind life," she found within the limits of the sitcom a way to explore a range of social issues.[23] The press, in turn, framed Harris as the sharp, talented (and, quite often, attractive) young writer behind these witty senior citizens.

Although *The Golden Girls* is her most famous show, it was not actually Harris's premise but NBC's. During a showcase for the 1984–85 season, Selma Diamond (*Night Court*) and Doris Roberts (*Remington Steele*) performed a brief introductory sketch in which Roberts kept misunderstanding *Miami Vice* as *Miami Nice*, thereby exasperating Diamond. The seasoned actors' skilled comic performances suggested to the NBC executives Brandon Tartikoff and Warren Littlefield that there was a rich potential in a sitcom starring older performers. Paul Junger Witt, Tony Thomas, and an unnamed third writer soon after met with Littlefield to pitch an idea they were working on. Although Littlefield passed, he mentioned possible interest in a show about older women. The unnamed writer declined, but Witt was intrigued, although he told Littlefield he doubted Littlefield would put it on the air.[24] Here accounts diverge: Witt said he knew his wife was perfect for the job, whereas Littlefield claims Harris was his recommendation. Either way, Witt himself pitched the concept to Harris, though she told him she did not want to hear any ideas. Even she had to admit it was promising, though she later revealed that the executives apparently meant women in their forties, whereas she wanted to write women in their sixties and older.[25] Harris was on board, but NBC was only promising the production team $200,000 of the $320,000 necessary to make each episode. They would need a business partner to cover the remaining expenses.[26]

Harris's representative approached Michael Eisner about coming aboard.[27] Eisner was well aware of Harris's reputation from his time at ABC, and her witty, timely scripts promised Touchstone Television exactly what Disney wanted: sophistication. Indeed, the film comedies that Eisner and Katzenberg had already put into production were often attempts at somewhat "elevated" fare: Paul Mazursky's *Down and Out in Beverly Hills*, for instance, was a loose remake of Jean Renoir's classic 1932 comedy of manners *Boudu Saved from Drowning*. While Eisner voiced hesitation about focusing on older characters, Harris assured him that mother-daughter relationships are the same regardless of age, and Eisner recalled one his projects at Paramount, *Terms of Endearment* (dir. James L. Brooks, 1983), as strong evidence to that fact.[28] Furthermore, her work—and the prestige that came with her name—would potentially provide the cultural capital Eisner sought to make his company relevant and competitive in television again. Disney agreed to deficit finance *The Golden Girls* via Touchstone Television in exchange for roughly one-third of the profits.[29] In addition to the atypically small percentage, Disney also afforded the production team a level of creative control it rarely afforded its other creative laborers—an unlikely gamble from a risk-averse executive team prone to micromanagement.

Writing *The Golden Girls*

A close analysis of two drafts alongside the final broadcast episode provides closer insight into Harris's creative process from inception to the eventual result. As I show later in this chapter, the pilot episode was revised along the way in a manner that suggests accommodations for censors, budgetary limitations and practicality, and improvements achieved in the rehearsal process. While the press as well as Harris and her co-producers presented her as the voice and mind behind the series, my comparative analysis demonstrates the inherently collaborative nature of television production, affirming Harris's oft-repeated assertion that television requires negotiation and compromise.

Dated March 1, 1985, the first draft of *The Golden Girls* teleplay is remarkably similar to the broadcast pilot, though there are some noticeable differences. The characters (five main: Blanche, Dorothy, Rose, and Sophia, as well as Coco) and three guest actors (Harry, the cop, and the minister) are the same, though some scenes are set outside of Blanche's house, including Blanche's wedding at the chapel and two scenes on the golf course. A joke about Mexicans taking siestas because of the food, a discussion mocking Rose's dietary idiosyncrasies, Coco lamenting a disappointing date with a cop (and consequently explaining to Rose that any profession can include gay men), and Sophia revealing to Dorothy that her deceased husband was a philanderer were all cut. So, too, are Sophia's casual references to Coco as "the fag in the kitchen," presumably explained away by the subsequent exchange between Blanche and Rose in which the latter insists that a "stroke destroyed the part of her brain that censors what she says."[30] (The slur got axed by the next draft; the rationale did not.) Most peculiarly, the episode ends with women affirming their kinship not on the lanai but on the golf course. While the final script ends with the women heading out for a celebratory lunch, Harris's original ending imagined a comically bizarre accident: Sophia drives the ladies' golf cart straight into a water hazard.[31]

The most obvious difference between the final script, dated April 12, and the broadcast pilot was the handling of the gay houseboy, Coco. As fans know, Coco did not make it past the pilot, allegedly because the four women were such rich sitcom characters that there was little for him to do. While Blanche borrows Coco's mink stole in the first and final drafts, it switches to Dorothy during production, and she gets Coco's witty retort, "It's Miami in June. Only cats are wearing fur."[32] Green-page revisions of Coco musing over the youth of his legs and then giving Rose and Dorothy a pep talk are also cut from air. A backstory about how Coco came out—his mother died of a heart attack from shock, while his father moved away and remarried without telling him—also ends up on the cutting-room floor. Later, when Dorothy throws Rose in the closet to prevent her from warning Blanche about her beau, Harry, it is Coco who lets her out. This is shown in the pilot, but what is removed is an exchange in which Coco tells an overwhelmed Rose, "You don't have to explain to me; I spent years in the closet."[33] Whether Coco's removal is a matter of timing or risk management is unclear, but in so doing, Harris's attempt to offer another endearing gay character in prime time (not unlike *Soap*'s Jodie Dallas) was effectively squashed.

Two other significant changes are evident between Harris's drafts and the final episode: the language and the sets. In the episode, when Harry departs, Sophia snarks, "The man is a scuzzball." The original insult, though, was "douche bag."[34] The most obvious rationale was the appropriateness of the line for prime-time audiences, revealing the likely negotiations among the producers and the network. Similarly, the early draft's use of multiple sets, including a golf course, was removed in favor of an episode that takes place exclusively at the house. Not only did this decision save money, but it speaks to the strength of the writing and the potential of Harris's characters to carry the show via dialogue alone. In this way, *The Golden Girls* allowed Harris to do not only what she did best—create memorable characters—but what she reportedly enjoyed doing most: writing dialogue.[35] The pilot episode adheres quite closely to a traditional sitcom structure, but its combination of sentiment and irony and its focus on relationships are Harris trademarks. Harris would go onto to write eight more episodes of *The Golden Girls*, including the failed backdoor pilot for *Empty Nest* with Paul Dooley and Rita Moreno (later reconceived with *Soap* star Richard Mulligan as a widower) and the two-part episode on chronic fatigue syndrome, which Harris based on her own experience (later rediagnosed as an adrenal issue).[36] Yet even today, *The Golden Girls* is more closely associated with Harris than with any other writer or even the showrunners who managed the day-to-day operations in her absence.

The Success of *The Golden Girls*

Touchstone Television's partnership with Witt-Thomas-Harris would pay off handsomely. When NBC showed the pilot episode to affiliates in New York, it received a riotous reception. *St. Elsewhere* showrunner Bruce Paltrow, who was in attendance, told Witt, Thomas, and Harris that they had produced the "perfect pilot."[37] Critics echoed the enthusiasm, and even Tom Shales, Harris's fiercest detractor, managed some measured praise: "This show is much better than *Soap* because the characters have human dimension. They aren't just snide cartoons. . . . Harris is shameless. She'll stoop to bathroom humor in a minute, but as rattled off by Getty, even these references have an authentic earthiness."[38] The show was not hampered by its scheduling on the usually sleepier Saturday night, and *The Golden Girls* was the clear star of the fall 1985 lineup. That December, Bob Knight of *Variety* deemed it the season of the sitcom, with *The Golden Girls* as the best of the new crop.[39] It won the Emmy Award for Outstanding Comedy Series in its freshman year, besting the ratings titans *Cheers* and *The Cosby Show*. Harris had her biggest hit yet, and Disney television was back in business—not with a family-friendly anthology show but with an adult-directed sitcom.

Situating *The Golden Girls* in Harris's much-longer career—and her reputation for sophistication and political awareness—underscores affinities that have gone unnoticed by earlier critics and scholars. For instance, in promoting *Soap*, Harris mused that although the Tates and the Campbells were "adorable Protestant" families, she usually writes "angry Jewish."[40] Dorothy and Sophia were originally written as Jewish characters, but when notes commented on their ethnicity, Harris just revised their names to "Petrillo" and said they were Italian without altering their personalities.[41] Dorothy and Sophia were played by American Jewish actresses, and commentators at the time noted that the humor often bears resemblance to Borscht Belt stand-up comedy routines.[42] While *The Golden Girls* followed a more traditional sitcom structure than the serialized *Soap* did, the characters bear some striking similarities: Rose Nylund's naïveté seems akin to Jessica Tate's, whereas Sophia's wisecracking links her to the butler, Benson. But *The Golden Girls*, of course, premiered to much less controversy, and its ultimate concentration on four principals (as opposed to two families) allowed for rounder characterizations than *Soap* does. Harris may have found the traditional sitcom to be confining compared to the storytelling she could do on *Soap*, but the template and formulas she forged in *The Golden Girls* nevertheless encouraged concise plots ending in a comforting return to stasis that clearly resonated with audiences then and now in ways *Soap* did not. It also made the series far more suited to success in syndication.

The Significance of *The Golden Girls*

The syndication market in the late 1980s was competitive, peaking with the sale of *The Cosby Show*, which commanded $4.4 million an episode.[43] *The Golden Girls* entered the market in 1990 during a downturn spurred by a glut in sitcom content. Although it did not command the price that *Who's the Boss?* had, reports suggest it was making $1.65 million an episode by March 1992.[44] Since 1988, Disney had been investing $100 million annually in television production, hiring *Roseanne*'s Matt Williams to cocreate *Home Improvement*, while *Charles in Charge* cocreator Michael Jacobs produced *Dinosaurs*.[45] Yet an economic recession further diminished demand for sitcoms in syndication, and in 1992, the Witt-Thomas-Harris team received a better deal to produce for Warner Bros., which allowed them to focus on features without giving up television. Consequently, Disney opted not to renew their contract in response to the changing market. The Disney executive Richard Frank noted, "It was a good relationship. . . . At the end of the day, this particular deal did not make sense for Disney—ultimately too costly in our projections."[46] The production company's final project with Touchstone Television was *The Golden Palace*, a Susan Harris–created spin-off of *The Golden Girls* without Bea Arthur. It premiered the fall after its parent series concluded, and it folded after one season. Witt-Thomas-Harris Productions returned to Touchstone Television in the 1998–99 season with *The Secret Lives of Men*, but it also was not renewed. Thereafter, the sitcom's "creator-deserter" officially retired from television producing. Touchstone Television found continued success with shows such as *My Wife and Kids* and *Alias*, but *The Golden Girls* remains perhaps its most profitable and influential show.

In a discussion of post-network television, Michael Z. Newman and Elana Levine discuss how "the showrunner-*auteur* functions as a commercial strategy of product differentiation and as a marker of quality."[47] Harris serves as an interesting example not only as a woman writer-producer of the network era but as one who really did not directly author many episodes of *The Golden Girls*: only nine over seven seasons. While Harris was not officially running the show, her persona allowed her co-producers and Touchstone Television to underscore the show's intelligence and originality.

Harris, in turn, leveraged that cultural capital into what she really wanted: artistic and industrial independence. Tony Thomas noted in 1987 that Harris was focusing on writing a feature for the production company, but "she reads all the scripts and is familiar with most of the stories."[48] Terry Grossman and Kathy Speer served as showrunners during the first four seasons, and Harris's partners, Paul Junger Witt and Tony Thomas, supervised read-throughs and rehearsals; but Harris remained the "face" in press coverage of what was going on behind the scenes at *Golden Girls*. In 1991, Harris admitted that she never wanted power, but, she said, "For me, it translates into being left alone, creatively."[49] In a time when women were denied creative opportunities and companies such as Disney micromanaged their contracted creative laborers, Harris leveraged her creative talent to redefine the "writer-producer" and give herself the time and space to work on her own terms. Her show also became an important platform for other women writers in television, including Winifred Hervey, Gail Parent, Liz Sage, and Kathy Speer, as well as the future showrunners Marc Cherry, Mitch Hurwitz, and Christopher Lloyd.

Furthermore, Harris's work on *The Golden Girls*, which Sofia Van Bauwel deems "the first successful series in the USA to focus on the lives of a group of women," provided a model for subsequent series such as *Desperate Housewives*, *Girls*, and *Sex and the City*.[50] Harris has dismissed the affinity between her work and *Designing Women* and *Sex and the City*, which she felt were less realistic and more formulaic.[51] Despite this resistance, the comedic power and alternative kinship found in women-centered ensemble comedies persist to this day—as does *The Golden Girls* through reruns and streaming.

Conclusion

That Disney of all companies was a relatively passive partner in *The Golden Girls* makes it an even more fascinating case study of television coproduction. It demonstrates how comedy—not animation—in film *and* television was central to Eisner and Katzenberg's early efforts at Disney, a strategy that clearly distinguished them from their executive predecessors. Touchstone Television achieved further success with *Empty Nest* (another Harris creation), *Blossom*, *Home Improvement*, and *Ellen*. Yet, from our current vantage, Disney is a company often associated with male-dominated media franchises, including Pixar, Star Wars, and the Marvel Cinematic Universe. But the fact remains that the company was revitalized and, in many ways, is still dependent on women and women's stories—not just the young, animated princesses in their castles but the mature, lively housemates sharing wisecracks and cheesecake at a kitchen table in Miami.

Notes

1. In media scholarship on Disney, Sean Griffin and John Wills have credited Eisner as the leader, whereas Douglas Gomery favors Eisner and Wells (but acknowledges Katzenberg); Thomas Schatz focuses on Eisner, Wells, and Katzenberg; and Janet Wasko points to "Team Disney" more broadly. Consult John Wills, *Disney Culture* (Rutgers University Press, 2017), 20; Sean Griffin, *Tinker Belles and Evil Queens: The Walt Disney Company from the Inside Out* (New York University Press, 2000), xv; Douglas Gomery, "Disney's Business History: A Reinterpretation," in *Disney Discourse: Producing the Magic Kingdom*, ed. Eric Smoodin (Routledge, 1994), 79–84; Thomas Schatz, "The Studio System and Conglomerate Hollywood," in *The Contemporary Hollywood Film Industry*, ed. Paul McDonald and Janet Wasko (Wiley-Blackwell, 2008), 23; Janet Wasko, *Understanding Disney: The Manufacture of Fantasy*, 2nd ed. (Polity, 2020), 34–37.

2. See, for example, David Landis and Jay McCormick, "Lotus Chief Leads in Pay; Top Execs' Pay Jumps 48% to $1.8M," *USA Today*, April 22, 1988; and Richard Turner, "Disney Seeks to End Big, Big Pictures as Executive Calls for Small, Small World," *Wall Street Journal*, January 30, 1991, B6.

3. Wasko, *Understanding Disney*, 20.

4. See, for example, Mark Potts, "New Team in Charge at Disney," *Washington Post*, October 28, 1984, G7.

5. *1985 Walt Disney Productions Annual Report* (Walt Disney Productions, 1985), 17.

6. For more on the dominant narrative of the Disney Renaissance, see Peter C. Kunze, *Staging a Comeback: Broadway, Hollywood, and the Disney Renaissance* (Rutgers University Press, 2023), 5–7.

7. David T. Friendly, "Team Disney—Flying High in Burbank," *Los Angeles Times*, July 28, 1985, T23.

8. Aljean Harmetz, "The Man Re-animating Disney," *New York Times*, December 29, 1985, SM16, SM18.

9. Susan Harris, in Robert Kubey, *Creating Television: Conversations with the People Behind 50 Years of American TV* (Lawrence Erlbaum, 2004), 127.

10. David Black, "Inside TV's 'Family Hour' Feud," *New York Times*, December 7, 1975, 37.

11. "Taming a Lusty Show: Censor's Memo Tells How," *Los Angeles Times*, June 27, 1977, C12.

12. Fred Silverman, quoted in Les Brown, "*Soap*, ABC's Explicit Comedy, Has Critics in Lather," *New York Times*, June 27, 1977, 40.

13. Susan Harris, quoted in Patrick Stoddart, "No Soft Soap for Susan," *Sunday Times*, July 28, 1985.

14. Paul Junger Witt, quoted in Aljean Harmetz, "NBC's *Golden Girls* Gambles on Grown-Ups," *New York Times*, September 22, 1985, H25.

15. Susan Harris, quoted in Tom Green, "Susan Harris: With Hits Like *Golden Girls*

and the New *Empty Nest*, She Has the Midas Touch in Creating Television Comedy," *USA Today*, October 19, 1988, 9D.

16. Tom Shales, "*It Takes Two* to Tangle but It's Just a Bore," *Washington Post*, October 14, 1982, D10.

17. Martha Bayles, "Old Folks, Old Jokes," *Wall Street Journal*, December 2, 1985, 18.

18. Noel Holston, "*Empty Nest* Is Funny, Has Crass Streak," *Star Tribune*, October 8, 1988, 6E.

19. Susan Harris, quoted in John Horn, "Still Playing Up to Men? Women Are Present Behind the Scenes, but They Have a Long Way to Go," *St. Louis Post-Dispatch*, June 4, 1990, 3D.

20. Susan Harris, quoted in Wayne Warga, "Susan Harris' *Soap*: Is the Bubble Going to Burst?," *Los Angeles Times*, October 23, 1977, O41.

21. Harris, quoted in Warga, "Susan Harris' *Soap*," O42.

22. Fred Rothenberg, "Her Scripts Are Golden," *The Record*, December 29, 1985.

23. Susan Harris, quoted in Harmetz, "NBC's *Golden Girls*," H25.

24. Harmetz, "NBC's *Golden Girls*," H25.

25. Stacey Wilson Hunt, "*The Golden Girls* Creators on Finding a New Generation of Fans and Giving George Clooney One of His Earliest Jobs," *Vulture*, March 3, 2017, www.vulture.com/2017/03/the-golden-girls-creators-on-finding-new-fans.html.

26. Ron Grover, *The Disney Touch: How a Daring Management Team Revived an Entertainment Empire* (Business One Irwin, 1991), 156.

27. Michael Eisner with Tony Schwartz, *Work in Progress: Risking Failure, Surviving Success* (Hyperion, 1999), 153.

28. Eisner with Schwartz, *Work in Progress*, 153.

29. Grover, *Disney Touch*, 156.

30. Susan Harris, *The Golden Girls* "Pilot" Script, First Draft, March 1, 1985, folder 3, box 1, Jay Sandrich Collection, American Heritage Center, Laramie, WY, 15–16.

31. Harris, *The Golden Girls* "Pilot" Script, First Draft, 51.

32. Susan Harris, *The Golden Girls* "Pilot" Script, Final Draft, April 12, 1985, folder 3, box 1, Jay Sandrich Collection, American Heritage Center, Laramie, WY, 3.

33. Harris, *The Golden Girls* "Pilot" Script, Final Draft, 36.

34. Harris, *The Golden Girls* "Pilot" Script, Final Draft, 19.

35. Harris, in Kubey, *Creating Television*, 134.

36. Hunt, "*The Golden Girls* Creators."

37. Bruce Paltrow, quoted in Kristen Baldwin, "How *The Golden Girls* Creator Susan Harris Changed TV Comedy Forever—and Why She Doesn't Watch It Now," *Entertainment Weekly*, October 15, 2018, https://ew.com/tv/susan-harris-golden-girls-soap-oral-history/.

38. Tom Shales, "*The Golden Girls*: Miami Spice," *Washington Post*, September 14, 1985, C1, C7.

39. Bob Knight, "Year of the Sitcom for TV Nets," *Variety*, December 4, 1985, 125.

40. Susan Harris, quoted in Sander Vanocur, "*Soap* in ABC's Eye," *Washington Post*, November 3, 1976, D6.

41. FoundationINTERVIEWS, "Executive Richard H Frank on 'The Golden Girls'—TelevisionAcademy.com/Interviews," YouTube, November 27, 2018, www.youtube.com/watch?v=dfZG6uyxXzo.

42. Jon Anderson, "*Girls* Series Is Solid Gold for Harris," *Chicago Tribune*, October 20, 1985, G3.

43. John Lippman, "Too Costly for Prime Time," *Los Angeles Times*, March 22, 1992, D1.

44. Lippman, "Too Costly for Prime Time," D1.

45. Bernard Weinraub, "Disney Now a Network TV Power," *New York Times*, December 9, 1991, D1.

46. Richard Frank, quoted in John Lippman, "Disney Lets Contract with TV Hit-Maker Team of Witt Thomas Harris Go to Warner," *Los Angeles Times*, March 12, 1992, OCD1.

47. Michael Z. Newman and Elana Levine, *Legitimating Television: Media Convergence and Cultural Status* (Routledge, 2012), 42.

48. Tony Thomas, in Nancy Mills, "*Golden Girls* Polishes It Scripts," *Los Angeles Times*, October 30, 1987, H28.

49. Susan Harris, quoted in Deborah Starr Seibel, "The Golden Touch," *Chicago Tribune*, October 13, 1991, F3.

50. Sofie Van Bauwel, "Invisible Golden Girls? Post-feminist Discourses and Female Ageing Bodies in Contemporary Television Fiction," *Feminist Media Studies* 18, no. 1 (2018): 22.

51. Baldwin, "How *The Golden Girls* Creator."

INTERVIEW

Creating *The Golden Girls*

How does *The Golden Girls* even happen? It seems so incredibly unlikely to have a sitcom centered around four old broads?

Marsha Posner Williams, Co-Producer
Susan Harris is one of the greatest half-hour writers ever. She wrote the first twenty-two episodes of *Soap* all by herself. I know, because I was her secretary. They're very convincing—[creators] Paul Junger Witt, Tony Thomas, and Susan Harris—when they want to be, and the fact that when they started casting and they have this astonishing cast, you know the network had to. They just had to give it a shot, and who knew?

And how did you become involved?

Marc Sotkin, Executive Producer
I came to the project because I had done four years of *It's a Living* for Witt/Thomas. We all knew we were only going to do one hundred episodes because it was in syndication. That's all they needed. So, I left to do a different project with another company, and I wasn't really happy in that situation. So, after only about two days, I called Paul Witt, and I said I knew they were looking for somebody for *Golden Girls*, and I said, "Have you found a new showrunner yet? How about Marc Sotkin?" He said, "That's interesting. Let me talk to Tony. Let me talk to the network. Let me talk to the ladies." So, the network was just fine with that, and then I went to lunch with the ladies. I chew with my mouth closed, I cleaned up pretty good, so I got their nod, and that's how I got the job.

Now, I didn't have a big vision for the show. When you take over a hit show, and they give you the keys, and they basically tell you "Don't f--k this up." So, the only thing I did was, I just said, "We're not making jokes about Bea's appearance anymore." That was the biggest thing I did. This isn't *Star*

Trek, and we're not putting appliances on a woman's face before she tells this joke. So, I didn't want to do those anymore.

I really hadn't watched the show that much. So, when I started, the first writers started handing in "picture it, Sicily" stories, and I didn't think they were that funny. And then Nina Feinberg, who was our line producer, came in and said, "No, no, no. Everybody loves those. We do these." I'm not stupid, so I said fine. We're doing "picture it" jokes. The jokes that come to my mind are different than the jokes that come into Barry [Fanaro] and Mort [Nathan]. So yeah, there was a difference in tone, and I know some fans prefer the first four years and some prefer ours.

Marsha Posner Williams, Co-Producer

I was doing a show with [Witt/Thomas/Harris Productions] called *Hail to the Chief*. Patty Duke played the first female president of the United States It went up and down in seven episodes, seven of the funniest episodes ever. By the way, ABC promoted it as the show that would offend everybody. That's how they actually promoted it, and I guess it did!

When I was finishing the last couple of episodes of that, they were doing the pilot of *The Golden Girls* with Charles Levin. I came in when we were doing some reshoots for changes on *The Golden Girls*, because, you know, the entrance to the patio used to be on that side of the set, then it moved to that side of the set, then they removed Charles Levin. He just disappeared. That's the power of the pencil! In the beginning, I don't think that the cast thought that young people could write this show. And I think they had a big problem with that. But after that first table read, they actually applauded.

Wayne Williams, Photographer

I was a photographer in Los Angeles, born and raised in LA. The industry was a door that I felt like, as a photographer, I could walk into if I needed work and started my career. I wanted to make it in more of the advertising world, but that was, for the most part, based in New York. So, even though I made lots of trips to New York with my portfolio, to knock on doors, and I got jobs out of New York, I found myself wanting to stay in Los Angeles, and the main industry here was television and film. I knocked on the door at ABC Television, and they said, "Well, you're overqualified for everything, but if you want, we need somebody to go onto a set and shoot pictures." . . . I remember walking onto one of the sets for ABC, which was a relatively well-known but new show called *Soap*. I always go up and introduce myself to the state manager and the camera guys because they're moving their cameras around, and I gotta get in between them, but I can't block them, and I don't want to get in their way. I go up to the stage manager, and I say to him, "Is there anything you need me to know?" and he, of course, tells me, "Just don't bump into the cameras, and whatever you do, don't piss that woman off over there!" And he points down about two or three sets, and there's this girl with a clipboard and about ten people standing around her, and she's directing them. And, well, little did I know that turned out to be my future wife. [So] when *The Golden Girls* came along, I had already done a number of the other shows that Marsha worked on shooting group shots and stage shots for Witt/Thomas/Harris, because they wanted to have the ability to promote the shows themselves.

How involved was Disney?

Marsha Posner Williams, Co-Producer
It was one of the first sitcoms that Disney ever got involved with, because Disney had a subcompany called Touchstone [now called ABC Signature Studios], which was the deficit financing company for the show. So, it was NBC and then Touchstone.

They said, "Here's the money, and here's some tickets to the park, and here's some special events at the park." . . . I still have a Disney Mickey Mouse watch that Disney gave us all during *The Golden Girls*, and I have a Mickey Mouse wooden statue that's about two feet tall. That's the only *Golden Girls* [stuff] I even have, besides what people just give me, merchandise, all that unlicensed stuff.

As someone there the whole run of the show, how did it change from beginning to end?

Isabel Omero, Production Associate/Script Supervisor, Writer
The early days were about discovery and creation. Witnessing the first St. Olaf story, the first "Picture it, Sicily" run, etcetera. That was one kind of excitement. In the latter days, it was about execution. After years of those bits, the challenge was to make them funny despite the audience's familiarity. It amazed me how our writers brought the funny every week.

CHAPTER 3

Miami Thrice

The Golden Girls in Rerun Syndication

TAYLOR COLE MILLER

In summer 2020, Hallmark announced the new Rose Nylund Christmas Keepsake ornament, the first launched in what would become an annual installment of *Golden Girls*–themed ornaments and a new line of merchandise eliciting for viewers both excitement and contempt in equal measure. That is because ardent fans of *The Golden Girls* have a strong love-hate relationship with Hallmark—an "eat dirt and die, trash" attitude. While *The Golden Girls* now appears variably in reruns on Paramount-owned cable channels (like TV Land, Logo TV, and CMT), Hallmark Channel has been the consistent, reliable cable home for the show since 2009, habituating viewers to prime-time and evening airings of the show that they have incorporated into their daily rituals.

Even if many fans report owning the DVDs or have a Hulu subscription with all episodes available to stream in full, as I discuss later in this chapter, they still claim that they prefer watching *The Golden Girls* live on Hallmark because of habit and the liveness of connection. They enjoy what Raymond Williams calls "televisual flow," liveness, and the commercials of the Hallmark Channel, which provide built-in breaks for tooth-brushing, face-washing, and bathroom-going without missing any of the jokes.[1] Hallmark was able to bank on its viewers' ritualistic connections to *The Golden Girls*—from years of them watching reruns on the channel—into a merchandising line not just of Keepsake ornaments but of numerous other products for a show whose original run ended decades ago. The company's successes with merch in its stores incentivizes Hallmark to continue to syndicate the show, and this example demonstrates one of the many ways in which the industry continues to leverage second-run syndication in new and exciting ways. With thirty-five years of successful syndicated runs in broadcasting, cable, and streaming and a fanbase so dedicated to those reruns that they have become daily rituals, *The Golden Girls* is an exemplary case study for historicizing how the industry sells its properties and appeals to broadcasters, cablers, and viewers, even long after its stars are gone.

The Golden Girls rerunning on cable channels means episodes play simultaneously across the nation—unlike in traditional broadcast syndication, in which stations air the show at whatever times they choose. And unlike the original airings, today's audiences can log in to one of dozens of different dedicated social media groups and connect with others who are also watching these cable reruns to chat in real time. But to fans, something dreadful comes to Hallmark Channel every October, interrupting this satisfying, dependable ritual of watching reruns of *The Golden Girls*: Christmas. Beginning in late October and running through January each year, Hallmark Channel's "Countdown to Christmas" TV movie marathons preempt the daily flow of *The Golden Girls*, and the tenor of camaraderie evident in social media posts by Hallmark viewers throughout the year changes to almost daily hate-posting about the channel and its Christmas movies.

Because *The Golden Girls* remains one of the best-performing and most dependably syndicated programs in American television history, fans in such groups commonly echo themes of ritual and comfort that the show brings into their everyday lives. In 2024, evidence of the show's unprecedented successes in broadcast, cable, and streaming syndication created a new cultural phenomenon, leading to a surge in *Golden Girls* merchandise (including action figures, bobble heads, chia pets, even skateboards), a *Golden Girls* cruise, *Golden Girls* kitchen pop-ups (in Los Angeles, New York, Miami, and Chicago), and even a dedicated fan convention: GoldenCon: Thank You for Being a Fan. Because of this late-in-life success coming in large part from the steady stream of *The Golden Girls* in syndication, so that a company like Hallmark would even benefit from a line of merch, considering its life after initial airing is both textually meaningful and illustrates the key role syndication continues to play in media production and audience cultures. Elsewhere, I have referred this analytical distinction as "retextuality," which argues that "in syndicated flows, the production labor endeavored by syndicators, executives, programmers, production staff, and all their marketing departments" may reauthor texts, resulting in new texts worthy of new critical analyses.[2]

Fans enjoying the show's iconic rattan fan-arm living room set as it was displayed at Golden-Con. (Photo by Taylor Cole Miller)

The project of studying *The Golden Girls* in its original run is certainly an important historical investigation, but studying the syndicated lives of episodes for a show that has structured many of its viewers' daily rituals for decades provides new ways of thinking about interactions among texts, audiences, and producers, especially given that syndicated shows are the texts through which some have their first contact with a show. In this chapter, I use *The Golden Girls* as a case study to demonstrate how the syndication industry crafts narratives about its properties to sell episode packages in syndication, how those narratives can retextualize programs to suit the needs of the marketplace over the course of decades, and how the industry's successes in syndication can now be studied through the publicly available social media labor of fans. Specifically, I argue that gender has come to play a material role in the syndication of *The Golden Girls* from its marketing materials to its audiences. And I focus on two different stages in the syndication of *The Golden Girls*: broadcast syndication and cable syndication, both of which contextualize the more substantive discussion of streaming in chapter 1. Before delving into the gendered strategies of syndicators of *The Golden Girls* specifically, it is important first to lay the groundwork with some basic definitions of television syndication and its industrial function.

Definitions

A core tactic of the television business is to repeat its successes. It certainly does so through reunions, reboots, sequels, and prequels, but it does so most profitably through reruns (properly called "second-run syndication"), where, the adage goes, the *real* money is. At the time of *The Golden Girls'* production, it was common for independent television studios to tape episodes of a show for more money than they would be paid by networks to air them, with the hope of building an audience that would make the show successful one day in reruns. This practice is called "deficit financing," and co-producer Marsha Posner Williams explained to me that *The Golden Girls* was deficit financed by Touchstone Television (for Witt/Thomas/Harris Productions) and distributed by Buena Vista, both separate arms of the Walt Disney Company, a more thorough discussion of which can be found in chapter 2.[3]

Independent studios' shows like *The Golden Girls* needed to "make it to syndication," meaning they had to become popular enough in their original network runs to justify taping at least one hundred episodes, known in the industry as a "hundred-episode package." That number of episodes is attractive to station programmers for reruns because with that big of a package, they can air the show every weekday for twenty weeks without repeating any episodes, a practice called "stripping." Thus, that old industry joke: if you want to strip, you'd better have a big package. Which, to quote Blanche Devereaux, reminds me, I gotta give Charlie Milburn a call.

With a big enough package in hand, the distribution arms of television studios go "door to door" to sell those episodes to local television stations, network affiliates, and station groups in different media markets across the country in a process called "broadcast syndication." These stations will then air the shows they syndicate at whatever time of day they choose. Unlike broadcast stations, cable channels, meanwhile, pick up exclusive cable rights to syndicate shows simultaneously on their national feeds, stopping

Co-producer Marsha Posner Williams; author of *The Golden Girls Forever*, Jim Colucci; and Taylor Cole Miller pose behind one of many photo displays at the 2023 Golden-Con. (Photo by Taylor Cole Miller)

competing national cable channels from syndicating the same packages they do. With 185 episodes, *The Golden Girls* has enough episodes that it might be able to syndicate one hundred episodes on Hallmark and nearly as many on Paramount channels (TV Land, CMT, Logo), and then the two entities swap contracted episodes, leaving viewers options to watch their favorite show on a variety of cable channels.

Typically, the more popular a show is on the original network, the higher, more competitive bids the syndicator will receive in broadcast and later cable syndication, pumping more money into the show, which pays off the production deficit and enriches profit participants. Despite a successful run on a network, however, the industry worries about racist, sexist, and queerphobic attitudes of local audiences, and small-town station managers sometimes have a chilling effect on the successful sales of shows featuring people of color, women, and queer folks. With Bea Arthur playing the eponymous role fifteen years earlier, *Maude* became just such a cautionary tale for Buena Vista when it came time to sell *The Golden Girls* in syndication, because *Maude* flopped—a big, floppy pancreas, Rose.

The Golden Girls Syndication Timeline

BROADCAST SYNDICATION

Despite *Maude* consistently rating in the top ten for network premieres, group and local station managers refused to buy reruns of the show for, according to Norman Lear, sexist reasons. "*Maude* had been a big hit on the network," Lear told me. "But the message coming back from guys buying for stations, and they were all guys, was 'I don't need that ballbuster on my station.'"[4] First appearing on *All in the Family*, Arthur's Maude Finlay was unapologetically liberal and a feminist foil to the "lovable bigot" Archie Bunker. In the show's most controversial episode, Maude decides to have an abortion. That episode aired just before the Supreme Court decided in *Roe v. Wade*, and it was penned by future *Golden Girls* creator Susan Harris.

After the *Roe* decision, and foreshadowing the show's flop in syndication, the expanding Religious Right called for harsh protests against the summer rerunning of "Maude's Dilemma." CBS affiliates in thirty-five regions declined to air it, and seven corporations also backed out of advertising.[5] The broadcast carried a disclaimer in the opening: "Tonight's episode of *Maude* was originally broadcast in November of 1972. Since it deals with 'Maude's Dilemma' as she contemplates the possibility of abortion, you may wish to refrain from watching it, if you believe the broadcast may disturb you or others in your family." Even with *Maude*'s high performances in the ratings, the fourth most popular network show that season, Lear believed that cultural perceptions about Arthur, gender, and the show's feminist overtones made for an unwelcome debut in the syndication marketplace. With this Bea Arthur–shaped problem characterizing *Maude*'s syndication, Buena Vista decided to be proactive in developing a comprehensive strategy to sell *The Golden Girls*, knowing that it, just like *Maude*, would be problematically gendered in the eyes of buyers, but, as Dorothy herself once quipped, "I am beautiful, men find me desirable, and people want to be my friend."

Reporting in the trades predicted a bright future for *The Golden Girls*, but Arthur and Harris's history with *Maude* and the show's association with older women incentivized Buena Vista to commission six hundred pages of research to persuade stations they had a "golden" opportunity if they purchased it.[6] "Buena Vista hopes to prove that the sitcom does not only skew to adults 50-plus and women, but that it also has attracted a wide range of demographic groups in a variety of time slots."[7] NBC immediately picked up the show for daytime reruns on weekdays at 11:00 a.m. (ET), where it rated highly in the prized female demographic and gave data buoying the show's strength as a syndicated show.[8] But its appearances in daytime, traditionally targeted to female viewers, further cemented the show's identity as a sitcom for women. Knowing that local station managers and buyers across the country were primarily white men, Buena Vista needed to creatively rebrand the show's appeal for men and ageist buyers, creating one of the oddest, queerest, and funniest syndicated advertising campaigns ever printed.

THE TOUGHEST BUNCH OF MOTHERS ON TV

With research in hand, beginning in the summer of 1988, months ahead of selling the show, Buena Vista began the "toughest mothers" campaign in industry trades that it knew male station managers would read, like *Broadcasting* and *Variety*. The campaign's ostensible goal was to demonstrate *The Golden Girls*' appeal for diverse audiences, although the ads really target men. Each of the ads features photo-realistic illustrations of Dorothy, Blanche, Rose, and Sophia dressed as the culture's stereotypically toughest characters, including mobsters, bikers, bank robbers, and gangsters. Each is paired with headlines asserting the powerful dominance of the show ("Selling like gangbusters!" "Golden Girls any night. Domination any day." "In this neighborhood, you need protection."), and most feature the same motto: "The toughest bunch of mothers on TV."

The descriptions included in each ad detail how *The Golden Girls* dominates other typically male programming. One ad, headlined "Meet the local muscle," features the women holding submachine guns and shotguns and reads, "They shot down everything the networks could throw at them. Action hours, sitcoms, the Olympics, the World Series, and even such blockbuster movies as *Superman* and *Rocky III*. . . . If they've got the firepower to blow away Superman and the World Series, imagine what they could do for you."[9] Another ad features the Girls dressed as leather-clad bikers and all holding their individual Emmy Awards.[10] It states, "They broke the backs of two networks with a wink and a smile," and describes the show going head to head with ABC and CBS and winning: "Just ask the two networks they left in tears . . . they took on the toughest programming, targeted at prime demos."[11] Another ad using the same image says, *The Golden Girls* "has never lost an award (or an audience) to the competition. That's why it will totally dominate any daypart, any audience, and every other station in town. . . . Its universal appeal cuts across racial, sexual and demographic groups, to deliver blockbuster audiences week after week."[12] One ad has the Girls dressed as mafia men in fedoras with the headline, "They'll make you an offer you can't refuse." This ad focuses on the show's proven appeal against all demographics because "it's the most wanted show in syndication. . . . Four funny ladies that mean serious business. Who can say no to that?"[13]

Perhaps my favorite ad from this campaign simply shows the women in silhouette walking down a dark alley after tagging "GG" on the side of a brick building. It is accompanied by the headline, "Meet the toughest bunch of mothers on TV."[14] These ~~godfathers~~ *godgrandmas* are parodying male media culture and making fun of "dangerous" masculinity—spilling way outside the contained gender roles they are expected to play. This campaign works to showcase *The Golden Girls*' appeal for straight men and to counter concerns about Arthur's troubled performance as the titular character on *Maude* in syndication. However, this very queer ad campaign perhaps ironically represents the Girls as hypermasculine and thus incredibly male dominating. After all, who needs a Clyde when you have four Bonnies?

After several months, Buena Vista switched up its *Golden Girls* campaign to target the yuppy egos of station managers and buyers with its "Golden Card" ads. This campaign focused on the show as an investment property with unrivaled flexibility, sure to make these executives part of a rich boys' club. "Join the exclusive group of discriminating programmers who will reap the benefits of carrying the Gold."[15] One ad features a young white male station manager on his private jet with aviators in hand. "Do you know me? My name isn't a household word, but with my NBC affiliate's lineup of top off-net sitcoms, households all over Atlanta are tuning in."[16]

Each of these ads features a Golden Card (with Dorothy, Sophia, Blanche, and Rose's faces) and the station manager's name. "Don't leave *your* homes without it." What both these campaigns illustrate are the ways in which the industry predicts a show's resonance with group and local station managers and their audiences and how they find ways to compensate for the systemic racism, sexism, and homophobia inherent in syndicating shows featuring women, people of color, and queer people. To successfully sell shows, syndicators become authors retextualizing the audience's understanding of a show, as with gendered appeal in the case of *The Golden Girls*.

Buena Vista's research, creative campaigns, and sales strategies were effective. Scoring early network daytime reruns on NBC—preempting *Wheel of Fortune*—demonstrated how nimble *The Golden Girls* already was in attracting female audiences while counterprogramming a variety of genres. NBC also swapped *Win, Lose, or Draw* with *227* to form a sitcom block in daytime, a natural match between the shows discussed in more detail in chapter 10.[17] Although *The Golden Girls* fell short of the syndicated successes of *The Cosby Show* on its first outing, it still dominated the broadcast syndication marketplace its first year in reruns as 1990's number-one off-network show.[18] After strong runs over the airwaves for several years, it was time for the show to try cable syndication, where it did quickly outpace *Cosby*.[19] As with its outing in the broadcast syndication marketplace, gender also became an important factor in selling the show for narrowcasting cable channels, but in a directly opposite way.

CABLE SYNDICATION: LIFETIME: TELEVISION FOR WOMEN

After several years in broadcast syndication, in 1997, *The Golden Girls* found a national cable home on Lifetime, a channel narrowcasting to women with the motto, "Lifetime: Television for Women." The show was rated TV-PG and aired afternoons at 5:00 and 5:30 p.m. (ET) as a lead-in to reruns of the channel's original program *Supermarket Sweep*. Hoping it would appeal to women, Lifetime used *The Golden Girls* to counterprogram *The Oprah Winfrey Show*, then practically unbeatable in the ratings for women audiences.[20] Months in with some success, Lifetime began also running *The Golden Girls* overnight in late fringe as a lead-in for paid programming.[21] As the show was a consistent and dependable performer there, Lifetime then added more episodes, running *The Golden Girls* as a reliable show in early late night, counterprogramming male late-night comedians and tucking its audience into bed each night with women instead of men on their screens, closing their nightly routines with the reruns. Lifetime syndicated *The Golden Girls* alongside pickups *Sisters*, *Martha Stewart Living*, and *Unsolved Mysteries*, all of which contextualized the channel's original programming aimed at women, including *Denise Austin's Daily Workout* (an exercise show), *Kids These Days* (a program about raising children), and *The Main Ingredient with Bobby Flay* (a cooking show). The channel also started a strategy greenlighting original made-for-TV movies like *Almost Golden: The Jessica Sanvitch Story* and *Chasing the Dragon*, while producing documentary specials on topics like child abuse, AIDS, breast cancer, and foster care.[22]

"It is my goal to make Lifetime and women synonymous," said Douglas McCormick, Lifetime's president and chief executive. "Just the way when you think of MTV you think of teens, when you think of Lifetime, you think of women."[23] To further legitimize the channel's feminist intentions, McCormick asserted that affiliation "through formal relationships with liberal feminist organizations, particularly the National Organization of Women (NOW) and the MS Foundation."[24] Embracing the feminist appeal of *The*

Golden Girls, McCormick used the show to inform women about the channel's brand and its original programming. By narrowcasting to women, Lifetime gained commercial marketplace novelty, appealing to advertisers also hoping to target women specifically. In a more liberal political climate, Bea Arthur's unapologetically feminist reputation was no longer a liability for selling the show but rather an asset that might be a life raft for Lifetime's original programming. This example illustrates how, in marketing the show, syndicators once again crafted gendered narratives to help it succeed in syndication, albeit in the opposite direction for cable. *The Golden Girls* remained a consistent performer on Lifetime, successfully attracting as many as thirteen million weekly viewers from 1997 to 2009.[25] In 2009, Lifetime's cable rights to the show quietly expired, and *The Golden Girls* moved to WE tv (Women's Entertainment) and Hallmark Channel, the latter on which it remains all year . . . at least until October.

So far, I have discussed syndication in relation to the larger television industry, highlighting two ways in which syndicators used gendered narratives to appeal to executives and buyers of *The Golden Girls* in both broadcasting and cable syndication. But how does the syndication industry create narratives and excitement for reruns specifically for fans? With DVDs and streaming making shows immediately and always accessible, how do syndicators incentivize viewers to turn to reruns on television at all, and why does gender continue to be a meaningful calculus in television for viewers when content is increasingly disconnected from platform?

Audiences and Syndication: Thank You for Hating Hallmark

In the digital era, beyond focusing on selling *The Golden Girls* to executives and buyers of programming within local markets and station groups, syndicators must also direct their efforts toward engaging with the show's fanbase directly. Syndicators for older programs often have a lot of new work to do to continuously add value to their intellectual property. Despite originating well before the social media era, the enduring success of *The Golden Girls* has been upheld by syndicators through the development and active management of a comprehensive social media presence across various platforms. These official profiles constantly create new knowledge about the show by offering never-before-seen content to continuously engage the fanbase, including the release of high definition photography such as stills from the set. They hope, in response, fans will share these posts in one of the dozens of dedicated fan groups, comment, and watch reruns of the show to engage with one another, too, in real time. They also make high-quality gifs available for social media users. Bea Arthur's signature long stare has undoubtedly been a reply to something stupid that all fans have commented at one point or another.

Although these strategies of habituating viewers to a show have taken on a new form through the use of social media, a history of *The Golden Girls'* own syndication demonstrates how syndicators and executives have long attempted to create the habit of watching for viewers and how that habit tended to be gendered. When *The Golden Girls* first cleared for syndication, NBC began rerunning episodes in daytime to appeal to women. Jacqueline Smith, NBC's vice president of daytime programs, said these network reairings do not hurt the prime-time showings of the series but instead begin to "develop a habit for the show."[26] Robert Jacquemin, then senior vice president of Buena Vista Television, acknowledged this tactic by syndicators and added that comedies work especially well as habit forming, given that "the stories are timeless and wear well over a long period of time. That's what the rerun business is all about."[27] While many prime-time sitcoms typically cater to male or at least gender-diverse audiences, *The Golden Girls* originally carved out an identity that uniquely resonated with women, making it a distinctive asset for daytime programmers looking for female-driven, safe comedy.

The practice of "rerunning" is not merely a benefit for the industry; it is also enjoyed by fans who take specific comfort in rewatching. Henry Jenkins argues that the experience of rereading texts "must be understood as a central aspect of the reception of both television programs and contemporary films," especially if every reading is already a rereading in an intertextual world.[28] Throughout the COVID-19 pandemic, numerous press articles covered the phenomenon of rewatching as a form of comforting self-care, creating listicles of comfort shows that quarantiners should watch, including *The Golden Girls*. The Girls' "whip-smart jokes complemented the cheesecake-heavy moments and became one of the few medicines I wasn't prescribed but so needed," wrote *Entertainment Weekly*.[29] A spokeswoman for Hulu told *The New York Times*, meanwhile, that "comfort viewing" was more popular than usual, adding that in April 2020 alone, its viewers streamed nearly eleven million hours of *The Golden Girls*.[30] And *Variety* created a graphic declaring *The Golden Girls*, *Schitt's Creek*, and *Tiger King* as the pandemic's winners.[31] Jenny L. Nelson argues that rewatching dislocates a text from time, allowing us to connect more to our memories of first experiencing a text. And truths about the comforts of rewatching specifically for reasons of gender and sexuality can be extrapolated from the work of several scholars, including Derek Kompare, Brett Farmer, Alexander Doty, Quinlan Miller, and me.[32] After Lifetime's dedicated campaign to appeal to women in 1997 at the same time the networks began greenlighting more gay programming, Lifetime would have discovered that it could lean into its acquired syndicated properties like *The Golden Girls* to appeal to supposedly lucrative LGBTQ audiences, hoping to capture some of its "Dorothy Dollars." But although such an appeal would certainly have been discussed by the channel, I have reviewed dozens of hours of Lifetime flow from that time but do not see any obvious direct appeals to gay men.

Occasionally, the joy in cable reruns on channels narrowcasting to specific audiences, then, is how the process of retextuality makes a program feel like it was created for a specific community. Logo TV, a Paramount cable channel targeted to LGBTQ viewers, for instance, aired *The Golden Girls* in blocks with similarly queer-friendly shows in a programming block it called "Sitcom Therapy," surely an obvious form of comfort TV, but one in which the Girls were surrounded by ads, bumpers, and teasers celebrating queer life and queer programming, particularly the show's appeal to gay men.[33] In collecting data on everyday viewers, Nielsen has not historically asked for data about sexual orientation. So, while channels geared toward women, Black audiences, or Spanish-speaking households have neutral ratings data about their target markets, Logo TV has had to rely on cultural discourses and vibes. Syndicators of *The Golden Girls* once again would have crafted gendered narratives to specify the appeal for certain kinds of audiences like gay men by using or publicizing statements from talent or in public or social media discourse. According to Betty White, for instance, while the show was still taping, it was not uncommon to find it playing live in gay clubs across the United States. "They'd all watch the show, and then at nine-thirty, they'd turn off the TV and start dancing again. [I] think that for some reason, gay men just like old ladies. I don't know why, but they do!"[34] Episodes on Logo TV were accompanied by "gayest moments" clips featuring montages of especially queer scenes from the show stitched up with bumpers for Logo TV that show images of gay men watching their television sets. While industry forces retextualizing shows may make them joyful for LGBTQ viewers, sometimes the joy of reruns is merely in the scheduling.

The Golden Girls is often programmed in two-episode blocks as viewers are settling in for the night. Instead of channel surfing as they get ready for bed, audiences can instead reliably tune in to Hallmark Channel to enjoy episodes selected by programmers, serving a soothing, maternalistic

Taylor Cole Miller hosts a panel featuring Monte Markham, who played Blanche's gay brother, Clayton. Here, with some help from the audience, they reproduce a beloved scene featuring Markham in "Sister of the Bride" (S06E14). (Photo by Taylor Cole Miller)

role for viewers seeking comfort and care—not just hardcore fans but also casual viewers. Through consistent rerunning and rewatching, viewers have ritualized *The Golden Girls* into a nightly habit, a comfortable, safe routine to make sense of a world turned upside down.

It is common in social media groups dedicated to the show to read viewers discussing the joy of reruns, suggesting that syndication provides a relief from decision fatigue. People make choices all day; syndication allows them to come home, turn on the TV, and not have to make decisions about what to watch. By making *The Golden Girls* a reliable and organic part of their evenings that happens with or without them, fans effectively ritualize the show as part of their daily habits—it becomes a structural part of their day-to-day lives.

To apply Dennis Porter's notion of "soap time" to syndication, in watching television "by appointment on every day of the working week, real time intersects with fantasy time. . . . [Fantasy] comes to occupy a structuring place" in a viewer's real life. Part of these viewers' days are constructed around the flow of syndication television. Porter refers to this concept as "cuddle literature" for grown-ups, which "takes place, like a bedtime story, according to a fixed routine and within a trusted setting. It raises problems, but it raises them in such a way and under such conditions that potential threats are effectively neutralized for the viewer."[35] One social media user on Facebook explained to me, "I have Hulu and the DVDs, but I still watch on cable. For

Drag queen Sadie Pines, a name-play on Sophia's former home, Shady Pines, hosts the Golden-Con costume contest. (Photo by Taylor Cole Miller)

me, watching on cable makes it seem like they are still on TV." Because many of these viewers have seen every episode multiple times and can even quote them, there is not as much insistence on close, active viewership. They can do other things and thus become programmers of an intersecting sequence of the show's flow—their own lives. They are so innately familiar with the intricacies of television programming that they have learned to hang their rituals on the skeletal structures of the television business.

On the one hand, these kinds of comments give scholars a chance to complicate fan identities, as we tend to think of fan engagement as an active practice when, through the lens of a rerun, we can see how the syndication business relies on the many passive ways that fans and casual viewers continuously engage with shows out of habit. On the other hand, social media like Facebook and Twitter allow for ritual viewers to deepen their engagement by connecting with other viewers as they watch episodes live on cable and comment live in one of dozens of dedicated social media groups, a practice not possible during the original airings or in broadcast syndication. By watching reruns airing on Hallmark together as an online community bolstered by industry tactics in social media, such viewers actualize what was once considered an imagined community of viewers. This practice of social engagement—connecting other fans on social media to the routine of rewatching, making connection with others during a ritual its own habit—is what becomes especially important every October when Hallmark preempts *The Golden Girls* for its original Christmas movies and daily hateposting begins, another form of social media camaraderie that fans of the Girls have found to comfort themselves. But the work of syndicators on habituating viewers to watch the show every night on Hallmark means that many viewers still continue to watch Hallmark live—or hate-watch Christmas movies—and they enjoy the delicious scorn of a cable channel by their companions in viewing.

Conclusion

HBO's half-hour dramedy series *Looking*, which explores the lives of a group of young gay men living in modern-day San Francisco, closed its first season not with a focus on the messy romance story lines of the leading character but rather with a loving nod to *The Golden Girls* and the Girls' place in the bonds of queer friendship. The series lead, Patrick (Jonathan Groff), finds his roommate, Augustín (Frankie J. Alvarez), curled up on the bed, heartbroken. Though they had been fighting, Patrick crawls into bed and comforts his friend by turning on an episode of *The Golden Girls* (the fifth-season episode "Dancing in the Dark"). As the scene dips to black and the credits begin to roll, Cindy Fee's voice begins singing that familiar theme: "Thank you for being a friend . . ." This simple, loving gesture of friendship inspired articles and tweets about how *The Golden Girls* became and remains an important text and a habit for queer people who considered this scene a kind of snapshot of their own lives, in which syndicated reruns can form a structuring place.

In a *BuzzFeed* article, Louis Peitzman explores the ritualistic relationship between *The Golden Girls* and its many queer viewers, who habitually finish their evenings tucked in and comforted by late-night reruns on channels like Lifetime and Hallmark. In the piece, Goff explains that during the taping of *Looking*, gay members of the cast and crew were talking about their "obsession with *The Golden Girls*": "we were saying how the characters are kind of like Rose and Blanche and Dorothy." Peitzman explores the common gendered resonance the show has especially with queer viewers, writing that "while some credit the raunchy humor and female characters for its appeal (surely part of the equation), . . . [*The Golden Girls*'] pervasive themes are innately queer, which is why the show has been and continues to be a comfort to men who are gay or just questioning. *The Golden Girls* isn't just a TV show: It's family."[36] The business of television syndication relies on the perpetual endeavor to establish and redefine the identities of its properties, tailoring specific narratives that can alter their significance for prospective buyers across independent television broadcasters, network affiliates, cable channels, and streaming platforms alike. Those narratives and appeals are often gendered in order to cater to or redefine the intended audiences, who, with more industry labor, will become so addicted to syndicated properties that they will continue to support them even when other opportunities for viewing are available. With enough luck, those viewers will make watching the show a habit, a nightly routine. Miami is nice, so we'll watch it thrice. *The Golden Girls* has been and will continue to be a comforting show in rerun syndication; again and again and again, it provides viewers a strong and comforting family structure guided by the *toughest bunch of mothers on TV.*

Notes

1. Raymond Williams, *Television: Technology and Cultural Form*, ed. Ederyn Williams (Routledge, 1997).

2. Taylor Cole Miller, "*Rewitched*: Retextuality and the Queering of *Bewitched*," *Camera Obscura: Feminism, Culture, and Media Studies* 36, no. 3 (2021), https://doi.org/10.1215/02705346-9349315.

3. Marsha Posner Williams, interview by Taylor Cole Miller, March 10, 2023.

4. Norman Lear, interview by Taylor Cole Miller, October 16, 2017.

5. Also, none of the six 30-second spots on the August 14th broadcast were picked up by a sponsor. *Broadcasting*. "'Maude' Dropouts Threatened by Boycott," August 20, 1973.

6. Kim Masters, "Syndication's Magic Kingdom," *Channels: The Business of Communication*, January 16, 1989, 40.

7. "On the Road to Off-Network," *Broadcasting*, October 9, 1989, 56.

8. "In Brief," *Broadcasting*, June 12, 1989, 88.

9. "Meet the Local Muscle," *Broadcasting*, June 20, 1988, 1–2.

10. At that point, *The Golden Girls* was one of only two shows in which all principal actors won an Emmy Award, the other being *All in the Family*.

11. "They Broke the Backs of Two Networks with a Wink & a Smile," *Broadcasting*, July 18, 1988.

12. "Make Them Laugh till It Hurts," *Broadcasting*, May 23, 1988.

13. "They'll Make You an Offer You Can't Refuse," *Variety*, May 4, 1988, 528–30.

14. "They'll Make You an Offer."

15. "The Opportunity to Carry Gold," *Broadcasting*, January 16, 1989, 15–17.

16. "Do You Know Me?," *Broadcasting*, July 24, 1989, 11.

17. "TV Briefs," *The Times*, August 13, 1989, 114.

18. Vicki Vaughn, "Players Could Win Millions with Disney Lottery Show," *Orlando Sentinel*, April 6, 1991, A-9.

19. David Bauder, "The Wild Women of 'Golden Girls' Are a TV Hit the Second Time Around," *Chippewa Herald-Telegram*, July 6, 2003, 13.

20. "TV Listings," *Daily Republican-Register*, March 28, 1997, sec. TV Register, 1–3; "TV Listings," *Austin American Statesman*, March 30, 1997, sec. Show World, 31.

21. "TV Listings," *Austin American-Statesman*, November 2, 1997, sec. Show World.

22. Jill Gerston, "Lifetime: A Network by, for and of Women," *New York Times*, June 29, 1997, sec. 12, 4.

23. Gerston, "Lifetime."

24. Eileen R. Meehan and Jackie Byars, "Telefeminism: How Lifetime Got Its Groove, 1984–1997," in *The Television Studies Reader*, ed. Robert C. Allen and Annette Hill (Routledge, 2004), 93.

25. Anna Maria Cruz and Stephen M. Silverman, "'Golden Girls' All Over Again," *People*, June 24, 2003.

26. Brian Donlon, "Daytime Reruns Bolster Network Ratings," *The Olympian*, August 30, 1989, 3C.

27. Donlon, "Daytime Reruns."

28. Henry Jenkins, *Textual Poachers: Television Fans and Participatory Culture* (Routledge, 1992), 69.

29. EW Staff, "EW's Favorite Feel-Good TV Shows, Episodes, and Characters to Quaran-Stream, *Entertainment Weekly*, April 18, 2020.

30. John Koblin, "Lockdown TV: Netflix Dominates, News Surges and Bea Arthur Is Still Golden," *New York Times*, April 30, 2020.

31. Rebecca Rubin and Marc Malkin, "From 'Golden Girls to 'Property Brothers,' What Hollywood Stars Are Binging During Coronavirus Lockdown," *Variety*, May 4, 2020.

32. Derek Kompare, *Rerun Nation: How Repeats Invented American Television* (Routledge, 2005); Brett Farmer, *Spectacular Passions: Cinema, Fantasy, Gay Male Spectatorships* (Duke University Press, 2000); Alexander Doty, *Making Things Perfectly Queer: Interpreting Mass Culture* (University of Minnesota Press, 1993); Quinlan Miller, *Camp TV: Trans Gender Queer Sitcom History* (Duke University Press, 2019); Taylor Cole Miller, "Syndicated Queerness: Television Talk Shows, Rerun Syndications, and the Serials of Norman Lear" (PhD diss., University of Wisconsin–Madison, 2017).

33. For a deeper discussion of this programming strategy, see Taylor Cole Miller, "Rewitched: Retextuality and the Queering of *Bewitched*," *Camera Obscura* 35, no. 3 (108) (2021).

34. Jim Colucci, *The Q Guide to "The Golden Girls"* (Alyson Books, 2006), 87.

35. Dennis Porter, "Soap Time: Thoughts on a Commodity Art Form," *College English* 38, no. 8 (1977): 782–83.

36. Louis Peitzman, "Why Gay Men Still Love 'The Golden Girls,'" *BuzzFeed*, March 9, 2014. www.buzzfeed.com/louispeitzman/why-gay-men-still-love-the-golden-girls.

The theme song in lights at the 2022 Golden-Con fan convention. (Photo by Taylor Cole Miller)

INTERVIEW

"Thank You for Being a Friend"

Marsha Posner Williams, Co-Producer

Taylor, did I ever talk to you about the main titles for *The Golden Girls*? We had shot four episodes. We weren't on the air yet, and Tony Thomas and Paul Witt, and I guess Susan, they were all interviewing main title companies. This is what they do. And Tony said to me, "Boy, you know, we're getting picked by these companies for twenty-five grand, thirty-five grand, even forty grand. And then, you know, we're going to take the women to Miami, and we're going to do a helicopter shot, blah blah blah. But," he said, "nothing's, you know, tweaking our propeller." We knew what the song was going to be—that was never an issue—and I said, "Why don't you let me take the song and go into editing for a day? And he said, "Go, go, go!" So, I took the song and went to the editor with the raw footage of four episodes, and frame for frame, what I came out with is what went on the air for forty years.

And wait, you did it in one day?

Yep. I was like editing to music, because I had a musical background. So, I know where . . . the downbeat goes, you know. And so, it was really fun for me, although a huge amount of work to go through the footage and make notes of every shot of it. Remember, every show was shot twice. In order to build that main title, I had to have every potential shot on paper and in my head as exactly what it was. So, when Blanche is walking out saying, "I'm as jumpy as a virgin at a prison rodeo!" I know that walk. And I want to put it to the beat. So those main titles, that was me. You know, every drag show or anything I've been to regarding *The Golden Girls*, when they play the main title, I get very emotional. I don't know why, but I do.

Is there a moment in the theme song you're proudest of?

When they throw Betty in the closet. And by the way, [I only cost] twenty-five hundred bucks instead of $40,000.

Do you remember Cindy Fee's recording session?

I was in that recording session. She did it in one take and said, "Okay, I'm done." And Tony said, "No, no, no, you can't just leave after one. Take two.... Please, please do another take." So, she acquiesced and did one more take. She had another gig to go to. "You've got it in one take," she said, and she was right.

Isabel Omero, Production Associate/Script Supervisor, Writer
I wasn't there for the recording, but I did once or twice pitch the idea of having the song's writer, Andrew Gold, on as a piano player. But no. He had a hit with it. But the show and the singer, Cindy Fee, made it immortal.

Cindy Fee, Main Titles Performer
It was one of four different themes I sang that year. (I don't remember the other theme songs, because none of the shows [were picked up].) I remember going into the studio. I asked what the show was about, and they said it was about older women. I am sure they told me the name, and they put a piece of music in front of me, which was Andrew Gold's song. I believe they played his version of it for me. But they also had a lead sheet in front of me. So, I listened to it a couple of times and looked at the music, and then I sang it a few times. And it was really quick. I am, generally speaking, very fast in the studio. It really came together quickly because it's a very good song, not difficult to learn, and not really that difficult to sing.

At the time, I was very, very, very busy. I'm not tooting my own horn, but I was the first-call female soloist in LA at that time, so I was doing everything from jingles to themes to movies to record dates, so I was just really busy. I think I literally had two other sessions that day as well.

Had they already done the instrumentation for the theme song and you just sang onto that?

Almost all leads in studio work, by the time the singers come in, for the most part, they've already done everything except for the background vocals [which there weren't any on *The Golden Girls*]. Occasionally, afterward, they may decide they want to change what the keyboard plays, but almost always the players will come in a couple of hours—it's very fast. My call would have probably been in the afternoon. They would have had all the instrumentalists in that morning, probably, and then had me come in after that.

After listening to Gold's version, how did you decide to make the changes you did for yours?

All of the little licks and things I sang, those were certainly things I put in. That's what I was hired for, the fact that I didn't just sing things straight ahead, that I would add what one of my friends calls my "Cindy sauce." I would add little things of my own. When I sing, I don't think too much about what I'm singing. I just get the song in my head, and then I open my mouth and sing and see what comes out. Like when I sang, "if you threw a part-aayyyy . . . ," that's called a lick. Or when I did, "invited everyone you knew-wwooo," that's a lick—things that are unique to a particular singer, and in today's world, there's a lot of that. Nobody things anything straight, but back then, it was different.

"Cindy sauce," I love that!

I did do a long version of the theme song, which they cut down. I would have sang the whole song so they would have had a ninety-second for promotional purposes. Part of that is just where it's sitting in the actual broadcast, commercials, and things like that. I at least sang the second verse because I remember that. . . . Next time I [sing at a *Golden Girls* event], I'm going to sing that gosh-darn second verse!

Besides *The Golden Girls*, what do most people recognize you from?

I did a long string of commercials, everything from Wheaties "What the Big Boys Eat" to Pontiac "Get on Your Pontiac and Ride!" to Hoover "Nobody Does It Like You." I did a ton of commercials that were on the air for a long time.

Do you still make residuals from the theme?

Oh, yes! Because of unions! I have a friend who sang the original *Gilligan's Island* theme, but there was no union contract when he did it, so he virtually made his day player's rate and that was it. I make a very nice living yearly as long as *The Golden Girls* is on the air. Even if I were to die, the money passes down to my heirs. So, very pro-union, I am!

CHAPTER 4

Golden Memories

Narrative Complexity and Flashback Episodes in *The Golden Girls*

JESSICA HOOVER

In the third-season episode "Three on a Couch," the women seek out a psychiatrist to address their domestic conflicts. Dorothy explains, "Doctor, we have been together for five years, and we're just getting on each other's nerves." Her comments allude to a narrative world not fully experienced by viewers, as this episode comes halfway through the show's third season. Through a series of flashbacks, the ladies share moments when their personality traits grated on one another. Dorothy accuses Blanche of being selfish, Blanche and Dorothy grumble about Rose's naivety, and Rose and Blanche complain that Dorothy is a perfectionist. Sophia mostly argues that she deserves the doctor's hourly rate for listening to their moaning. Their reminiscences and bickering are so convincing that the doctor concludes they are completely incompatible as roommates. The ladies return home and mull over the doctor's advice. Sophia points out that disagreements are a normal part of life. "Just because you have some rough times doesn't mean you throw in the towel. You go on living," she tells them. Resolved to stay together, they decide to share some cheesecake.

The flashback as a narrative device should be familiar to most sitcom viewers, especially fans of *The Golden Girls*. While it has a long history in the genre, *The Golden Girls* made extensive use of the technique, featuring fifteen flashback episodes across its seven-season run. There are two types or forms of flashbacks utilized. First, there are episodes that use the *flashback as a narrative device* to present events that occurred in the past but that are new to the viewer. In narrative theory, this is referred to as "external analepsis" and is used to reveal unseen moments from the characters' history. Second, there are *clip show* episodes. These make use of the flashback to remediate previously aired footage and would be considered "internal analepsis." I make these distinctions because there are important variations between the two—creative and industrial differences that mark their different functions for the program, which I discuss in more detail later in this chapter. These episodes also invoke differing responses from the audience. For example, *Variety* includes "Three on a Couch" among its twenty-five favorite episodes from the series, while other fans were more critical.[1] Across various online discussion boards, fans complain about such episodes, considering the flashback to be a hackneyed writing technique. When discussing clip shows specifically, the response is even more antagonistic, with people pointing to the use of previously seen material as laziness or blaming their frequent occurrence on the age of the stars or creator Susan Harris's struggle with chronic fatigue syndrome. In this chapter, I offer an alternate view on *The Golden Girls*' recurrent use of the flashback. The scholar Christyne Berzsenyi describes the role of story exchange in *The Golden Girls* as offering "structure and substance for each episode" in a way that "constructs character identities and create[s] intimacy and community among the characters and their viewers."[2] Building on Berzsenyi's work, I am interested in other ways this device manifests itself in the program. I argue that memory is one of the primary themes of *The Golden Girls*, that it undergirds the entire program, and that the writers underscore the importance of memory through the repeated use of the flashback. I argue, then, that the show's use of the flashback, through both external and internal analepsis, creates narrative complexity.

Narrative Complexity

The kind of televisual narrative complexity described by the scholar Jason Mittell begins in the 1990s and includes elements like temporal play, high levels of viewer engagement, and "a redefinition of the episodic form under the influence of serial narration."[3] This increasing complexity is viewed as ushering in a new golden era of television, of legitimating the medium. But, as Michael Newman and Elana Levine note, this "legitimation of television is premised upon a rejection and denigration of 'television' as it has long existed."[4] Up to the 1990s, most television narratives were episodic, meaning each episode came to a tight resolution, which was better for reruns, while serialization tended to be the domain of soap operas. But with narrative complexity, Mittell identifies the increasing use of ongoing story lines across multiple programs, with *Lost*, *The West Wing*, *The X-Files*, and *The Wire* being demonstrative of this mode. When select sitcoms like *Arrested Development*, *How I Met Your Mother*, or *My Name Is Earl*, for example, have been considered sufficiently complex, it is often because they share characteristics with these more dramatic shows, like single-camera production style, temporal play, or a frequent focus on male protagonists. And as Newman and Levine indicate, the rise in status of individual programs such as these is accomplished through the denigration of past television, with gendered implications. Television has long been considered a feminized medium because of its place within the private sphere of the home. Newman and Levine state, "that television has been classified as feminine, and thereby as a less worthy, significant, and serious medium, has been a fact of its history." The attempt to legitimate television through the identification of these narratively complex programs is an attempt to masculinize it "by rejecting the feminized medium that 'used to be.'"[5]

Mittell is correct that various technological and media industry factors indicative of this time period affected the forms and types of television narratives produced going forward. However, tying narrative complexity to an increase in serialization overlooks how some of the aspects ascribed to this mode were already present in television narratives. In analyzing the importance of the flashback as a narrative device in *The Golden Girls*, I trouble this notion of narrative complexity by exploring the use of temporal play in a female-centric episodic sitcom, a text that stands in contrast to the example programs listed previously. *The Golden Girls* writers use the device to manifest the show's central theme of memory. Their use of the flashback as external analepsis is representative of the sharing of individuals' memories. In the form of the clip show, or internal analepsis, they are representative of characters', and the viewers', shared memories. Using the narrative technique of the flashback, *The Golden Girls* increases characterization, providing additional context for the interrelationships of the four women while reinforcing the creators' preferred readings of the overall text, as well as strengthening viewers' relationship with the show.

The Way They Met

While the majority of scholarship on such temporal play and the use of flashbacks in television has been focused on dramas, that does not necessarily mean that some of this work cannot be applied to the sitcom format. Amanda Lotz's work on narrative complexity in the medical procedural *House* is helpful here. Seeking to "better understand attributes of episodic television storytelling and techniques of characterization," Lotz analyzes a single episode from late in the first season, despite its being "arguably the least routine episode" of the series. Lotz finds that through the use of narrative techniques including flashback, the episode conveys crucial character information in its basic plot, while it "reaffirms a central theme of the program."[6] *The Golden Girls*' repeated use of flashbacks functions to accomplish similar goals. The first-season finale, titled "The Way We Met," uses the flashback to provide narrative information that viewers might expect in a sitcom's pilot. Centered around the way Blanche, Dorothy, and Rose became roommates, the framing story is that the women cannot sleep after watching *Psycho* and decide to partake in their ritual of late-night talks with a side of cheesecake. Blanche mentions that she never did anything similar with her old roommates, and Dorothy is surprised to learn that she had prior roommates. Blanche remembers that she actually met Rose the day she kicked her old roommates out, and a circle-wipe transition takes viewers to the moment Blanche and Rose meet in front of the grocery store bulletin board. The episode temporally bounces between the current day kitchen and the past. Present-day Rose observes that they were fast friends, but Dorothy reminds her of their first grocery shopping trip together, in which they disagree about the cost of smoked oysters, the appropriate size of pepperonis, and the best method for finding a ripe cantaloupe. Ultimately, these disagreements lead them to conclude that they should not be roommates after all. However, their conflict is resolved when Rose shares one of her famous "St. Olaf" stories. Her tale of the "Great Herring War" has them all laughing such that they decide to continue cohabitating.

The ladies celebrate their decision over cheesecake, providing the origin story of the treat that would become synonymous with the show. In this first example, the flashback is utilized to provide viewers with crucial new narrative information. It deepens understanding of the characters' relationships and explains how they came to live together. And for viewers wondering why Dorothy and Blanche tolerate all of Rose's stories, the flashback presents those stories as a core moment in their relationship's growth, bringing them together through laughter and enabling them to imagine the possibilities of future friendship. This episode may be seen as so representative of the *Golden Girls* storytelling style as a whole that in 2024 the publisher Penguin Random House selected "The Way We Met" for the *Golden Girls* contribution to its *Little Golden Book* children series.

Feminizing the Flashback

While not exclusively identified with masculine genres and forms, male-centric narratives seem to dominate many of the television programs considered "complex." And the use of temporal play itself may be utilized more often along gender lines. Julianne Pidduck notes in her work on costume drama films that "the temporal gap afforded by the flashback allows a deepening understanding of character developing through time," most commonly in the service of a male protagonist who "is afforded a depth and complexity that come with ageing and regret, whereas the female object of desire remains frozen in time."[7] In previous examples of narratively complex sitcoms like *My Name Is Earl* or *How I Met Your Mother*, while the flashback is often used for humor, it is still most often in service of a male protagonist, with the latter's narrative being structured entirely around remembrances of the central character. However, in examining the second-season episode of *The Golden Girls* "A Piece of Cake," we can understand how writers use the device to the benefit of female characters instead.

In this episode, the women are throwing a birthday party for a friend, which prompts them to reminisce about their own past birthdays. Dorothy's and Blanche's flashbacks are played purely for humor, but Rose's and Sophia's flashbacks involve more pathos and serve to deepen viewer understandings of each of their characters while asserting the importance of memory. Rose flashes back to St. Olaf as she remembers the last birthday cake she baked there. While her many stories of her hometown usually feature a plenitude of colorful characters, in this moment she is alone in her kitchen. Via a monologue in which she speaks to an absent/deceased Charlie, she confesses that she has decided to sell their home and move to Miami, saying, "This place is too filled with memories for me to get on with my life. I need to start over without you, Charlie." The scene closes with her acknowledging that she knows he will be with her wherever she goes. In this instance, memory is both comfort and curse. And similar to Pidduck's observations, it is Charlie who has become frozen in time for Rose as she acknowledges that she must move forward without him.

Then we're transported to Brooklyn, 1956. Sophia and her husband, Salvadore, are fighting when a young Dorothy arrives to drive them to Sophia's birthday party. Sal has informed Sophia that a mistake was made on her birth certificate, and it is her fiftieth birthday, not her forty-eighth. She laments the loss of those two years, which confuses her daughter. "You don't understand, Dorothy," she tells her. "I always had plans, dreams, things I wanted to accomplish by the time I was fifty." She acknowledges that those two years would not really make a difference, but she explains, "That's not the point. I'd still have two more years to dream. I can't believe it. I'm fifty. I'm an old woman who hasn't accomplished a thing in her life." Dorothy reminds Sophia that raising three kids through the Depression is hardly nothing. Sal, through a closed door (as he is never seen in this flashback), tells Sophia that she is as beautiful as the day he married her, and Sal and Dorothy both convince Sophia that she need not be upset. This flashback does much in the service of the characters as well as the deeper meaning of the program. Viewers see Sophia and Dorothy as younger women and, importantly, their relationship in another time and place. Taken together, the flashback strengthens viewers' understanding of their connection in the diegetic timeline of the series. This flashback helps explain the older Sophia's desire to remain active by exploring her past concerns about aging. And it allows viewers to see her as we see the other three women. In this flashback, she is roughly the same age as the other characters in the present-day series. Young Sophia expresses some of the same concerns that viewers see present-day Dorothy, Rose, and Blanche struggle with. Sophia's presence in the household serves as an example to the three that they too can continue enjoying life into their later years.

The Golden Girls feminizes the flashback, bringing these aspects of Rose's and Sophia's history into the present as defining moments that shaped their characters while relegating their husbands to the past. Although through these memories we have traveled to places and times when their husbands featured heavily in their lives, the men are not physically present, with Sal relegated to the offscreen bedroom and Charlie relegated to the spiritual beyond. Pidduck points out in her discussion of the narrative technique's gendered implications that "the nostalgic device of flashback . . . preserves the timeless pleasures of the female image as displayed for the male gaze."[8] But in "A Piece of Cake," the men are removed from our gaze altogether, leaving the focus on the women and their subjective memories of love and loss at pivotal moments in their lives.

Memory and Motherhood

The familial setting for most sitcoms results in female characters historically being positioned as wives and mothers. Many scholars have discussed this limited representation of women across the genre's history (Mellencamp, Spigel, Liebman, Rabinowitz). Programs like *Father Knows Best, Ozzie and Harriet*, and *Leave It to Beaver*, among others, offer common examples of such genre limitations for sitcom women in early television. Alongside the circumscribed roles of wife and mother, there was an additional tendency to eliminate these roles altogether, often in response to concerns about the influence of mothers in larger society. Single-father television programs were popular during the 1950s and '60s, making up nearly 30 percent of TV families at one point.[9] In contrast, single-mother sitcoms were uncommon, with *The Lucy Show* and *Julia* being the earliest examples that featured widowed women. These single-father depictions were reflective of a cultural rhetoric that blamed suffocating mothers for raising children, predominantly sons, to be "simpering homosexuals or delinquent monsters" and encouraged men to relocate their masculinity outside of the bureaucratic workplace by reinvesting in fatherhood.[10] There is a reemergence of this type of sitcom in the 1980s and '90s, coinciding with the run of *The Golden Girls*. Mary Desjardin writes that although programs like *The Golden Girls* "continue the [sitcom] trend of the 1970s in representing working women, female friendships . . . non-traditional family formations, etc., television producers during this period persisted in creating family sitcoms that banished mothers."[11] In Bridget Kies's work on what she refers to as "Mr. Mom sitcoms," she notes that the elimination of mothers from many of these shows, like *My Two Dads* and *Full House*, for example, should be seen in relation to "the tensions between 'new man' ideology and Reaganesque machismo in response to the women's movement."[12] When mothers are present in contemporary sitcoms, their familial roles are often center stage, despite having occupations outside the home. Sitcom mothers Claire Huxtable, Elyse Keaton, Maggie Seaver, and Roseanne Connor from *The Cosby Show, Family Ties, Growing Pains*, and *Roseanne*, respectively, were working women, but it was their roles as wives and mothers that provided the bulk of their story lines. In comparison, the women of *The Golden Girls*, through their age and their either widowed or divorced status, are allowed to be independent characters with their own interests and concerns. Indeed, Sophia often plays mother to them all, but even she is offered unique story lines that do not center on familial responsibility. But the women do not have to relinquish their roles as mothers or daughters in service of this, which helps create more complex characterizations for each of them.

The season 3 episode "Mother's Day" integrates motherhood into the program's core theme of memory by depicting the act of remembering and the importance of being remembered. The women plan to take Sophia to a Mother's Day lunch but insist on waiting for their own children to call before leaving. As they wait, each shares a Mother's Day memory. Rose tells the story of a long wait in a Minnesota bus station on her way to visit her children. She befriends an older woman who says she is on her way to visit her daughter. It is eventually revealed that the woman's daughter is dead; but she always visits her daughter's grave on Mother's Day, and this year, she has escaped her nursing home to do so. When the sheriff shows up to take the woman back, Rose intervenes and claims the woman as her own mother. She boards the wrong bus to help this woman keep her daughter's memory alive, highlighting the importance of the mother-daughter bond, even beyond the grave.

Blanche remembers a visit to her elderly mother's nursing home on the last Mother's Day they spent together. This segment increases the episode's narrative complexity through layered storytelling, highlighting memories of memory sharing, as during the visit she recounts another previous Mother's Day when her parents prevented her from eloping with an older man. "Don't you remember that, Mama," Blanche asks. Her elderly mother replies, "Well, I thought that happened to Virginia [Blanche's sister]." Blanche is visibly upset at her mother's failing memory, but then her mother corrects her: "Blanche, that didn't happen on Mother's Day. That happened on Christmas Day, nineteen . . . 1949." Blanche is surprised when she realizes that her mother is right and touched that she remembers. Her mother says, "Blanche, there are days when I can't remember who I am. But trust me, I remember every stunt you ever pulled." Blanche's relationship with her father is referenced often throughout the series, with "Big Daddy" Hollingsworth appearing in two episodes and a third centering on his death, but in this segment, Blanche's bond with her mother and her joy that even though the elderly woman's memory is fading, she still knows and loves her daughter is on full display.

Sophia recounts the Mother's Day she asked her mother to move in with her and her husband. In an entertaining bit of stunt casting, Bea Arthur plays her own grandmother, Sophia's mother, while the same actress who played young Dorothy in "A Piece of Cake" returns. At one point, Sophia complains as her mother begins yet another story from Sicily, and as they argue over her moving in, Sophia turns to young Dorothy and says, "If I ever

Dorothy's family. (Photo © Wayne Williams 1984–87. All rights reserved.)

do this to you, I want you to take me out to a field and shoot me." Dorothy asks if she can get that in writing. Similar to "A Piece of Cake," viewers get a deeper sense of their mother-daughter relationship, which is central to the show, as well as a glimpse of Sophia not just as a mother but as a daughter. The importance of being remembered is reinforced again as, after they have all shared their stories and Dorothy and Rose have both spoken to their children, Blanche announces that they might as well go to lunch because she knows that her daughter Janet is unlikely to call. In true happy-ending sitcom fashion, the phone rings just as they are exiting the kitchen. Blanche answers and is ecstatic to find her Janet on the other end.

Each segment focuses on the mother-daughter relationship as integral to the characters' past and present, without it being any of the women's sole purpose. The focus on the matrilineal connection is at odds with sitcoms that either pigeonhole women as only wives and mothers or separate them from the familial through workplace settings, as well as the wave of Mr. Mom sitcoms of the 1980s and '90s that Kies describes.

As (Previously) Seen on TV

The clip show as an episode form arises out of the regime of television repetition identified by Phil Williams and Derek Kompare. Williams and Kompare both explore how the economic usefulness of the rerun resulted in its quickly becoming an integral feature of television programming. Williams notes that by 1956 networks turned from testing out new programming during the off-season to airing reruns instead.[13] This allowed production companies and networks to increase the cost value of their programs. Kompare argues that television is a "machine of repetition, geared toward the constant recirculation of recorded, already seen events."[14] The clip-show format internalizes the logic of the rerun. If television viewers are willing to watch the same episode in reruns, why would they not watch an episode that contained previous footage? Additionally, utilizing preexisting footage reduces the production costs for clip shows compared to a new episode. If viewers consume both reruns and clip shows in roughly the same numbers, then both make financial sense.

However, instead of seeing the clip show as a purely economic cop-out, I argue that it offers value to both the creators and viewers by enabling the former to reinforce their preferred readings of the overall text while strengthening the latter's relationship with the program and its characters, accomplished within the context of shared memories. Jonathan Gray focuses on how paratexts (texts that are not within the diegesis of a text but surround and support it, such as posters, advertisements, trailers, and opening sequences) contribute to the meaning and understanding of that text. Gray notes that television programs stretch out over years, and "since our process of textual 'actualization' remains open, . . . paratexts are free to invade the meaning-making process."[15] He argues that paratexts "often tell us how producers or distributors would prefer for us to interpret a text, . . . how they want us to make sense of their characters and plots, . . . offer 'proper' and 'preferred' interpretations."[16] In exploring in media res paratexts that "inflect or redirect the text following initial interaction," he specifically identifies recaps as "arguably the most clear-cut [in media res] example."[17] I argue that the clip show functions like the recap as it remediates past events to encourage a preferred reading.

Consider the two-part clip show from season 3 titled "Golden Moments." The premise concerns Sophia's decision to move out, introducing the idea that their group dynamic may be torn apart and threatening the core narrative of the show. In the first two and a half minutes, the basic attributes of each character are clearly defined. Rose is tenderhearted, demonstrated by her feeding the neighborhood stray cats. Blanche is hypersexual, and Dorothy is sarcastic, established by her joke comparing noises from Blanche's bedroom to the howling of the strays. Sophia is quick with a caustic remark comparing her past nursing home meals to the cat food. Viewers are reminded of each woman's essential qualities. Sophia announces that she is moving in with her son, Phil, to help after his wife has left him. The women are worried what this could mean for their lives and relationships, which prompts clips from past episodes as they reminisce about all they have shared. Trying to dissuade Sophia from leaving, Blanche points out that she is unlikely to get any privacy in Phil's trailer home. Sophia argues that there is not much privacy in their house, via clips in which two or more of the women are sharing a bed together. While humorous, clips showcasing the physical intimacy of sharing a bed represent the emotional intimacy these women share with one another.

In the second installment, Sophia goes to bed, leaving the girls to discuss their problem over cheesecake. Dorothy wonders aloud how often they have talked things over this way, and Rose asserts that most of those talks have been about sex. Blanche replies, "Oh, well, of course we do talk about sex, but we talk about other things too. We console each other, we help each other, we advise each other, . . . and then we talk about sex again." This dialogue transitions to the clips, including one in which the women discuss their first sexual experiences. While some of the humor is bawdy, it also mediates the women's bond through sharing personal memories. Li Guan and Qi Wang suggest that "sharing memories serves important social functions by facilitating relationship closeness between conversation partners. . . . The partners re-experience past events together. . . . These processes further contribute to the development and maintenance of relationship closeness."[18] Additionally, the humor of the moment does not distract from the sentimentality of the clips but reinforces another defining characteristic of the program: that sexuality and explicit repartee are integral to the show's humor.[19] Another set of clips reinforces the humor and the episodic nature of the program as viewers see some of the zany situations in which the ladies have found themselves: for example, Rose nearly shoots Blanche's date when she mistakes him for a burglar, and Blanche's inflatable bra backfires on her as she is competing for the attentions of a gentleman. Just when they decide they are going to demand that Sophia stay, she enters the kitchen and announces that Phil's wife has already returned. This example highlights that, similar to other types of in medias res paratexts, the clip show can "reaffirm what a show is about, how its characters are interrelated, and how we 'should' make sense of them."[20] Each character's identity has been firmly reestablished, the importance of their relationships has been reaffirmed, and the show's narrative and comedic style have been clearly conveyed while returning the program to stasis.

Shared Memories

The clip show also strengthens parasocial relationships between audiences and characters. A "parasocial relationship" is defined as an ongoing "one-sided mediated form of social interaction between the audience and media characters."[21] The parasocial relationship seems particularly suited to defining the possibility of a relationship built through television. As Gray notes, the television schedule results in texts that unfold over weeks and years, which allow for viewer-character connections that build over time. John Weispfenning argues that the rerun may strengthen the "possibility for long-term para-social relationships between the audience and the fictional characters."[22] If we understand the clip-show format as an internalized form of the rerun, then it similarly helps build parasocial relationships between viewers and the characters within the program. In particular, the clip show's dominant framing device of reminiscence combined with previously seen footage invites viewers to understand the clips not only as memories within the diegesis but as reflective of experiences that they themselves have shared with these characters. As Guan and Wang note, the reexperiencing of past memories together strengthens relationships, and this can apply to parasocial relationships as well. A viewer who has built a relationship with *The Golden Girls* over the past two and a half seasons might reflect on their own connection with the characters through the various shared memories in the "Golden Moments." They may feel they also benefit from the motherly advice Sophia offers or the way they all, to paraphrase Blanche, console, help, and advise each other. The clip show can reinforce not only the producer's preferred reading but the meaning viewers themselves make from the text. The proliferation of fan-created videos in the modern digital age may support this assessment. Gray describes viewer-created videos as paratexts that allow fans to "further build the para-social relationships."[23] These classic clip shows may be part of the genealogy of such creations.

Conclusion

Sitcoms have often been referred to as "amnesia television," where each installment seems to start anew with little connection to the past. But the flashback as a narrative device, and its use via clip shows, offers a way to understand how memory plays a larger role in episodic programs than assumed. The legitimation of television through increased serialization requires the dismissal of episodic sitcoms from concepts of narrative complexity. I argue that we should reassess the sitcom's use of the flashback as a narrative device. *The Golden Girls* serves as an example of how the concept of narrative complexity functions in episodic programs and contests the gendered implications of legitimization that Newman and Levine identify. Temporal play in *The Golden Girls* enables writers to increase characterization, shape a preferred understanding of female interrelationships, and help viewers build engaging parasocial relationships with the women by increasing the length and depth of narrative time we spend with them, all serving to reaffirm the program's central theme of memory.

Notes

1. BreAnna Bell, "'The Golden Girls': 25 Best Episodes Ranked," *Variety*, August 26, 2020, https://variety.com/lists/golden-girls-best-episodes-ranked/.
2. Christyne A. Berzsenyi, "The Golden Girls Share Signature Stories: Narratives of Aging, Identity, and Communal Desire." *Americana* 9, no. 2 (2010): 1–3, https://americanpopularculture.com/journal/articles/fall_2010/berzsenyi.htm.
3. Jason Mittell, "Narrative Complexity in Contemporary American Television," *Velvet Light Trap*, no. 58 (2006): 32.
4. Michael Z. Newman and Elana Levine, *Legitimating Television: Media Convergence and Cultural Status* (Routledge, 2012), 2.
5. Newman and Levine, *Legitimating Television*, 10.
6. Amanda Lotz, "*House*: Narrative Complexity," in *How to Watch Television*, ed. Ethan Thompson and Jason Mittell, 2nd ed. (New York University Press, 2020), 34.
7. Julianne Pidduck, *Contemporary Costume Film: Space, Place and the Past* (BFI, 2004), 57.
8. Pidduck, *Contemporary Costume Film*, 57.
9. James D. Robinson and Thomas Skill, "Five Decades of Family on Television: From the 1950s through the 1990s," in *Television and the American Family*, ed. J. Alison Bryant and Jennings Bryant (Lawrence Erlbaum, 2001), 154.
10. James Gilbert, *Men in the Middle: Searching for Masculinity in the 1950s* (University of Chicago Press, 2005), 75; Lynn Spigel, *Welcome to the Dollhouse* (Duke University Press, 2001), 192.

11. Mary Desjardins, "Gender and Television," in *Encyclopedia of Television*, vol. 2, ed. Horace Newcomb, 2nd ed. (Routledge, 2013), 674.

12. Bridget Kies, "Television's 'Mr. Moms': Idealizing the New Man in 1980s Domestic Sitcoms," *Feminist Media Histories* 4, no. 1 (2018): 147.

13. According to the *I Love Lucy* wiki on Fandom.com: https://ilovelucyandricky.fandom.com/wiki/The_%22I_Love_Lucy%22_Christmas_Show#Trivia.

14. Derek Kompare, *Rerun Nation: How Repeats Invented American Television* (Taylor and Francis, 2006), xi.

15. Jonathan Gray, *Show Sold Separately: Promos, Spoilers, and other Media Paratexts* (New York University Press, 2010), 43.

16. Gray, *Show Sold Separately*, 72–73.

17. Gray, *Show Sold Separately*, 35, 43.

18. Li Guan and Qi Wang, "Does Sharing Memories Make Us Feel Closer? The Roles of Memory Type and Culture," *Journal of Cross-Cultural Psychology* 53, nos. 3–4 (2022): 344.

19. Nicole S. Krypker, "Sex and Death and St. Olaf: Deconstructing the Magic of *The Golden Girls*," *Comedy Studies* 10, no. 2 (2019): 205.

20. Gray, *Show Sold Separately*, 76.

21. Nicole Liebers and Holger Schramm, "Parasocial Interactions and Relationships with Media Characters," *Communication Research Trends* 38, no. 2 (2019): 4–5.

22. John Weispfenning, "Cultural Functions of Reruns: Time, Memory and Television," *Journal of Communication* 53, no. 1 (2003): 168.

23. Gray, *Show Sold Separately*, 144.

The Weekly Schedule

Taping Seasons 1–3

Marsha Posner Williams, Co-Producer
The Golden Girls was a Monday to Friday show.

Monday: We would have a table read with the cast, the director, the head writer, the writers, and myself and the department heads. And that is a very, very important time, the table read. You don't read the script just for the writers to hear it for the first time—which is really important to see what works, what doesn't work—but also there is a discussion of each scene with the wardrobe people, the lighting people. They may ask, "What time of year is this?" "What kind of wardrobe are they going to be wearing?" . . . After the table read, everybody would leave, and then the director would usually start rehearsing right away. . . . It might be a short day, maybe not. Who knows?

Tuesday: Rehearse, rehearse, rehearse. . . . You're dry blocking, which means just actors and no cameras or anything, no equipment. And then, at the end of Tuesday, we would have a run-through for the writers. And again, we ask what works, what doesn't work, and a discussion with the director and all that.

Wednesday: Again, dry blocking, dry rehearsing, and at the end of the day, a run-through for the network. And then, the network just goes off, and they talk about things and blah, blah, blah—whatever, a lot of hot air.

Thursday: You bring in all the equipment, all the engineering, so now you're on camera for the first time, and you're camera blocking all day. And the director is doing shots with the assistant director, and you're just blocking everything for camera now. At the end of the day Thursday, we had a run-through, and in the '70s and '80s, we used to do run-throughs in wardrobe, so we could actually see how the wardrobe works. Everything Bea Arthur wore was custom-made and designed for her.

Friday: Rehearse. You come in a little later, because it's going to be a longer day, but you do a quick run-through. And then the schedule says, "Okay, we're breaking for makeup, hair, and wardrobe. And while they're putting everyone in makeup, hair, and wardrobe, we bring in the first audience for a five o'clock shoot. The idea of the first show was, really, it's like a test; you're testing with an audience. There's no reason to stop and reshoot unless something just goes terribly wrong where an actor just really f-cks up a line. So, it's basically just go through it and us sitting in the booth and watching it on the monitors. And we got a great sense of what worked and what didn't work. Okay, now we let the audience go. Now we're in between shows while we're bringing in the later audience. We're giving the cast and crew a meal and giving the cast notes.... Okay, now we go back and we do the 7:30 show, and the 7:30 show was always, *always* a better audience because the people are done with work.... The earlier audiences were a lot of older people, and you know, you pay an audience service to bring people in.... We were lucky

Behind the scenes of the iconic kitchen. (Photo © Wayne Williams 1984–87. All rights reserved.)

Marsha Posner Williams in her office on the set of *The Golden Girls*. (Photo © Wayne Williams 1985. Used with permission. All rights reserved.)

because we had three hundred people in our audience, not seventy-five or one hundred. We had three hundred people, and it was joyful to hear that laughter like that.

So, then you take all that footage, and you edit the best of both together. So, during the late show, when we're doing something, the director might say that's better, that's better, or that's better, and the script supervisor is making notes of the best—take the best takes. The editor still has a choice of a lot of material. By the way, at the late show, sometimes we would stop if somebody screwed up something, and we would redo it right away. But if it was too big of a thing we needed to redo, we wouldn't bore the audience with it. We would just wait until after the audience was gone, and we would do a reshoot. Usually, when it's with an audience, we call it a restart and without a reshoot, but everybody has their own lingo for this stuff.

PART II

Text

CHAPTER 5

Enquiring Minds

The Golden Girls and Tabloid Culture

CLAIRE SEWELL

Nearly forty years after the 1985 network television premiere of *The Golden Girls*, the cast was featured on the November 22, 2022, cover of *Closer Weekly* with headlines that promised "new stories from the set!" and "untold tales of trauma, tears, laughter, and love." This phrasing mirrors language that has long been used by tabloid publications like the *National Enquirer*, well known for manufacturing shock-value headlines and articles. The *Enquirer* billed itself as having the "largest circulation of any paper in America" at the time, and the phrase still most associated with it, "Enquiring minds want to know," originated on its television commercials, which ran from 1982 until 1988.[1] The *Enquirer* featured *The Golden Girls* several times over the years during the show's original broadcast run, sometimes even creating drama between the cast members with headlines such as "Golden Girls Storm Off Set." Two other prime-time shows of the 1980s, *Dynasty* and *Dallas*, were the only other ones of the period to receive similar levels of coverage, their soap-opera-like story lines generating their own real-world headlines. The pastime of celebrity gossip was frequently used as a punch line in episodes of *The Golden Girls*, and this chapter creates an intertextual timeline to analyze references in the scripts alongside stories published in the *Enquirer*. As first defined by the feminist philosopher Julia Kristeva, intertextuality is the literary theory that "specifies the passage from one signifying system to another," but it has since been expanded more broadly to encompass the variety of media in today's highly interactive landscape.[2] Often derided as anti-intellectual, the tabloids both onscreen in *The Golden Girls* and off in viewers' real lives prove to be as much a valuable source of cultural significance as the topics featured throughout the series. In other words, fasten your seatbelts.

Journey to the Center of Tabloid Valley: Scandalous Origins

> *Blanche*: I almost forgot. I need a *Globe* and a *Tatler* and a *Midnight Star* and an *Enquirer*, and I guess maybe one serious news magazine so we know what's going on in the world. One *People*! ("The Way We Met," S01E25)

It is a curious phenomenon that a sitcom that premiered in 1985 could still be turned into front-page news, but it also reflects the marketability of the multigenerational fanbase that continues to interact with *The Golden Girls* today. According to the magazine's official Facebook page, *Closer Weekly* is "an entertainment magazine for readers 40+ that focuses on the stars you grew up with and love."[3] While that age range probably skews a little on the younger end, it is a tagline that nonetheless indicates that readers will find less scandal and more sentimentality within its pages. *Closer Weekly* tends to focus on positive celebrity content alongside tributes and remembrances.[4] In this way, the content is closer to *People* magazine, one of Blanche's favorite reads. In contrast to tabloids like the *Enquirer* and others, *People* cultivated itself as a trustworthy source from its debut 1974 issue. Bea Arthur was popular enough thanks to *Maude* that she even made *People*'s cover in 1975. *People* is also known as the magazine with which celebrities welcome interaction, granting it the coveted exclusive interview after marriages, divorces, or scandals, whereas the *Enquirer* and other tabloid publications often fabricate stories based on dubious sources.

A wealth of scholarship is dedicated to gender, celebrity, and media studies, alongside historical treatments of the development of tabloid culture. In *Extraordinarily Ordinary: "Us Weekly" and the Rise of Reality Television Celebrity*, Erin A. Meyers discusses another magazine within the tabloid milieu. Launched in 1977, *Us Weekly* also highlights the "intertextual . . . tension between [the] public and private selves" that the tabloids work to exploit.[5] Although there is a tendency among the literary intelligentsia to view the *Enquirer* and similar publications as less worthy of scholarly study than other publications are, still, the *Enquirer* provides a broad level of insight into twentieth-century American culture, values, and social mores. The indexers of a database of entries on articles in *Enquirer* issues starting in 1977 and held on microfilm at the Library of Congress provided this summary: "The *Enquirer* was a staple of grocery store checkout lines. No one escaped the front cover headlines, and millions took home the occasional copy to peruse on the couch.... You might imagine old issues of the *Enquirer* are readily available at any research library. This is not so.... There is no [complete] index to this content. Researchers interested in searching the back issues must travel to a holding library, and then search the microfilm frame-by-frame in the hope of finding an article of interest."[6] Meyers also notes this "ephemeral" challenge in "researching celebrity media gossip."[7] Perhaps owing to the increased popularity of *The Golden Girls* in recent years, vintage copies of *Enquirer* issues featuring the show are somewhat easy to locate on websites like eBay. This chapter is an expansion of a blog post I wrote after I discovered and purchased the issues discussed herein.[8] I was drawn to them first because this facet of *Golden Girls* lore has somehow faded into obscurity, and I wanted to critically examine this microcosm of 1980s pop culture. On a more personal level, I felt a connection to this aspect of fandom as someone who grew up reading *People* with my mother and sneaking glances at the tabloids every week in the grocery store checkout line. The culture writer and gossip industry scholar Anne Helen Petersen chronicled the interconnected history of the *Enquirer* and *People* during the 1970s that cultivated the interest in celebrity news that continues today. Petersen's analysis fills a gap in "mainstream examinations of the celebrity and gossip industry, the majority of which treat... celebrity-focused journalism as [a phenomenon] without precedence."[9] The *Enquirer* issues that featured *The Golden Girls* offer a particularly fascinating picture of the expansion of tabloid culture.

Like the Golden Girls themselves, the *Enquirer* became a Florida transplant in 1971 when Generoso Pope Jr., the paper's owner since 1952, moved the publishing offices from New Jersey to the town of Lantana, Florida, just a little over an hour and a half up the coast from Miami. The area later came to be known as "tabloid valley" after five other rival tabloids also set up shop in the Palm Beach area.[10] While it is certainly possible that being in such close proximity to the fictional setting of *The Golden Girls* helped keep it in the minds of reporters at the *Enquirer*, there are more factors at play here. Pope's personal history is like something out of one of Sophia's classic "picture it" tales—Italian heritage, Mafia connections, and all. Like Sophia, he was always scheming to make more money, although his efforts proved more successful than selling bacon-lettuce-and-potato sandwiches and water from the hose out back. One of his innovations, "specially designed pedestal racks, all labeled *National Enquirer* and built to sit exactly at eye level on the checkout counter," has perhaps kept the paper in the public's consciousness more than any other.[11] Further, Pope also "shifted the paper's focus . . . into something that housewives would feel comfortable bringing into the house."[12] In its previous incarnation as the *New York Enquirer*, the paper covered sensationalist crime and gore stories with headlines like "I Cut Out Her Heart and Stomped on It" throughout the 1960s.[13]

Beginning in the 1970s the *Enquirer* steadily included more pop culture stories, along with diet and lifestyle articles and pieces featuring everyday people in extraordinary circumstances. Certainly, another way to court the "housewife" market at the time was to feature highly rated television shows. This made sense in print alongside the "inclusion of women's concerns within mainstream programming on television rather than in specifically labeled 'women's programming'" blocks.[14] Uniquely, *The Golden Girls* provided a level of broad crossover appeal since it proved popular with audiences across the gender divide from the start.[15] And so, the *Enquirer* featured *The Golden Girls* on its cover for the first time on February 18, 1986.

The cast is shown in what is now a well-known promotional photo from the pilot episode, with the headlines "Hit of the Season!" and "'Golden Girls' Speak Out Candidly . . . About the Show and Their Lives." There are no lies detected on this cover, as the show earned top ratings following the September 1985 premiere and would later win three Emmy Awards for its first season.[16] A March 1986 article for *The Washington Post* noted that "America loves to watch these four, feisty, single over-fifties scrap and cope and spat in the sunny Miami house they share and share alike."[17] Indeed the article inside the *Enquirer*, spread over two pages, highlights Rue, Bea, Betty, and Estelle in turn.

Rue is pictured in a photo with her fourth husband, Gus Fisher, and the *Enquirer* would go on to capitalize on her volatile love life on future covers. A photo of Betty and her husband, Allen Ludden, on a game show he hosted is also featured, and the article notes that she was a widow like Rose. The similarities of the characters' fictional lives to those of the cast in real life also conveniently dovetailed with the human-interest stories sprinkled throughout the paper that included everything from "self-help pieces; quizzes; mazes; cute photos, especially of dogs and children; and accounts of good Samaritans and heroes."[18] Many of those stories have such a "back in St. Olaf" appeal that, for me, seeing them for the first time as I looked through each issue was a jarring, almost uncanny, experience. Still, this was all a part of the formulaic approach employed by Pope to sell papers to as wide an audience as possible and one that *People* has capitalized on as well, albeit through a "classier, less trashy, less tabloid-ish" lens.[19]

The cast's appearance on the December 22, 1987, cover is more typical of the type of content the *Enquirer* notoriously thrived on. A large photo with the headlines "Golden Girls Storm Off Set" and "Feud with Writers Could Shut Down Show" is paired with an article titled "The Grumbling Girls." It details a "brief walkout on December 4 [that] capped a series of bitter skirmishes between the stars and writers as both sides battle over the content of the scripts." An unnamed "staff member" is the source, who also described Rue as having complained that her part in an episode from November was "so small" that she didn't "even have to show up for the taping!"—even though she had just won the Emmy Award for Outstanding Lead Actress in a Comedy Series that September. A *Los Angeles Times* article from October 1987 quoted executive producer Tony Thomas, noting that "a good comedy requires a lot of teamwork," providing a more likely summary of what went into making an episode of *The Golden Girls*.[20] Curiously, the conflict described by the *Enquirer* is quite similar to the plot of "Three on a Couch," which just so happened to have aired not long before, on December 5. By this time, "celebrity quotes became next to impossible for the *Enquirer* to get firsthand," so covering popular television shows in this manner certainly made for cheap and easy reporting.[21]

So Much Tawdry Trash

Blanche: Now, Dorothy, if you're saying you can't get stimulating conversation around this house, I beg to differ.
Rose: I can't believe it! It says since Michael Jackson can't buy the Elephant Man, he's now put in a bid for the remains of the Big Bopper!
Blanche: Rose, you can't believe everything you read in that rag! It caters to people of the lowest intelligence.
Rose: Then why do you buy it?
Blanche: Because it's the only newspaper Elvis will talk to from beyond the grave! ("Dorothy's New Friend," S03E15)

Elvis was also an obsession of both *The Golden Girls* and the *Enquirer*. In 1977, the *Enquirer* infamously published "the last picture" of Elvis lying in his casket.[22] A 1978 article even backs up Blanche's claim word for word with the headline "Elvis speaks to relatives from beyond the grave."[23] Stories questioning his death and more claims of him communicating with various psychics for decades remained popular cover stories that the *Enquirer* could always count on for a bump in circulation numbers. Such "conspiracy theories and paranoia, especially regarding the death of a celebrity, are a built-in feature of the architecture of the modern cult" of celebrity worship.[24] Similarly, the sustained level of fanatic devotion toward Elvis made him a frequent punch line on *The Golden Girls.*

Dorothy's characterization as the smart one of the group was often used as a foil for Rose's and Blanche's intelligence, so a reference to their habit of reading the tabloids made perfect sense after Dorothy befriended the "snooty" author Barbara Thorndyke, in the season 3 episode "Dorothy's New Friend." Rose enters the scene reading from a paper resembling the *Enquirer* as she describes a real-life, straight-from-the-tabloids story about Michael Jackson's supposed attempt to buy Joseph Merrick's bones in 1987.[25] Dorothy then hides the paper under a couch cushion in preparation for Barbara's visit. After continued efforts to befriend Rose and "Madge" stall because they would rather discuss fashion over Faulkner, Barbara tells Dorothy to "face it, . . . Blanche and Rose are limited." Never mind that her "artistic inspiration" is a brooch. Of course, at the end of the episode, Barbara discloses her antisemitism, and Dorothy gets her comeuppance for prioritizing the friendship. The repartee throughout the episode is what makes it a fan favorite, but the setup of supposed intellectual contrasts among the characters also reveals "the differences between trash culture and high culture" that sustain popular culture.[26] Further, as in the *Enquirer* and on *The Golden Girls,* "any time someone exceeds the boundaries of perceived propriety or defies expectations in some way, they can be perceived as acting like trash."[27] Blanche, of course, is known for deploying "trash" as an insult to signify her perception of herself as being of a higher status than others.

A small promotional cast photo next appeared on the September 13, 1988, *Enquirer* cover alongside a large photo of Burt Reynolds and Loni Anderson with a headline that announced a "6-Page Special Section Fall TV Preview." Although there was no further mention of the show inside the issue other than within a TV listings guide, this would seem to be a clear intertextual call back to Reynolds's popular guest appearance on the "Ladies of the Evening" episode in the second season. The paper was back to its usual tricks with the November 22, 1988, cover, making a "shocking" headline out of Sophia's quickie marriage to Max Winestock in the fourth-season "Sophia's Wedding" episodes. This time another large photo of the cast on set was featured, taking up fully half of the cover space. Spoiler alert: the pizza-and-knish stand burns down, and they get an annulment, however, not before

Dorothy is kicked "outta" Rose and Blanche's unauthorized Hunka Hunka Burnin' Love Fan Club for making a joke about their "genuine Elvis artifact." Sophia and Max are also married before a group of Elvis impersonators because Rose "mixed the Elvis list with the wedding list." The King (or Kings, in this case) again functions as a gag that pits Blanche's and Rose's intelligence against Dorothy's, but this scene also points to the conflict between "the Establishment" and trash culture that was carefully maintained at the *Enquirer* and on *The Golden Girls.*[28]

An example of this tension is the April 25, 1989, *Enquirer* cover with the headline "Once Friends . . . Now Jealousy Is Ripping Apart 'Golden Girls.'" Featuring the same promotional photo from 1986 (except cropped against a red background this time for emphasis), this cover also hit newsstands just ahead of the show's one hundredth episode, "Foreign Exchange," which aired on May 6. Inside, a photo of the cast superimposed onto a $10,000 bill leads the article, which describes the "chilly atmosphere on the . . . set" due to supposed disparities in salaries. A "set insider" provided plenty of gossipy tales of cast conflicts, notably that all the publicity following Estelle Getty's Emmy win had "gone to her head" and that "Bea goes crazy when Estelle blows her lines." Another unnamed source reported that "Bea and Betty . . . [were] hopping mad" because Rue "kept everyone waiting while she went to her dressing room and touched up her makeup in the middle of a scene." Such alleged behavior is closer to something viewers would expect more of Blanche and reveals a creeping tone of misogyny that would come to dominate tabloid journalism into the twenty-first century.

Wake Up! Miami: The Tabloids Take TV

> *Dorothy*: I want to thank you all for holding this event on a night when my hang glider is in the shop and Congress is in recess and the lepers are on *Geraldo.* ("What a Difference a Date Makes," S06E22)

By the late 1980s and early 1990s, tabloid journalism had found a welcome home on television, with talk show hosts like Phil Donahue's, Sally Jessy Raphael's, and Geraldo Rivera's featuring scandalous guests and topics on their eponymous daytime talk shows. Matt Browning's *The Definitive Golden Girls Cultural Reference Guide* comprehensively links "the sizable cache of dated references that were topical for the time period" on the show, but greater context is sometimes necessary to grasp the full intent of a joke and its place within the pop culture lexicon.[29] This phenomenon is on display on the same *Enquirer* cover from 1988 that also featured Rivera. Interestingly, Browning's guide points to the very episode of *Geraldo* that the cover highlights, although there is much more to the story.

The episode, titled "Young Hate Mongers," aired on November 3, 1988, and "the guests included white supremacists and Black activists [and] led to a brawl that resulted in [Geraldo's] nose being broken."[30] Although Dorothy's joke came a bit later in the series, this curious moment is also representative of the shifting sands of popular culture recollection. In fact, the reference comes not from any actual guests that were on *Geraldo* but from an exposé that defined Rivera's early career as an investigative journalist. In 1972, Rivera hosted a series of reports about the Willowbrook State School in Staten Island, New York, that exposed the horrific abuse endured by the children with intellectual disabilities who lived at the facility.[31] He referred to it as a "leper colony" because conditions there had long been ignored and left to deteriorate far beyond what should have been acceptable. The report won a Peabody Award, but it has by now almost been lost to the annals of pop culture history, even if it still could have been recalled by viewers in the early 1990s.

Further, leprosy is uncommon enough today in developed countries that many young people are probably unfamiliar with the disease, which "causes severe, disfiguring skin sores and nerve damage" if left untreated.[32] It is therefore understandable when many fans of *The Golden Girls*, especially those born in the twenty-first century, have little to no grasp of what made jokes like Dorothy's work. Here, the reference to "the lepers" functions as both a sly allusion to the *Merriam-Webster's Dictionary* definition of the word for "a person shunned for moral or social reasons" and to the guests frequently hosted on *Geraldo* and other tabloid talk shows, those "whose voices [were] often excluded from U.S. commercial media discourse . . . and other socially marginalized 'abnormals.'"[33] Both formats had to maintain a careful mix of "the ingredients of sin and scandal" in their stories.[34] Such plot devices also factor into the tendentious balance of humor and seriousness on *The Golden Girls* that made it such a hit with audiences and supermarket shoppers alike.

In what seems to be the last instance that *The Golden Girls* was on the cover of the *Enquirer* while it was originally on television, a "sneak preview" of the season 6's "There Goes the Bride" episodes appeared on January 15, 1991, alongside "world exclusive" coverage of none other than Vanna White's wedding. Vanna was first mentioned on the "It's a Miserable Life" episode back in the second season, but by 1991, she had become such a pop culture fixture turning the letters on *Wheel of Fortune* that the term "Vannamania" was coined.[35] After *Playboy* magazine published a lingerie photo shoot that Vanna did before she became famous, her 1987 autobiography, *Vanna Speaks*, became a best seller.[36] Dorothy's reference to it being "just a helluva book" in the fifth-season episode "Sisters and Other Strangers" not only helped to fuel the talk-show-like atmosphere of the scrambling customers in the bookstore scene but was an indicator that even she had acquired an appreciation for those lesser than "great literary figures of our time." The *Enquirer* cover here also provides a satisfying conclusion to the publication's intertextual engagement with the show.

> *Blanche*: Rose Nylund, every man I know is watchin' this show, this live show, this live show about lesbian lovers of Miami!
> *Rose*: Every man you know is watching? Hey, we could beat *The Price Is Right*! ("Goodbye, Mr. Gordon," S07E15)

Finally, worlds collide in the season 7 episode "Goodbye, Mr. Gordon," when Dorothy and Blanche agree to appear on *Wake Up! Miami*, a morning talk show on which Rose has become an unlikely associate producer. Her first assignment is to find two "women who live together," but, predictably, there is a misunderstanding, as the topic was supposed to be about lesbian couples. Such mistaken-identity plots have long been a popular way to include "a gay-affirmative message" in sitcoms.[37] As on *Geraldo*, this story line is also typical of the Reagan and George H. W. Bush eras that ensconced the years in which *The Golden Girls* was on the air. While these administrations worked to instill their state-sponsored heteronormative, homophobic, and evangelical politics, tabloid talk shows often featured guests from the so-called fringes of society, even if their aim was often still more scurrilous than sympathetic. This overlap with the print tabloids illustrates "how the lines between normal and abnormal sexual beings are drawn and redrawn" in mainstream media.[38] Later, Blanche tells Rose, "Well, I don't mind being labeled a lesbian, honey, but since I'm not, you just ruined my social life!" This line does not often get as much attention as others in the episode, but it is emblematic of how the show "explore[d] complex social and cultural shifts emerging in the late twentieth century."[39] After all, back in the season 2 episode "Isn't It Romantic?," Blanche was not even quite sure what a lesbian was, mistaking the term as meaning Lebanese people.

Fans and scholars have continuously acknowledged the groundbreaking story lines featured on *The Golden Girls*. For the most part, its characters were portrayed with a sensitivity that stands out in stark contrast to the tabloid papers and talk shows that had become just as popular. A notable comparison is the *Enquirer*'s treatment of the actor Rock Hudson and the "72 Hours" episode of *The Golden Girls*. The August 13, 1985, cover of the *Enquirer* features a full-page photo of a gaunt Hudson with several headlines, one of which states, "Linda Evans & *Dynasty* Cast Terrified—He Kissed Her on Show."[40] Hudson was diagnosed with AIDS in 1984 and had been guest starring on *Dynasty* at the time. He died of AIDS-related complications on October 2, 1985. Just a few days later, on October 5, the first-season *Golden Girls* episode "Transplant" aired, containing the coded references to "Nancy Reagan's decorator" in the shadow of President Reagan's refusal to acknowledge the AIDS crisis.[41] While more information was known about HIV and AIDS by the time "72 Hours" aired in 1990, a topic that Andrew J. Owens explores in this volume, dialogue from the episode, such as "AIDS is not a bad person's disease," reflects both the stigma that still surrounded it and the show's ability "to present a controversial and complicated topic without judgment," which still resonates today.[42]

Twice . . . in a Lifetime

By the 1990s, the "tabloid valley" would give way to a "tabloid decade" that included a slew of "more media outlets and more vulgarity."[43] Further, *The National Enquirer: Thirty Years of Unforgettable Images*, published in 2001, offers a visual who's who of celebrities featured in the paper and referenced on *The Golden Girls*. The gang's all there—from Martha Raye to Zsa Zsa Gabor, Sonny and Cher, and more. Most of those stars shine less brightly in our collective memory today, but it's fascinating to think about how *The Golden Girls* has been on television and remained consistently popular through it all. Over the years, the stars of *The Golden Girls* also contributed to the gossip surrounding the show. Most notably, Betty White stated several times in later years that she and Bea Arthur did not get along, although this contradicts her earlier portrayals of the set as "a happy ship."[44] Their personality clash was corroborated by one of Arthur's sons in 2019, and their on-set differences are still a popular topic even after White's death in 2021.[45] If imitation remains the sincerest form of flattery, then this story continues to travel down the road and back again in the reporting style of the *Enquirer*. The Hollywood casting director Joel Thurm got yet more mileage from it by sharing that "Betty was not loved by her *Golden Girls* co-stars, especially by Bea Arthur, and not exactly adored by Rue McClanahan."[46] Thurm even included a tabloid-worthy bit of name-calling from Bea about Betty when he worked with Bea in 1999, which grabbed still more headlines when he used it to promote his book on the podcast circuit.[47] *Page Six*, the gossip outlet of the *New York Post*, also continues to recycle this story.[48]

While the *Enquirer* is still in print, it no longer wields the kind of influence it once did, and many of its other print competitors have ceased publication. The same is true of talk shows like *Geraldo*, which went off the air in 1998. Only *People* maintains its reputation and position at the top of the check-out stand. But in the celebrity gossip game, all have unquestionably been eclipsed by the culture created by *TMZ* and the "rise of digital media since the 1980s and the spread of the internet since the 1990s."[49] Yet, the more things change, the more they stay the same, as the saying goes, and *The Golden Girls* continues to shine on its own hilarious and heartfelt merits to connect with ever-younger audiences (even if they don't remember Merlin Olsen).

This chapter is dedicated to my mother, who instilled in me a lifelong love of celebrity gossip through our weekly readings of People *magazine, among many other valuable life lessons.*

Notes

1. Jack Vitek, *The Godfather of Tabloid: Generoso Pope Jr. and the "National Enquirer"* (University Press of Kentucky, 2008), 230.

2. Julia Kristeva, *The Kristeva Reader* (Basil Blackwell, 1986), 111.

3. Closer Weekly (@closerweekly), Facebook, accessed March 17, 2023, www.facebook.com/closerweekly.

4. "Bea Arthur's Amazing Untold Story," *Closer Weekly*, September 20, 2021.

5. Erin A. Meyers, *Extraordinarily Ordinary: "Us Weekly" and the Rise of Reality Television Celebrity* (Rutgers University Press, 2020), 19.

6. Library of Congress, "National Enquirer Index and Database Files, 1977–", comp Mike Handy (2018–), data set, www.loc.gov/item/2018487908/.

7. Meyers, *Extraordinarily Ordinary*, 13.

8. Claire Sewell, "Tattle Tales: Tabloids and The Golden Girls," *The Golden Girls Fashion Corner* (blog), December 16, 2022, https://goldengirlsfashion.com/2022/12/16/tattle-tales-tabloids-and-the-golden-girls/.

9. Anne Helen Petersen, "Towards an Industrial History of Celebrity Gossip: The *National Enquirer*, *People Magazine* and 'Personality Journalism' in the 1970s," *Celebrity Studies* 2, no. 2 (July 2011): 132.

10. Paula E. Morton, *Tabloid Valley: Supermarket News and American Culture* (University Press of Florida, 2009).

11. Morton, *Tabloid Valley*, 38.

12. Petersen, "Towards an Industrial History," 145.

13. S. Elizabeth Bird, *For Enquiring Minds: A Cultural Study of Supermarket Tabloids* (University of Tennessee Press, 1992), 26.

14. Virginia Nightingale, "Women as Audiences," in *Television and Women's Culture: The Politics of the Popular*, ed. Mary Ellen Brown (Sage, 1990), 30.

15. "'Golden Girls' Tops Ratings," *Los Angeles Times*, September 17, 1985.

16. "The Golden Girls," Wikipedia, last modified March 10, 2023, https://en.wikipedia.org/wiki/The_Golden_Girls.

17. "Out to Lunch with the Golden Girls," *Washington Post*, March 14, 1986.

18. Vitek, *Godfather of Tabloid*, 165.

19. Petersen, "Towards an Industrial History," 138.

20. Nancy Mills, "'Golden Girls' Polishes Its Scripts: Daily Revisions Geared to Sharpen Story and Hone Those Laugh Lines," *Los Angeles Times*, October 30, 1987, www.latimes.com/archives/la-xpm-1987-10-30-ca-11702-story.html.

21. Vitek, *Godfather of Tabloid*, 144.

22. "Exclusive . . . Elvis the Untold Story . . . the Last Picture," *National Enquirer*, September 6, 1977.

23. "Elvis Speaks to Relatives From Beyond the Grave," *National Enquirer*, September 19, 1978.

24. John David Ebert, "The Weird and Fantastic Tale of the Pixellation and Disintegration of Elvis Presley," in *Dead Celebrities, Living Icons: Tragedy and Fame in the Age of the Multimedia Superstar* (Praeger, 2010), 47.

25. "Hospital Refuses to Sell Elephant Man Skeleton to Pop Star, " *AP News*, June 18, 1987, https://apnews.com/article/9de819de75426320002fa7ad0a0a2f92.

26. Richard Keller Simon, *Trash Culture: Popular Culture and the Great Tradition* (University of California Press, 1999), 2.

27. Jill E. Anderson, "Eat Dirt and Die, Trash: Tacky, White Southerners in *The Golden Girls* and *Murder, She Wrote*," in *The Tacky South*, ed. Katharine A. Burnett and Monica Carol Miller (Louisiana State University Press, 2022), 108.

28. Ebert, "Weird and Fantastic Tale," 40.

29. Matt Browning, *The Definitive Golden Girls Cultural Reference Guide* (Lyons, 2021), v.

30. Browning, *Definitive Golden Girls*, 339.

31. John O'Connor, "TV: Willowbrook State School, 'the Big Town's Leper Colony,'" *New York Times*, February 2, 1972.

32. "Leprosy (Hansen's Disease)," WebMD, November 12, 2022, www.webmd.com/skin-problems-and-treatments/guide/leprosy-symptoms-treatments-history.

33. Kevin Glynn, *Tabloid Culture: Trash Taste, Popular Power, and the Transformation of American Television* (Duke University Press, 2000), 185.

34. Vitek, *Godfather of Tabloid*, 145.

35. Peter H. Brown and Jim Pinkston, "Vanna-mania . . . You Ain't Seen Nothing Yet!," *Los Angeles Times*, December 7, 1986, www.latimes.com/archives/la-xpm-1986-12-07-ca-1008-story.html.

36. "Bio-Book Mania: All About Vanna and Her Afghan," *New York Times*, May 23, 1987.

37. Stephen Tropiano, *The Prime Time Closet: A History of Gays and Lesbians on TV* (Applause Theatre and Cinema Books, 2002), 223.

38. Joshua Gamson, *Freaks Talk Back: Tabloid Talk Shows and Sexual Nonconformity* (University of Chicago Press, 1998), 18.

39. Kate Browne, *The Golden Girls* (Wayne State University Press, 2020), 8.

40. *National Enquirer*, "Enquirer Classic Covers: 1980s," accessed March 17, 2023, www.nationalenquirer.com/photos/national-enquirer-classic-covers-1980s-part-one/.

41. Claire Sewell, "Pride and Prejudice: Nancy Reagan's Decorator," *The Golden Girls Fashion Corner* (blog), June 3, 2022, https://goldengirlsfashion.com/2022/06/03/golden-girls-transplant-nancy-reagans-decorator/.

42. Claire Sewell, "Deconstructing HIV and AIDS on The Golden Girls," *Nursing Clio*, December 4, 2018, https://nursingclio.org/2018/12/04/deconstructing-hiv-and-aids-on-the-golden-girls/.

43. David Kamp, "The Tabloid Decade," *Vanity Fair*, February 7, 1999, www.vanityfair.com/culture/1999/02/david-kamp-tabloid-decade.

44. Alan Carter, "A Rose by Any Other Name," *New York Daily News*, February 8, 1987, www.newspapers.com/image/492071158.

45. Stephanie Nolasco, "Bea Arthur's Son Recalls Growing Up with 'The Golden Girls' Star, Addresses Alleged Betty White Feud," *Fox News*, April 25, 2019, www.foxnews.com/entertainment/bea-arthurs-son-golden-girls-maude.

46. Joel Thurm, *Sex, Drugs, and Pilot Season: Confessions of a Casting Director* (BearManor Media, 2023), 265.

47. Molly Claire Goddard, "Casting Director Joel Thurm Reveals Betty White's 'Golden Girls' Costars Called Her the C-Word, Allegedly Did Not Like the Beloved Actress," *OK! News*, February 10, 2022, https://okmagazine.com/p/joel-thurm-reveals-betty-whites-golden-girls-costars-called-her-the-c-word/.

48. Nicki Gostin, "Bea Arthur Called Betty White a Shocking Name for Being 'Unkind' to Co-star," *Page Six*, January 23, 2023, https://pagesix.com/2023/01/23/bea-arthur-called-betty-white-a-shocking-name-for-being-unkind-to-co-star/.

49. Johannes Fehrle, "Introduction: Adaptation in a Convergence Environment," in *Adaptation in the Age of Media Convergence*, ed. Johannes Fehrle and Werner Schäfke-Zell (Amsterdam University Press, 2019), 7.

INTERVIEW

The Weekly Schedule

Writing Seasons 5–7

Marc Sotkin, Executive Producer
Okay, so we are going to do twenty-two to twenty-four episodes. That's a lot of scripts. It's about four and a half feature films that we will have to write, create, think up, shoot, edit, and deliver in nine months. So, I have to worry about, first of all, getting enough paper, getting enough stories early on. So, I tended to start earlier than most showrunners, just because I like to have a lot of paper when we started. And so, I'm listening to pitches from people who are going to write stories and deciding yes or no whether we're going to tell those stories. Then, they will go off and write a draft, and I'll read that. And I'll give them notes, send them off to do a second draft. That'll come in, and if it's an outside writer, we'll usually go, "This is fabulous. This is great. Thank you. We've never seen better than this. Good-bye," and then that's going to change anywhere from 25 to 90 percent in the writer's room. Others will find out when we've gathered the family around to watch their script. So . . . in the rewrite process, I'm handing out scenes to different writers who, I know, you know, maybe someone stronger with Blanche or someone stronger with Dorothy or someone does certain stories better than other people. And so I'll hand out those sort of piecemeal to different writers, and then we'll create another draft. And we'll keep doing that until we're pretty much happy with it.

Friday, the week before: If we decide, "Okay, so this is good. We're going with 'sperm bank' next week," I will sit down in a room with Gail Parent, [James] Vallely, Tracy Gamble, maybe one or two of the other writers, and we will go line by line and ask, "Is there any way to make this funnier?" If Blanche goes, "What time is it?" then someone has to say, "Why, is it time for Mel

Bushman's sponge bath?" It has to be something. No one can just say, "What time is it?" So, we go line by line and get that as close as we can get.

Monday: We go to a table read, hear the cast read the script, and decide what kind of shape we're in. And it's never—you don't get a perfect paper. Nobody ever goes, "Oh! We're shooting this one." I'll talk to the director, and early on, it was Terry, or whoever is directing, and say, "Okay, here's the scenes you can start working on. [Then the writers go to work if] there's a hole in the story that has to be fixed or something's not funny enough or whatever.

Tuesday: We're going to go to another table read first thing in the morning Tuesday and see how we did on Monday. And then we're going to go to [start] . . . seriously working on the script for the next Monday and the script that's going to be ready the week after that. So, I am working on those scripts and giving writers notes on those scripts. Tuesday afternoon, we're going to go down to the stage, and we're going to see the actors still [reading from their scripts]. There are things sometimes you think are great on the page, but when you see them on the stage, they're not working, or there's problems. So, we will do a pretty big rewrite Tuesday night. On *The Golden Girls*, that was pretty much our biggest rewrite.

Wednesday: In the morning, go to a table read, see how we did, go back to the office and continue working on next week's script and the script after. We're figuring out what's going into that third position the next Monday. So, the biggest part of my job is juggling all those stories and scripts and stuff. If there's a short, small outside part, we'll probably cast those on a Wednesday, and they may be in the run-through. If it's a big role, we've already cast them or done some stunt casting, then they're going to be there Monday morning. If it's a big actor, they'll be at the table read Monday morning. Wednesday, we are also going to see another run-through, and that's the first time anybody is going to get any acting notes. But those are generally in terms of "Hey, do a cross here," not necessarily line stuff. Film is a director's medium. Comedy is a writer/producer's medium. So, I am actually giving notes to the ladies. If I see something I think they can do funnier or different or whatever, I would start giving those notes on a Wednesday.

Thursday: It's camera blocking day. So, they're working on figuring out their marks on the stage and how the director is going to shoot that and all that. The writing staff, meanwhile, is working on a different script heading

Stage manager Tom Carpenter gives the cast notes. (Photo © Wayne Williams 1984–87. All rights reserved.)

towards Monday and getting it ready for Friday. They do a run-through Thursday that they shoot, because that's when their director gets to see whether all the cameras are in the right place, and I get to watch that with the director because, let's say, we're three minutes long. Okay, I can say to the director, "Then give me a clean shot of when Dorothy comes in, because we're going to take out the three minutes from three minutes ago to that her entering the door." I'm not going to tell the ladies that because I don't want them thinking, "Oh, they're cutting my jokes" or any of that stuff. But I've already started planning editing, and I know those three minutes are coming out.

Friday: I'm in the room with the posse going line by line in the script. We get ready for the four o'clock run-through, which is the dress rehearsal. So, we have an audience there. We see that, then we all go to dinner together. The cast and the writing staff and some key departments are there. And I've watched the four o'clock run-through on camera. I'm in the booth with the other people, and so then I can give actual acting notes. And I will give notes to the actors at that point during dinner. It could also be just "Hey, you want to hold on this line. We didn't expect a big laugh. There, you need to hold for that laugh" or "Just watch the pacing here" or "Lighten up a little bit there." And then we go into the seven o'clock show, and we shoot it. I'm in the booth for that. I make sure we're happy with everything that we shoot, that we don't have to go back and get anything because I think they can get a line better or whatever. Also, I should point out that after the four o'clock dress rehearsal—this is how great the ladies are—a joke that we thought was funny all week, this audience will tell us is not so funny. We will go and write new jokes, which the ladies—other than Estelle, because she's always nervous—don't freak out about. They're ready. They're going to do that joke when we shoot the seven o'clock.

Some of the stuff with Estelle we would do what's called pickups, after the audience leaves. We may go back and shoot something. You don't want the audience to get too tired, so if you are having trouble with a scene, you may move on and go back to shoot the problem after the audience leaves.

Saturday and Sunday: I go home and heal. I say "Hi!" to my wife. And then it's time for Monday-morning table again. We usually shoot three or four in a row, and then we go down for a week. The writers get to catch up during that week, and the cast is off that week. And so that's an easier week, because we're not working nights.

As a general rule, how many writers were on a staff?

That was probably the largest staff I've ever had. And some of them were teams, but there might be ten to twelve individuals, which is a big staff. It was a great staff; it's one of the best staffs I've ever done between that and *Laverne and Shirley*'s staffs. It was like top to bottom great. As a company, Witt/Thomas is the best place I ever worked in terms of supportive writers and supporting writers and believing in writers.

I only wrote, I think, five or six [episodes] because I was busy rewriting other people and doing all the other stuff. I'm known as the guy who killed everybody because I killed Big Daddy, and I killed Phil. I killed everybody.

Did you ever hear from network censors?

I'm not sure who our network representative was for *The Golden Girls*. We never heard from them. I never had to talk to them! It was such a hit, and my guess is that even before we got there, Paul and Tony just didn't want to deal with that. They'll take care of it: don't bother our writers. I've never been on a show that had that much leeway. And *The Golden Girls* is four old ladies doing dick jokes! That's what the show is!

Isabel Omero, Production Associate/Script Supervisor, Writer
[In the beginning] a Broadcast Standards person would attend table reads and watch the midweek network run-through. In the early days, they'd point out words or jokes that they'd ask the writers to change. But I don't recall any big battles. Besides, our producers were really skilled when it came to handling all kinds of network notes. Paul, Tony, Susan, and Marsha had all been through the real wars with Susan Harris's previous controversial creation, *Soap*. I remember "the pool was pizwarm" being replaced with "you're no good at disdam game" [in "The Break-In," S01E08]. I recall the network learning to trust us by the latter years.

Can you tell us about titling episodes?

Marc Sotkin, Executive Producer
One of the first shows I get there, it's the one where Rose gets a new job. I didn't think we were getting anything out of Rose being the grief counselor. So, it's where she goes to work, and I titled it "Rose's New Job." Tony Thomas calls me and he goes, "No, no, no, no, this show is different. It's a hit. People love this show. It's disrespectful to name it 'Rose's New Job.'" And he changed the name to "Rose Fights Back" [S05E04] because there was a real reporter in Los Angeles, a consumer reporter, and his segments were called "Fight Back." When I wrote my next show, which may have been when I killed Big Daddy, I named it "Ebbtide," which has no meaning whatsoever. But, I figured, f-ck these people, I'm going to name it "Ebbtide," and everybody was like, "Oh, fine, 'Ebbtide'!" They love it, and that's why there is an "Ebbtide" [S05E11] and an "Ebbtide's Revenge" [S06E12] and "Ebbtide VI: The Wrath of Stan" [S07E18]. They all mean nothing.

CHAPTER 6

I Need a Cheesecake

1980s Diet Culture and *The Golden Girls*

ASHLEÉ CLARK

A trip to the grocery store almost dissolved the chosen family at the center of *The Golden Girls*. In the sitcom's season 1 finale, lead characters Blanche Devereaux, Rose Nylund, and Dorothy Zbornak cut into a double-fudge chocolate cheesecake as they remember their first feud at the supermarket the day after Rose and Dorothy moved into Blanche's Miami home.[1] In a flashback, we watch the women attempt to shop together for their household. They bicker over one another's expensive food choices, methods of testing a cantaloupe's ripeness, and Rose's commitment to checking the cashier's pricing. They decide to shop separately. In the next scene, they return home in a huff and continue to argue as they put away groceries.

"Girls, let's face facts," Dorothy says. "The three of us just can't agree on anything. It's obvious we were not meant to live together."

Blanche and Rose agree.

"This is exactly what happened during the Great Herring War," Rose says.

With that intro, the audience realizes we're in for a ubiquitous Rose story from the daffiest member of the bunch. By this point in the show's run, we know Rose for her rambling and nonsensical tales from her hometown of St. Olaf, Minnesota, that she tells with so much sincerity that the other characters can't help but let her tell them time and time again. But in the grocery flashback, this is the first time Rose tells her roommates one of these stories. Rose recounts how the Lindstroms and the Johanssons, controllers of the most fertile herring waters off the coast of Norway, couldn't agree on what to do with the fish: pickle them or train them for the circus? It's hard to tell where the characters end and the actors begin as Blanche and Dorothy giggle and ask probing questions about the technicalities of a herring circus ("Do they ever shoot a herring out of a cannon?"). The group ends up collapsing in laughter (see "The Myth of Ad-Libbing the Great Herring War" in this volume).

"Do you think it was just a fluke, or do you think we could learn to like each other?" Rose asks.

"Well, I think it might take time," Dorothy says, "but I think it could be worth it."

Rose pulls a bright-pink baker's box from a grocery bag. Her new roommates learn that it's a chocolate cheesecake.

"I think this could be the beginning of a beautiful friendship," Dorothy says.

Cheesecake could've been the fifth main character on *The Golden Girls* with all the screen time it received in the show's seven seasons. Blanche, Rose, Dorothy, and Sophia, Dorothy's mother, would bring out the dessert late at night when there was a big problem that the group needed one another to solve. Comfort food like cheesecake was an integral part of the characters' lives on *The Golden Girls*. It was also a catalyst that sparked story lines in which the characters followed, internalized, and upheld the norms of 1980s diet culture throughout the run of the show. *The Golden Girls* debuted in the middle of the 1980s, the decade that gave us Jenny Craig, Jane Fonda workout tapes, and Lean Cuisines.[2] Guidance about weight loss at the time focused on low-fat eating and aerobic exercise as the keys to attaining the slender body that American society deemed ideal for women.

The characters on *The Golden Girls* were contemporaries of the real women who watched the show. Like the audience, the fictional women tried fad diets. They worried about how they looked in bathing suits. They weaponized one another's insecurities about their bodies to gain power within the group. The show's writers could have avoided story lines and jokes about food and body image that were reflective of the decade's diet culture in the same vein that the creators of the show *Schitt's Creek* never had story lines about homophobia for its queer characters.[3] The show's actresses, who each had their own impressive lists of credits, had enough star power at the show's inception to push back against stories that centered dieting and amplified the insecurities of these middle-aged women. Instead, the show's creators and actresses reflected the real world of womanhood by embracing the characters' contradictions in their interactions with and attitudes toward diet culture. The Girls knew that the key to problem-solving involved a late-night cheesecake pickup from a bakery, no matter how much time they spent fretting over their waistlines during the day. They turned to fat jokes to put one another in their place, but they more often supported one another through challenges big and small. In their own ways, these middle-aged women rebelled against the negative influences of diet culture in favor of loving one another and, ultimately, themselves. Real women are complicated, and so were the Girls.

"We all draw on other people in our lives—parents, grandparents," said Terry Grossman, co-executive producer and head writer during the show's third season. "Part of the reason for the show's popularity is that these are very vital people. The very same story you've seen 100 times on every sitcom takes on new light with characters in this age group. That makes life easier for us."[4]

The writers' decision to reflect the internal conflicts of real women of the era and their navigation of the decade's diet culture made *The Golden Girls* relevant to its audiences. Thirty years later, American women still struggle with societal expectations that dictate how they are supposed to look—and the foods they need to eat to achieve the ideal. In grounding the show's four main characters in the messy reality of being American middle-aged women, *The Golden Girls* writers and actresses created a classic show that's relatable to new generations of female viewers who still have to contend with the cultural pressure to be thin.

Dieting in American History

Women's bodies and what they eat have been the subject of much hand-wringing in the United States for almost two hundred years. The actions of women, specifically how they cooked for their families, was the impetus for the first group of Americans who recorded their weight somewhat regularly: disciples of the Reverend Sylvester Graham, who, beginning in the 1830s, sought to reform gluttony in the American diet.[5] Rather than focusing on fatness and weight loss, Graham's teachings centered a spiritual call to remove the sin of gluttony from Americans' lives. "In simplest terms, this was the theory: Gluttony, arch sin, was born of civilization, which seduced the natural appetite and played digestion false."[6] Graham claimed that fighting gluttony began in the kitchen—the woman's domain. It was a woman's job not only to feed her family but to rescue her household from the sin of gluttony with the food that she cooked.

By the late nineteenth century, societal changes in the United States led to the idea of gluttony being bound to fatness: "fatness to inefficiency,

inefficiency to lack of energy and loss of balance, and imbalance to overweight."[7] Unlike the Grahamites, the focus was less on the family and more on the self. And with fatness villainized, America had a full-blown dieting culture as we entered the twentieth century, especially among middle- and upper-middle-class white women—the demographic of the four main characters on *The Golden Girls*.[8]

By the 1980s, much of weight-loss ideology in the United States was focused on reducing or eliminating fat from one's diet. Doctors and scientists began promoting the low-fat diet for cardiovascular health in the 1950s, but in 1977, the U.S. Senate Select Committee on Nutrition released its first national guidelines, including recommendations that codified this approach: "increase carbohydrate consumption to between 55% and 60% of the energy (caloric) intake," and "reduce fat consumption from over 40% down to 30% of energy intake."[9] Even though the data were limited, an expert panel at the National Institutes of Health Consensus Development Conference on Lowering Blood Cholesterol to Prevent Heart Disease in 1984 cosigned the idea that Americans needed to reduce dietary fat. The National Cholesterol Education Program did the same in 1987.[10]

Diet and Exercise in 1980s Popular Culture

By the time *The Golden Girls* premiered on September 14, 1985, on NBC, fat was the enemy of good health, an idea that would last through the 1990s.[11] The 1980s gave us the birth and peak popularity of weight-loss programs, fad diets, low-fat food products, and meal replacements. The Jenny Craig weight-loss program opened its first center in the 1980s.[12] Los Angeles Dodgers manager Tommy Lasorda became a spokesperson for the meal-replacement "shake" SlimFast and lost thirty-five pounds when he followed the beverage's companion diet plan.[13] Host Oprah Winfrey rolled a literal red wagon filled with sixty-seven pounds of fat onto the stage of her talk show to show just how much weight she had lost adhering to the Optifast diet, another liquid meal plan.[14]

Along with the diet trends of the 1980s, working out at home also saw a rise in popularity because of the video cassette recorder (VCR) and celebrity exercise videos. Television as a workout tool had existed for decades before. In 1948, WEWS in Cleveland hired a television personality named Paige Palmer to host what would become the United States' first daily fitness television show. *The Jack LaLanne Show*, which premiered in the 1950s, was the first nationally syndicated workout program in the country and popularized the guided at-home fitness genre.[15] In the 1970s, tech companies began selling consumer devices, including the VCR, for recording television programs.[16] VCRs didn't gain broader appeal until 1982 with the debut of the *Jane Fonda's Workout* tape, an aerobic workout led by the Academy Award–winning actress that was geared toward women.[17] At the time, only 5 percent of American households had a VCR.[18] By the end of the decade, Fonda's tape sold seventeen million copies and helped to popularize the VCR, the only way to access the workout.[19]

The Golden Girls was steeped in the culture of its time. Story lines tackled the news, people, and cultural phenomena of the moment: a well-intended letter from Rose to Mikhail Gorbachev, the final leader of the Soviet Union; visits from prominent figures like President George H. W. Bush, Pope John Paul II, Michael Jackson, and Burt Reynolds; references to films and TV shows like *Teenage Mutant Ninja Turtles, Ghostbusters, On Golden Pond, The Cosby Show*, and *America's Funniest Home Videos. The Golden Girls* even engaged with current events that challenged its audience, such as the episode when Rose has an HIV scare. The fith-season episode "72 Hours" aired the same year that the Centers for Disease Control adopted the HIV-prevention counseling model that focused on the patient instead of the disease (as the episode did by focusing on how waiting for a potential diagnosis impacted Rose and her roommates).[20] With American women giving more attention to diet and exercise, coupled with *The Golden Girls*' attempt to engage with contemporary issues, the focus on dieting was ripe for exploration on a series starring four women.

Dating and Dieting

The three younger characters of *The Golden Girls* household—Rose, Dorothy, and Blanche—often participate in story lines related to dieting for weight loss. The show depicts dieting as a part of womanhood as much as menopause, hearing loss, and chronic illness. The series also tethers weight to ideals of feminine beauty and desirability; all of the characters are active in the dating scene, which often acts as a motivator for the women's weight-loss efforts. For example, Blanche begins a regimen of exercising, taking supplements, and changing her eating habits after her much-younger Jazzercise instructor, Dirk, asks her on a date.[21] In another instance, the Girls are gathered for a late-night snack after helping Rose with her résumé;

Dorothy discusses the merits of eating so much food right before her high school crush, Barry Glick, comes to visit: "I'm so glad my date with Barry is tomorrow—the fat won't have time to show," Dorothy says. She tells the Girls she wants to be "svelte for Barry."[22] The women are willing to give up delicious calorie-laden food (or at least schedule their bingeing so the effects aren't apparent) in order to appear thin and therefore attractive to their male suitors.

Thinness is especially synonymous with desirability for Blanche. The writers most often make her the subject of story lines related to dieting and weight loss. Blanche's contradictions make her one of the most fascinating characters on *The Golden Girls*: She has seemingly endless confidence in the bedroom yet the most blatant insecurities about her looks. For Blanche, maintaining her weight is connected to her sex appeal, and sex appeal is everything to her. In the second-season episode "End of the Curse," Blanche meets with a psychiatrist after she discovers she is beginning menopause:

> *Dr. Barensfeld*: All right, it is not just menopause. It's what it represents to you: growing older.
> *Blanche*: Yes.
> *Dr. Barensfeld*: And growing older represents a loss of attractiveness.
> *Blanche*: Yes.
> *Dr. Barensfeld*: And is that all there is to you, sex appeal?
> *Blanche*: Yes![23]

Blanche is the most willing of the Girls to turn to fad diets and exercise to meet what she perceives as an almost immediate way to lose weight. She often partakes in crash dieting, the practice in which a person severely restricts what they eat in order to lose weight quickly.[24] In the first season's "Job Hunting," Blanche fixes herself a raw vegetable plate because she has gained three pounds, a fall from grace from a character who, in the same conversation, brags about how she used to have an eighteen-inch waistline like Scarlett O'Hara, the heroine of the book *Gone with the Wind*.[25] While Blanche prepares for her date with Dirk from Jazzercise, Rose tells Dorothy that Blanche looks terrible. "That's because all she eats is wheat grass and bee pollen," Dorothy says. When Blanche finally makes it to her date, she begins the night with an order of a duck à l'orange (a dish that derives much of its deliciousness from the high fat content of the bird),[26] escargot, and a tossed salad with blue cheese dressing but changes her order to a watercress salad with two lemon wedges to mirror what Dirk is having. In another episode, Blanche throws out her junk food and attempts to stick to a SlimFast-like diet of shakes and small "sensible meals" so she can fit into her wedding dress, a garment she first wore at least twenty-five years and several children ago. But Sophia knows what happens when Blanche goes on a diet, which happens often enough for Sophia to observe, "The last time you went on a diet, you turned into that guy from *Silence of the Lambs*."[27] Because Blanche is the character who puts the most focus on her appearance and sex appeal, she is also the character most likely to go to extremes to achieve the body she believes she needs to keep her attractive to men.

When Weight Becomes the Butt of the Joke

Blanche's desire to control her weight extends to her children, as when Blanche's daughter Rebecca comes to visit after a four-year estrangement. This episode, called "Blanche's Little Girl," is pivotal in understanding not only Blanche's relationship with diet culture but also how the show's creators confront the issue of women's weight. Blanche sees Rebecca, a model, as a reflection of herself; before her daughter arrives, Blanche tells her roommates that her daughter has "a figure men would mortgage a house for": "we were always so much alike." But when Rebecca arrives, she is noticeably bigger than she was the last time that she saw her mother. Sophia's fat jokes about Rebecca begin immediately. "What did she model, car covers?" Sophia asks.[28]

Sophia's put-down and the litany of others that follow are a type of disparagement humor in which jokes are intended to belittle people in a marginalized group on the basis of stereotypes that reflect societal beliefs about this "other."[29] Disparagement humor reflects how "individuals are likely to compare themselves with others who are in a less prestigious social position related to a specific characteristic (e.g., body weight)," which may result in an increase in the subjective well-being of the person who's making the comparison.[30] In other words, we feel better about our own insecurities when we put down another person for those same insecurities. We see this in many exchanges between Blanche and Dorothy:

Dorothy: Blanche, I hope you don't mind, but I borrowed your rhinestone necklace.

Blanche: No, that's fine, but I should point out that it was designed for a dainty neck.

Dorothy: Yes, Blanche, but I don't know Mike Tyson well enough to borrow his jewelry.[31]

Fat jokes on *The Golden Girls* give the characters an outlet to express their own insecurities without making themselves vulnerable; they allow the women to lift themselves up in comparison to the women around them; and, because of societal attitudes toward fatness, they make the audience laugh.

Throughout *The Golden Girls*, the writers put some of the show's more mean-spirited quips in the mouth of Sophia, an octogenarian grandmother. The juxtaposition of an older woman whom the audience assumes would be a sweet old lady with the barbs she often trades with other characters adds to the humor of many of the scenes. In "Blanche's Little Girl," the writers put the weight-related jokes in Sophia's mouth to give us permission to laugh. But the writers expect the audience to villainize the character of Jeremy, Rebecca's boyfriend, who also makes Rebecca the subject of fat jokes. When the couple talks about how they met at a sidewalk café in Paris, Jeremy says, "There weren't any tables left, so I just sat at Becky." Even Jeremy's proposal is couched in a fat joke: "Blanche, I'd like to ask for your daughter's hand in marriage. I'd take the rest of her, but I have a bad back." The writers want the audience to think that it's funny when Sophia makes fat jokes; it's offensive when Jeremy does the same. With this turn, *The Golden Girls* writers capture what it's really like to be a part of a tight-knit group of women. The four women love one another (and in "Blanche's Little Girl," that love extends to Blanche's daughter), but they will also put one another down. But if an outsider (in this case, Jeremy) does the same thing, the women unite in their rejection of this individual. They have earned the right to make fun of one another thanks to years of intimacy, trust, and vulnerability; someone new has not.

Blanche walks this fine line when confronting her daughter's weight gain in "Blanche's Little Girl." Blanche wants to fix what she views as the problem of her daughter's bigger size. In their first conversation after their reunion, Blanche tells Rebecca that she is going to put her on a diet. But Blanche hasn't earned the right to criticize Rebecca's life choices after their four-year estrangement. Blanche's suggestions about her daughter's weight end when Jeremy arrives (since he takes over the bulk of the episode's fat jokes and critiques about Rebecca). When Blanche finally breaks her silence about her dislike of Jeremy, Rebecca pushes her away, but she acquiesces when she realizes that her mother was right about her now-fiancé. It's at this point, after reestablishing their relationship, that Blanche can return to addressing Rebecca's weight: At the end of the episode, Blanche steers Rebecca away from the kitchen, where a cheesecake awaits. Blanche is ultimately a product of the society in which she was raised, which places a high value on a woman's looks and, therefore, her weight. In trying to get her daughter in line with what is considered a typical female body, she is at once perpetuating diet culture while protecting her daughter from becoming an "other" in this society.

Subverting the Narrative

Even though the show's writers made Rose, Dorothy, and Blanche fret about their weight, *The Golden Girls* ultimately challenges the norms of 1980s diet culture and prioritizes the women's relationships with one another and themselves through choices in story structure, character choices, and motifs throughout the series's seven seasons.

Television writers illustrate a story line's importance through the structure of an episode. Each episode of *The Golden Girls* was written with the same formula: "the idea, the act break and the resolution," Grossman said in 1987. "Usually there's an 'A' story and a 'B' story going. It's the natural structure."[32] The A story is the main story line of an episode. An episode can also contain a secondary, or B, story. This story line does not have the importance of the A story. Rather, it is a way to involve other characters who are not involved directly in the A story. B stories can still, in the context of sitcoms, be funny, but they do not concern the main conflict around which the majority of an episode is built. *The Golden Girls*' writers often relegated plotlines about dieting and weight loss to B stories, which demonstrates that the subject does not warrant the attention or gravitas of the main story line.

A notable exception is the fourth-season episode "Rites of Spring." Both the A and B plots are about dieting: the Girls try to lose weight for a party as Sophia tries to gain weight for her own peace of mind after losing weight. However, this episode is a compilation, in which the Girls' dieting is used as a framing device to contextualize flashbacks. While the episode uses a mixture of new and previously aired footage, the episode ends with the Girls remembering that the party for which they are losing weight has been moved from Saturday to Sunday, which gives them an extra day before they need to start dieting. They end the episode digging into the cake that Sophia baked in her effort to gain weight. Even in an episode in which both the A and B stories focus on dieting, the Girls choose comfort food over their vanity (even if it's only temporary).

The writers also use the characters to voice opposition to diet culture. Dorothy is the most outwardly defiant toward diet culture. She often verbally dismisses attempts from Blanche and Rose to diet. For example, Dorothy wants no part of a "healthy" pizza:

> *Rose*: Should we go healthy and get whole-wheat crust and low-fat cheese?
> *Dorothy*: Why don't we go really, really high fiber and spread ketchup on cardboard? Pizza, dammit, get pizza![33]

When the Girls turn to comfort food, Dorothy is often the one who initiates the emotional eating or, at least, dives wholeheartedly into it. When Dorothy and Rose are having a hard time trying to find entertainment for a charity gala and Rose asks what they will do about their problem, Dorothy says, "I tell you what we're going to do, Rose: We're going to eat a cheesecake."[34] Dorothy readily recognizes that a solution is not immediately available, so they might as well get a slice of cheesecake to soften the dilemma or at least give them time to figure things out. Or when Dorothy discovers that her son-in-law cheated on her daughter, Kate, Dorothy makes the Girls pause their *I Love Lucy* marathon to join her in the kitchen, where she immediately gets ice cream from the freezer so they can start talking about the situation.[35] Dorothy is often shown as the logical, practical woman of the foursome, so the writers' choice to have this character be the voice of reason when it's time to give up healthful eating in favor of something fatty and delicious is a deliberate way to give more credence to the idea that dieting is not the smartest option for the characters.

Let's Talk About Cheesecake

The food often at the center of the *Golden Girls* kitchen table is cheesecake. For the Girls, it seems impossible to solve a problem without the decadent dessert. And that choice of dessert is the most blatant rejection of 1980s low-fat diet culture. Cheesecake as we know it in the U.S. was first introduced through recipes for English "curd cheese" cakes. In the 1850s, a cookbook author from Philadelphia replaced the curds with local cream cheese, which had a reputation for "full cream" cheese that was made from unskimmed whole milk.[36] Cheesecake was created to be full of fat, which is still reflected in ingredient lists of modern recipes for the dessert. One such recipe specifically calls out the need to use full-fat cream cheese: "Cheesecake is not the time to skimp."[37]

For the characters on *The Golden Girls*, cheesecake is also a good example of comfort food. The term has been around since as early as 1966, when *The Palm Beach Post* used it in a story on obesity: "Adults, when under severe emotional stress, turn to what could be called 'comfort food'—food associated with the security of childhood, like mother's poached egg or famous chicken soup."[38] The label of "comfort food" can apply to anything that a person uses to feel better; the warm fuzzy feelings don't come from a dish's caloric value but rather from the associations that the food calls to mind for the person eating it.[39] As we saw in the episode "The Way We Met," the inaugural cheesecake after the disastrous trip to the grocery store provides Rose, Blanche, and Dorothy with the opportunity to bond over a shared interest after resolving their first conflict. By the time we see the pink cheesecake box, the characters' hostile feelings toward one another have moved toward humor and fondness. With each subsequent slice of cheesecake, each of the characters calls on that original high of their first shared dessert, therefore bringing comfort to stressful situations.

Putting cheesecake at the center of the Girls' most intimate moments with one another, when they are the most vulnerable, shows that the cheesecake fellowship is ultimately stronger than the cultural urge to be thin, as the women return to the dessert when there is a predicament. A cheesecake is there when Dorothy thinks a priest wants to leave the church to marry her, when the girls are trying to figure out how to keep Sophia from moving in with her son, Phil, when Blanche debates selling the house.[40] Eating the cheesecake gives the group the time to examine an issue, exchange personal stories and quips, and, hopefully, solve their problem.

Conclusion

The four main characters of *The Golden Girls* regularly participate and perpetuate the diet culture of the era throughout the run of the show. By making this choice, the show's writers and actresses reflect the real lives of women in the show's audience. We watch and commiserate as the Girls try fad diets to lose a few pounds quickly, exercise to stay fit for the dating scene, and lob fat jokes at one another to make themselves feel better about their own insecurities. Ultimately, the writers enabled their characters to question and challenge the societal norms that kept them in want of an ideal body. The characters' love of one another and, as a result, a love of themselves proved to be more important than staying thin. In other words, fellowship around a cheesecake was the subversive response to the diet culture of the 1980s.

Notes

1. "The Way We Met," S01E25.

2. Alex Beggs, "Diet Foods of the '80s Are Out. But Has Anything Really Changed?," *Bon Appetit*, January 10, 2022, www.bonappetit.com/story/diet-food-in-america.

3. Devon Ivie, "Dan Levy Explains Why Homophobia Will Never Infiltrate *Schitt's Creek*," *Vulture*, November 18, 2018, www.vulture.com/2018/11/dan-levy-explains-why-schitts-creek-has-no-homophobia.html.

4. Nancy Mills, "'Golden Girls' Polishes Its Scripts: Daily Revisions Geared to Sharpen Story and Hone Those Laugh Lines," *Los Angeles Times*, October 30, 1987, www.latimes.com/archives/la-xpm-1987-10-30-ca-11702-story.html.

5. Hillel Schwartz, *Never Satisfied: A Cultural History of Diets, Fantasies, and Fat* (Free Press, 1986), 27.

6. Schwartz, *Never Satisfied*, 25.

7. Schwartz, *Never Satisfied*, 81.

8. Ann F. LaBerge, "How the Ideology of Low Fat Conquered America," *Journal of the History of Medicine and Allied Sciences* 63, no. 2 (2008): 141.

9. Cara B. Ebbeling, Ian S. Young, Alice H. Lichtenstein, David S. Ludwig, Michelle McKinley, Rafael Perez-Excamilla, and Eric Rimm, "Dietary Fat: Friend to Foe?," *Clinical Chemistry* 64, no. 1 (2018): 34.

10. LaBerge, "How the Ideology of Low Fat," 153.

11. LaBerge, "How the Ideology of Low Fat," 147.

12. Jenny Craig, "Our Story," accessed September 5, 2023, www.jennycraig.com.au/about/.

13. Kellie Kreiss, "How SlimFast Became a Billion-Dollar Diet Craze and Faded Away into Health Fad Heaven," *Ranker*, September 23, 2021, www.ranker.com/list/slim-fast-history/kellie-kreiss.

14. "Oprah's Top 20 Moments," *O, The Oprah Magazine*, October 2005, www.oprah.com/oprahshow/oprahs-top-20-moments.

15. Corinne Purtill, "A Short History of Home Fitness, from 600 BC to Today," *Quartz*, April 26, 2020, https://qz.com/1845146/from-discus-to-peloton-the-history-of-home-fitness; Carrie Battan, "Thank You, Jane Fonda: A Brief History of America's Obsession with Workout Videos," *Grantland*, April 14, 2015, https://grantland.com/hollywood-prospectus/thank-you-jane-fonda-a-brief-history-of-americas-obsession-with-workout-videos/.

16. Jake Rossen, "A Brief History of the VCR," *Mental Floss*, April 1, 2021, www.mentalfloss.com/article/642374/vcr-history.

17. Bryan Lufkin, "The Evolution of Home Fitness," *BBC*, May 4, 2020, www.bbc.com/worklife/article/20200504-covid-19-update-quarantine-home-workouts-during-coronavirus.

18. Rico Gagliano, "Jane Fonda's Workout and the VHS," *The Dinner Party Download* (podcast), May 24, 2013, www.dinnerpartydownload.org/jane-fondas-workout-and-the-vhs/.

19. Lufkin, "Evolution of Home Fitness."

20. "A Timeline of HIV and AIDS," HIV.gov, accessed September 4, 2023, www.hiv.gov/hiv-basics/overview/history/hiv-and-aids-timeline/#year-1990.

21. "Blanche and the Younger Man," S01E09.
22. "Job Hunting," S01E22.
23. "End of the Curse," S02E01.
24. Jacqueline Jacques, "The Risks of the Crash Diet," Obesity Action Coalition, Fall 2014, www.obesityaction.org/resources/the-risks-of-the-crash-diet/.
25. "Job Hunting," S01E22.
26. Daniel Gritzer, "Duck à l'Orange Recipe," *Serious Eats*, December 12, 2018, www.seriouseats.com/duck-a-lorange#toc-what-is-duck--lorange.
27. "What a Difference a Date Makes," S06E22.
28. "Blanche's Little Girl," S03E14.
29. Romeo Vitalli, "The Problem with Fat Jokes," *Psychology Today*, July 7, 2014, www.psychologytoday.com/us/blog/media-spotlight/201407/the-problem-fat-jokes.
30. Jacob M. Burmeister and Robert A. Carels, "Weight-Related Humor in the Media: Appreciation, Distaste, and Anti-Fat Attitudes," *Psychology of Popular Media Culture* 3, no. 4 (2014): 223.
31. "Dorothy's New Friend," S03E15.
32. Mills, "Golden Girls' Polishes Its Scripts."
33. "That Old Feeling," S05E08.
34. "Diamond in the Rough," S02E22.
35. "Son-in-Law Dearest," S02E23.
36. Stella Parks, *BraveTart: Iconic American Desserts* (Norton, 2017), 78.
37. Emma Christensen, "How to Make Perfect Cheesecake," *The Kitchn*, updated October 5, 2021, www.thekitchn.com/how-to-make-perfect-cheesecake-recipe-cooking-lessons-from-the-kitchen-110760.
38. Cari Romm, "Why Comfort Food Comforts," *The Atlantic*, April 3, 2015, www.theatlantic.com/health/archive/2015/04/why-comfort-food-comforts/389613/.
39. Romm, "Why Comfort Food Comforts."
40. "Forgive Me, Father," S02E18; "Golden Moments (2)," S03E19; "We're Outta Here (1)," S04E25.

The cast. (Photo © Wayne Williams 1984–87.)

INTERVIEW

Memorable Moments with the Girls

Isabel Omero, Production Associate/Script Supervisor, Writer
From table read to taping, Bea never let go of the script. It was her security blanket. Betty, on the other hand, let it go as soon as she read it once. Rue saw the script, and you could just see her wheels start turning, sizing up juicy acting opportunities. Estelle, sadly, was often afraid of the script. She'd open it up, and all she could see was the number of lines she had to memorize.

Marsha Posner Williams, Co-Producer
As early as the third episode, one of the notes we gave Estelle between scenes was to wash her hands. Do you want to know why? Understand, nobody knew in those days what Alzheimer's or dementia was for her, but obviously it was the start of that, because that's ultimately how she died. But we're doing a scene, and we were in the early show [5:30 p.m.], and the camera cuts to Estelle to do a line, and they're doing a medium close-up of her, and she makes a hand gesture, and the line was written on her hand. So, we said, "Please wash your hands. It's a little giveaway, right there." Her notes and lines were written everywhere on that set—everywhere, even from the beginning.

We got an episode in which they are sitting around the kitchen table, and there was a cigar box in the middle of the table, and the cigar lid was open. And we all knew... Estelle had a big speech, and we knew that that speech was written on the inside of that cigar box. But you know she delivered it perfectly, so nobody gave a shit, right? Just do it as long as it works. So, we do the early show, and the cigar box is open, like it's supposed to be. She does the speech. Okay good. Now we get to the late show. And we get to that speech, and you can see in her eyes that she's saying, "I'm going to show them that I know this speech," and in the middle of the taping, she closes the lid and does the speech. Well, now we're screaming in the booth, "Nothing is going to match now!" We can't edit between both shows because the lid would be open, closed, open, closed.

Wayne Williams, Photographer
Bea had purchased a BMW 650 or 850 or something like that, and she was frustrated as all get out because this audio cassette wouldn't play. And so, she calls me. "Hello, darling. I've got this problem with my car. Can you come over here?" And so, I said, "Sure, why not? It's Bea Arthur calling me!" You're gonna go, right? So, I drive over to the house, and I said, "What's the problem?" and she said, "You get in the driver's seat, and I'll get in the passenger's seat." So, now we're in the carport, and I say, "Okay, so what's the problem?" And she says, "This cassette, it won't play. I put it in, and nothing happens." And I said, "Do you have the keys to the car?" And she said, "Yes." She hands me the key, I put it in the ignition, I turn the car on, I put the cassette in, and it starts to play.

And then I get one of those looks from her: "Go home."

Marsha Posner Williams, Co-Producer
Wayne and I were having breakfast one morning, and the phone rings. "Hey, Bea, what's happening?" She said, "Marsha, I saw you on HBO last night on a show called *Real Sex*." I said, "Oh, you know, Bea, that segment that you saw is so popular, it's run dozens and dozens and dozens of times." And she said, "I know, that was the second time I'd seen it." And I just lost my shit, because I'm picturing Bea Arthur—this was a late-night show—and she's in bed channel surfing, going, "Oh my God, there's my producer, on *Real Sex*." That episode was shot in my house, by the way.

Marc Sotkin, Executive Producer
When I killed Phil in an episode, after the Tuesday-night run-through, Estelle calls me at home, and the ladies have never called me at home. And she says, "I don't want to do this episode." And it's like, well, let's figure out what the problem is. So, we really talked it out, and the problem was when they go up to the casket and they're looking at Phil in the casket and doing jokes about what Phil was wearing. Estelle just said, "I can't do that. I can't go up there—my son is dead—I can't go up and do those jokes." So, when you watch that episode, she remains seated. And that was it. The respect for the writing was amazing. We got so few notes from the ladies wanting to change things.

So, Estelle calling me was a big deal, because they never complained, and they never had a lot of input. I go down to the stage one day, and Betty wanted to change the word "this" to "that." "I don't want to say 'this one.' I want to say 'that one.'" And I said, "Just this once, Betty. But let's not make a habit of this," and she laughed because they all do.

Bea asked me to change a joke only once. I wrote a joke hoping she would deliver it like Bert Lahr when he was the Cowardly Lion. She was pissed off at Stan, and I wanted her to say [with Lion's accent], "I'll murderize him!" And she didn't want to do that. And once, we did a fund-raiser episode and wrote a joke saying "tuna sandwiches," and she wanted to change that. She didn't want to say "tuna" because of marine life trapped in nets. So she didn't want to say "tuna" or do Bert Lahr. And those are the only things I remember she ever wanted to change.

We treated them with respect. We knew who they were. I think my only really emotional good-bye was with Betty. Betty loved to do the little dirty jokes, and she loved that we got them in, and we just connected on a comedic level that was great. And I had watched her—you know, Betty invented television—so growing up, I was like, "I like her." And I got to work with her.

CHAPTER 7

"AIDS Is Not a Bad Person's Disease, Rose"

Contagion and Comedy on *The Golden Girls*

ANDREW J. OWENS

On June 17, 1982, *NBC Nightly News* ran a report considered to be one of the first U.S. television broadcasts about HIV/AIDS. Under the title banner "Cancer Study," before HIV or AIDS were ever officially named as such, anchor Tom Brokaw stated that "scientists at the National Centers for Disease Control in Atlanta today released the results of a study which shows that the lifestyle of some male homosexuals has triggered an epidemic of a rare form of cancer." Reporting for NBC, correspondent Robert Bazell grimly noted a surge in a "mysterious newly discovered disease which affects mostly homosexual men. . . . One-third have died, and none have been cured. . . . Researchers are now studying blood and other samples from the victims trying to learn what is causing the disease. So far, they have had no luck."[1] Such an enigmatic, ominous tone was typical of nearly all media reporting during the early years of this public health emergency. Indeed, what would come to be known as the HIV/AIDS crisis of the 1980s and early 1990s, in the words of David Skal, "weirdly echoed the classic motifs of vampire legends. A blood-borne wasting malady appears, each victim capable of creating others through vein-puncturing or unconventional forms of sex. Science is baffled. Self-appointed moral guardians come forth, waving religious talismans, insisting that the affliction is the work of the devil."[2] As James Kinsella maintains, making this disease as "spooky as possible helped make AIDS a national issue, but it also fed on Americans' fears and did little to inform them."[3] AIDS was, for many Americans, both a literal and metaphorical nightmare out of a horror movie come true. So how, then, did what would seem like one of our country's most prominent "no laughing matter" issues of the second half of the twentieth century come to be thematized and narrativized not only on scripted television but on, of all formats, the sitcom? How might its on-screen appearance reflect broader changes within the U.S. television industry during an era of rapid deregulation? And if HIV/AIDS became paradoxical fodder for televisual comedy, in whose direction were such jokes pointed?

As Matt Sienkiewicz and Nick Marx argue, "moments of great trauma have, historically, often led simultaneously to serious introspection and comedic interpretation, . . . offering Americans opportunities to debate and interpret social and political upheaval beyond the realm of traditional 'serious' media."[4] And indeed, on February 17, 1990, toward the end of season 5, NBC's juggernaut sitcom *The Golden Girls* aired one of its most socially significant episodes vis-à-vis national trauma: "72 Hours" (S05E19). After Rose has received a letter that the blood she was given during a routine cholecystectomy (gallbladder removal) may have contained HIV antibodies, she returns to the hospital for the recommended precautionary screening. Much to her chagrin, a doctor informs her that her results, only available at that time via a standard western blot blood test, would not be available for three days—or seventy-two hours.

In this chapter, I argue that this episode, and *The Golden Girls* more broadly, helps us reconsider both the scope and significance of what Ron Becker famously terms U.S. network television's "Gay '90s" in order to bring to the critical foreground a more capacious and illuminating set of texts that have yet to be given their full scholarly due.[5] Although beloved by queer audiences since its original airing, *The Golden Girls* did not indiscriminately applaud the "We're here! We're queer!" ethos that championed "positive" media representation through identity politics as its end goal, one that became central to both industrial and popular discourses attached to successful LGBTQ+ programming like *Ellen* and *Will & Grace*. Instead, both the series writ large and "72 Hours" most markedly were sporadically haunted by polymorphously queer specters of contagion that mainstream U.S. media had previously tethered to representations of HIV/AIDS patients in "must-see TV" movies like *An Early Frost*, *Go Toward the Light*, and *The Ryan White Story*. Aired in the middle of George H. W. Bush's presidential administration, which continued predecessor Ronald Reagan's near total disregard of this public health crisis, *The Golden Girls* sat at the intersection between increasingly empathetic viewers and a wider American populace and media culture that remained fundamentally uneducated and prejudiced about the infection/syndrome.

Premiering on September 14, 1985, *The Golden Girls* became an almost immediate, if somewhat improbable, breakout hit for NBC. Among the inevitable ebbs and flows that the series experienced over its seven-season run, industry trades consistently attributed its success primarily to two factors. First, as Miles Beller of *The Hollywood Reporter* noted in September 1987, Bea Arthur, Betty White, Rue McClanahan, and Estelle Getty worked together as one of American television's best "well-oiled ensembled cast[s]. . . . The girls and their series improve with age, character and nuance deepening, personalities more fully rendered." Second, as Beller also argued, the series was no stranger to "*sturm und drang*," referencing a late eighteenth-century German literary movement characterized by societal turmoil and character revolt against the status quo.[6]

Indeed, this penchant for timely cultural critique and even courting controversy lay largely at the feet of the series's creator: Susan Harris. Having previously written episodes of critically and popularly lauded series such as *Love, American Style*, *All in the Family*, and *Maude*, in addition to being the showrunner of the serial sitcom *Soap*, Harris and her writers' room latched on to the 1970s' "turn toward relevance" and adapted it for what was a decidedly different sociopolitical moment.[7] In this spirit, *The Golden Girls* and the HIV/AIDS crisis actually made opportune bedfellows. As many critics were quick to point out, the series's take on women of a certain age was original insofar as it centered the agency of its main characters, who were given a second lease on their romantic and sexual lives after marriage and child rearing. In addressing the contagious paranoia engendered by HIV/AIDS through the lives of older, sexually active straight women, the series significantly demystified what many Americans thought they knew about exactly who could be affected by the disease and how it was spread.

On June 18, 1982, the day after Robert Bazell's earlier-cited *NBC Nightly News* report, Lawrence K. Altman wrote in *The New York Times* that what had become colloquially known across the country as "gay cancer" was now officially recognized as such by Centers for Disease Control (CDC) scientists, who designated the immune disorder GRID, or "gay-related immune deficiency."[8] Potential homophobia notwithstanding, this official medical classification was engendered more by the fact that the CDC simply didn't have any answers as to why the national uptick in cases of Kaposi's sarcoma

(KS), pneumocystis pneumonia, and their attendant immunosuppression seemed only to afflict gay men. Yet just two months later, finally acknowledging that these conditions could in fact be tracked from any one person to another and were also spreading among nonqueer populations including intravenous drug users, blood-transfusion patients, and impoverished communities of color, the CDC settled on a new name for this mysterious illness: AIDS (acquired immune deficiency syndrome). In May 1986, after American researchers at the CDC and National Institutes of Health (NIH), along with French scientists at the Pasteur Institute, finally managed to isolate AIDS's etiological agent, the viral malady that activated the syndrome was also officially named: HIV (human immunodeficiency virus).

By the time *The Golden Girls* premiered in the fall of 1985, then, it was clear to the international medical community that what was previously known as GRID was a complete misnomer. HIV/AIDS had no causal relationship to sexual identity. Yet this knowledge grounded in scientific fact was not the primary picture painted and propagated by mainstream U.S. media. As James Kinsella argues, "As long as AIDS seemed to be confined to fringe groups like gays, . . . it was simply a medical curiosity. The closer the threat of AIDS seemed to move toward the lives of the 'average American,' . . . the bigger the story became."[9] And in fact, such "this could happen to you" paranoia was ironically facilitated at least partially by the deregulation of the U.S. television industry during the 1980s.

In May 1981, President Ronald Reagan appointed Mark Fowler as chairman of the Federal Communications Commission (FCC). Agreeing with Reagan that the federal government should "get out of the way with respect to regulating the broadcasting industry, allowing for a marketplace approach instead," Fowler's laissez-faire FCC began a campaign of eliminating most existing regulatory prohibitions for television.[10] By the end of 1985, the FCC had reviewed, changed, or abolished 89 percent of the agency's approximately nine hundred mass media rules.[11]

Many of the broadcasting guidelines revisited by the FCC during this period centered on the ability of the federal government to regulate programming content, specifically regarding what was and was not permissible vis-à-vis on-air violence, profanity, and sex/sexuality. While constitutional protection under the First Amendment has always guarded against "governmental interference with 'the press' and the FCC is specifically prohibited from preemptory censorship of broadcasts," free-for-all protections on speech have never applied directly to radio or television, "owing to the government's role in licensing all broadcast stations." Since broadcasters transmit signals via publicly owned over-the-air spectrums, networks and their affiliates have always been bound by FCC regulations, including content indecency standards, if they wish to be granted and retain broadcast licenses. These licenses are "issued for and held accountable to the public good or, more specifically, ill-defined community standards—a constantly changing and highly variable target." With self-censoring Standards and Practices divisions at each of the major networks diminishing during the mid-1980s and early 1990s, "the network censor's role in broadcast television also diminished, as a result of budget cuts at the networks and competition from cable TV, which offered far more risqué programming."[12]

Indeed, U.S. network television had long adhered to a voluntary code of broadcasting standards (the National Association of Broadcasters [NAB] Television Code) that became increasingly burdensome in the late 1970s and early 1980s when cable and syndicated programming began pushing the boundaries of on-screen content. To keep up, networks began to loosen their grip on the content they aired and started addressing more sexually relevant topics. More often than not, however, those risqué programs that dealt with the creeping sexual contagion of HIV/AIDS did so in somewhat surreptitious, elusive fashion. Take, for example, "Valentine's Day" (S04E15), a clip-show episode wherein the girls recollect various Valentine's Days gone by. Preparing for a weekend away with gentlemen friends, Blanche, Rose, and Dorothy find themselves confronted with a dilemma inside a local drug store:

Blanche: Well, we are going away for a romantic weekend to the Bahamas with Jeff and Rich and Randy. In this day and age, it might be a good idea to take along some [beat] protection.
Rose: What kind of protection?
Dorothy: Two armed Pinkerton guards. [beat] No, Blanche is talking about . . . um . . . [gestures toward product display]
Rose: A Nestle's Crunch?
Dorothy: One over.
Rose: An enema bag?
Dorothy: To the right.
Rose: Dentugrip?
Dorothy: Condoms, Rose! Condoms! Condoms! Condoms!
Cashier: Calm down, lady! You just get out of prison?

While this scene is often quoted as one of the series's most memorably side-splitting exchanges, it also reveals what had become deeply rooted cultural anxieties surrounding sex. Blanche's warning to her friends begs an obvious question: Protection from what? Just a few years before, this cautionary line might have been interpreted as the need to pack condoms for the purposes of contraception. However, such a deliberate reminder of protection "in this day and age" is a masked yet unmistakable reference to the burgeoning climate of "safe sex" that the HIV/AIDS epidemic had engendered. In fact, Blanche practically says as much to the entire drug store as she wrenches a microphone from the cashier's desk after he price checks each of the women's condom purchases over the loudspeaker:

> *Blanche*: All right, just what in the hell are all of you staring at? Haven't you ever seen three vibrant, healthy, sexually active women before? Now, we are embarking on a little weekend cruise with some longtime gentlemen friends, and if we decide to be intimate, then we'll be prepared. We are not embarrassed. We're not uncomfortable. We are not humiliated. We're going to walk out of here today with our heads held high, secure in the knowledge that what we have done is morally and socially responsible. Isn't that right, girls?
>
> *Dorothy*: I have no idea who this woman is. I bought these for my brother.

The scene does predicably end with a laugh, but Blanche's ad hoc public service announcement more significantly exposes the extent to which this culture of "safe sex" had indeed begun to reach ordinary, "average" Americans.

While there's admittedly nothing especially queer about this scene, it reflects one of the many tragic ironies of this public health crisis during the 1980s and early 1990s. Famously chronicled by the journalist Randy Shilts, disabusing the American public of the idea that HIV/AIDS was a "gay disease" was, to say the least, a tough sell when so much of its media coverage seemed to corroborate exactly that.[13] Look, for example, at how reports of the Hollywood heartthrob Rock Hudson's death from AIDS complications in October 1985 also served as the final confirmation of his long-rumored homosexuality. As the Reagan administration joined with evangelical Christians to force U.S. politics radically to the right, federally funded organizations like the Centers for Disease Control and National Institutes of Health were given little, if any, money to study exactly how HIV/AIDS worked on a biologic level and how a cure might be developed. Simply put, the U.S. government was not helping those who were most intensely affected by this epidemic, so LGBTQ people decided to help themselves from situations in which, as the voice-over in Marlon Riggs's 1989 experimental documentary *Tongues Untied* famously puts it, "this nut could kill us." As Douglas Crimp recalls of public health campaigns spearheaded mostly by gay men during this period, "We were able to invent safe sex because we have always known that sex is not, in an epidemic or not, limited to penetrative sex. Our promiscuity taught us many things, not only about the pleasures of sex, but about the great multiplicity of those pleasures. It is that psychic preparation, that experimentation, that conscious work on our own sexualities that has allowed many of us to change our sexual behaviors—something that brutal 'behavioral therapies' tried unsuccessfully for over a century to force us to do—very quickly and very dramatically."[14] Ironically, then, those who were treated by mainstream U.S. media as contagious pariahs were exactly the same people whose educational efforts took sexual prophylactics to the front of drug stores nationwide and allowed the "Valentine's Day" condom gag to land so effectively.

Yet, even while the risqué nature of addressing HIV/AIDS on television frequently meant recourse to inference and allusion, *The Golden Girls* famously took the epidemic head-on. As previously noted, the season 5 episode "72 Hours" revolves around Rose anxiously awaiting the results of an HIV screening after being informed that blood she was given during a routine gallbladder removal may have contained infectious antibodies. In terms of form, this episode adheres to sitcom norm, following the "problem of the week" formula that has been de rigueur since the genre's inception without verging into the territory of the "very special episode."[15] However, in both content and context, the episode mixes the series's trademark humor with unambiguous social commentary.

> *Dorothy* [*to Sophia*]: Why were you using my bathroom?
> *Sophia*: There's something wrong with mine.
> *Dorothy*: What?
> *Sophia*: Rose used it.
> *Dorothy*: Ma, that is just ignorant paranoia.
> *Sophia*: Hey, I'm making progress. Yesterday I was using the bathroom down at the Shell station.
> *Dorothy*: You know, it's attitudes like that that add to the panic about this. Now what is wrong with you?
> *Sophia*: Look, I know intellectually there's no way I can catch it. But now that it's so close to home, it's scary.[16]

While audiences might smirk at imagining Sophia slowly shuffling her way down to the local Shell station with trademark wicker purse in tow, this exchange is nevertheless a textbook example of Kinsella's claims that making this disease as "spooky as possible helped make AIDS a national issue" and that "the closer the threat of AIDS seemed to move toward the lives of the 'average American,' . . . the bigger the story became." Indeed, all four women are forced to confront the social stigma that had been tethered to HIV/AIDS patients for nearly a decade when it's supposed threats loom large on their very own doorstep.

"72 Hours" is perhaps best remembered for the climactic exchange between Rose and Blanche, in which tempers and frustrations finally boil over:

Rose: Why does everyone keep saying that? I don't feel like taking it easy. I might have AIDS, and it scares the hell out of me. And yet every time I open my mouth to talk about it, someone says, "There, there Rose, take it easy."

Blanche: I'm sorry, honey.

Rose: Why me, Blanche? I'm tired of pretending I feel okay so you won't say "take it easy." And I'm tired of you saying "take it easy" because you're afraid I'm gonna fall apart. Dammit, why is this happening to me? I mean, this isn't supposed to happen to people like me. You must have gone to bed with hundreds of men. All I had was one innocent operation.

Blanche: Hey! Wait a minute! Are you saying this should be me and not you?

Rose: No, no, I'm just saying I'm a good person. Hell, I'm a Goody Two-shoes!

Blanche: *AIDS is not a bad person's disease, Rose! It is not God punishing people for their sins!*

Rose: You're right, Blanche.

Blanche: Well, you're damn straight I'm right![17]

While I wouldn't go so far as to claim that this scene is singular in the history of U.S. television, several prominent features are especially worthy of attention. First, as alluded to previously, this episode and climactic moment in particular are one of few instances in this period wherein the threat of HIV/AIDS is placed at the feet of straight women rather than gay men made out as either victims or villains. Moreover, the fact that *The Golden Girls* did lean in so intently to the older age of its ensemble cast creates a double-down effect, in which not only are straight women threatened by HIV/AIDS but especially ostensibly wholesome little old ladies (although anyone familiar with the series knows that there is much that humorously complicates that particular stereotype, from Rose's supposed ability to kill men in bed in the first-season episode "In a Bed of Rose's" to Blanche's long-standing reputation as resident slut).

Second, it is especially significant that this scene's powerfully didactic message is delivered by Blanche, southern belle and Georgian debutante and, perhaps most meaningfully in this context, Baptist. "AIDS is not a bad person's disease, Rose. It is not God punishing people for their sins," Blanche indignantly states. However, that was precisely the verbatim rhetoric espoused by New Right evangelical leaders such as Pat Robertson and Jerry Falwell, both of whom took such fire-and-brimstone homophobia to the U.S. broadcast airwaves during the 1980s and 1990s. "AIDS is not just God's punishment for homosexuals," Falwell was famous for saying: "It is God's punishment for the society that tolerates homosexuals."[18] And while Blanche did have some queer tolerance of her own to gain throughout the series, learning in the series's fourth season that her brother Clayton is gay, she emphatically disabuses both Rose and the viewing audience of the notion that gay individuals are both "bad people" and deserving of the HIV/AIDS epidemic that befell so many of them.

Finally, the episode's penultimate scene finds Dorothy, Blanche, and Sophia pondering future next steps and what-might-bes based on Rose's impending test results. Sophia, who had earlier marked several of the kitchen coffee mugs with an "R" for Rose out of fear of contagion, decides to overcome her prejudice and paranoia with a sip from an R mug as the girls vow to stand by Rose whatever the outcome. The next day, the three women accompany Rose back to the hospital to the welcome news that she is HIV-negative and that the previous balance of their lives has once again been restored.

While this episode's engagement with the HIV/AIDS crisis was direct and unquestionably topical, its treatment of the subject did fall in lockstep with rising critical takes on the series. As one *Variety* writer put it, *The Golden Girls*' fifth season gave every indication that the series was "sliding past its prime, . . . the usually well-oiled machine creaking with all-too-familiar jokes." Additionally, it was the opinion of this same reporter that the series's writing was getting "far too preachy. . . . It's a shame a program that broke down a number of TV's taboos doesn't know the limits."[19] While the moralizing message of "72 Hours" may have been too heavy-handed for some, the episode nevertheless gave American viewers a different lens through which to view the HIV/AIDS crisis, one decidedly different from the occasionally tragic made-for-TV movie or stunting drama-series episode that found an (almost inevitably) gay male character and the people around him coming to terms with what seemed tantamount to a death sentence. Indeed, the episode has remained a popular one for queer audiences in particular, winking at them then and now in loving approval.

If, as Horace Newcomb and Paul M. Hirsch famously assert, television is a "cultural forum" for the circulation of ideas, then its narrativizing and thematizing of national traumas like HIV/AIDS is one of the most prominent ways in which publics make sense of their historical moment, regardless of genre.[20] As Crimp argues of the relationship between AIDS and its cultural mediation,

> AIDS does not exist apart from the practices that conceptualize it, represent it, and respond to it. We know AIDS only in and through those practices. This assertion does not contest the existence of viruses, antibodies, infections, or transmission routes. Least of all does it contest the reality of illness, suffering, and death. What it *does* contest is the notion that there is an underlying reality of AIDS, on which are constructed the representations, or the culture, or the politics of AIDS. If we recognize that AIDS exists only in and through these constructions, then the hope is that we can also recognize the imperative to know them, analyze, them, and wrest control of them.[21]

Even if *The Golden Girls* became increasingly preachy and moralistic in the eyes of some critics, "72 Hours" and the series writ large were able to harness the kind of "piercing point" comedy that can make the sitcom genre both relevant in its contemporary moment and historically significant.[22] In an era when HIV/AIDS patients were more or less left to fend for themselves, *The Golden Girls'* appreciative refrain of being a friend may have meant more than many of us could possibly fathom.

Notes

1. "Cancer Study," *NBC Nightly News*, June 17, 1982.
2. David J. Skal, *V Is for Vampire: The A-to-Z Guide to Everything Undead* (Plume, 1995), 5. See also Andrew J. Owens, *Desire After Dark: Contemporary Queer Cultures and Occultly Marvelous Media* (Indiana University Press, 2021).
3. James Kinsella, *Covering the Plague: AIDS and the American Media* (Rutgers University Press, 1989), 54.
4. Nick Marx and Matt Sienkiewicz, "Volume Introduction: Comedy as Theory, Industry, and Academic Discipline," in *The Comedy Studies Reader*, ed. Nick Marx and Matt Sienkiewicz (University of Texas Press, 2018), 11.
5. See Ron Becker, *Gay TV and Straight America* (Rutgers University Press, 2006).
6. Miles Beller, "The Golden Girls," *Hollywood Reporter*, September 18, 1987.
7. For a full analysis of U.S. network television's "turn toward relevance," see Todd Gitlin, *Inside Prime Time* (Pantheon Books, 1983).

8. Lawrence K. Altman, "Clue Found on Homosexuals' Precancer Syndrome," *New York Times*, June 18, 1982.

9. Kinsella, *Covering the Plague*, 58.

10. David S. Silverman, *You Can't Air That: Four Cases of Controversy and Censorship in American Television Programming* (Syracuse University Press, 2007), 21.

11. Jennifer Holt, "Vertical Vision: Deregulation, Industrial Economy and Prime-Time Design," in *Quality Popular Television: Cult TV, the Industry and Fans*, ed. Mark Jancovich and James Lyons (British Film Institute, 2003), 14.

12. Kinsella, *Covering the Plague*, 3–4.

13. See Randy Shilts, *And the Band Played On: Politics, People, and the AIDS Epidemic* (St. Martin's, 1987).

14. Douglas Crimp, "How to Have Promiscuity in an Epidemic," in *Melancholia and Moralism: Essays on AIDS and Queer Politics* (MIT Press, 2002), 64.

15. For recent examinations of the "very special episode," see Jonathan Cohn and Jennifer Porst, eds., *Very Special Episodes: Televising Industrial and Social Change* (Rutgers University Press, 2021).

16. "72 Hours," S05E19.

17. "72 Hours," S05E19 (emphasis added).

18. Christopher Reed, "Obituary: The Rev. Jerry Falwell," *The Guardian*, May 17, 2007, www.theguardian.com/media/2007/may/17/broadcasting.guardianobituaries.

19. "Television Reviews: The Golden Girls," *Variety*, October 18, 1989, 84.

20. Horace Newcomb and Paul M. Hirsch, "Television as a Cultural Forum: Implications for Research," *Quarterly Review of Film Studies* 8, no. 3 (1983): 45–55.

21. Douglas Crimp, "AIDS: Cultural Analysis/Cultural Activism," in *Melancholia and Moralism*, 28.

22. Beller, "Golden Girls."

The cast. (Photo © Wayne Williams 1984–87. All rights reserved.)

INTERVIEW

Photographing the Girls

Wayne Williams, Photographer

Before the networks would do something for marketing *The Golden Girls*, Witt/Thomas/Harris wanted to get a leg up in the publicity. And so, at one point, Tony and Paul asked the ladies to do it, and Bea said, "No f-cking way. I don't want to do any pictures." Marsha came to me and said, "We've got a problem, and I think you can help us out. We need to promote the show. We've only done one episode, and we're getting ready to do a second and a third, and the network isn't doing anything. And so, we need some stills to put out in *Variety* and the *Hollywood Reporter* and start getting some buzz going. Can you talk to Bea?" I said, "Okay," and went down to the stage.

I walked up to Bea, and I introduced myself to her, and I said, "Look, I understand they want to promote the show because the network isn't doing it, and they want to give it some legs."

And she said to me, "I don't."

I said, "Can you explain to me what you're thinking and why?"

And she said, "Look, I come out of theater, and when you do a show, it either lands on its feet and it runs or it doesn't. You don't have to promote it."

If you think about it, almost all pictures of stage shows and theater are just shots of people on the stage. There's not something special done, but television and movies are different. And you've got to sell it before it lands.

And I said, "Bea, what else is the problem? What else doesn't work for you?"

She says, "I hate getting in, going on a special day, and having to get into wardrobe and makeup and hair, and it's a half day, and it's a lot of bullshit."

And I said, "I've got an idea. Tomorrow night, when you're finished taping the second show, you're already going to be in in makeup and hair. You're already going to be in wardrobe. If I set up my stage with lights all set right next door to where you're shooting and taping, and immediately after you wrap and you're cleared, I walk the four of you over, I shoot the shots, and

Left: Bea Arthur as Dorothy (Photo © Wayne Williams 1984–87. All rights reserved.)
Right: Betty White as Rose (Photo © Wayne Williams 1984–87. All rights reserved.)

you're gone in five minutes, will you let me do that and let you go? And I'll still get the shots, and you'll be able to go home really quickly and not have to go through all that other bullshit?"

"All right, darling."

And that was the start of what got the candle lit for what turned out to be another six, eight, ten photo sessions that almost always happened immediately after a taping was done so that Bea "didn't have to deal with any of the bullshit."

So that very first session, I walked the four ladies over. I had a stool set up for Estelle to sit on, and I was going to put the other three ladies right behind her. I'd shoot a Polaroid, walk it over to them. They'd all see they were beautifully lit and looked really clean and really nice. And I said, "Everybody okay with this? Let's do this." And they all said, "Yeah!" I could tell they were tired, and I walked back to the camera, and I looked at them, and I said, "I'm ready to go. Do me a favor, just pretend like you all like each other." I would bring them in and say, "Anybody have a joke they want to tell?"

Click, click, click, click, click, click, click. "Thank you very much!" They were gone in two minutes.

And those first two minutes are probably the bulk of the pictures that most people see of the ladies laughing, because it was just the right moment for them to be exhausted and relieved that they could just laugh at each other and go.

I have noticed a lot of the unlicensed merch uses photos. Is there an easy way we can tell your photos of the Girls from the network's?

One of the keys you can tell with my shots is, if they were a studio shot, there would never be a hair light—a light from above. I never like hair lights. I would beauty light the front so that their faces look good, and especially with ladies with gray hair, I don't want to make their hair go bright white so you could see their scalp. So, if you look at network shots, they always shot with a hair light. And I hated that. It just wasn't my style.

I just pulled up a Google search of shots, and you're right. In a few of these, Estelle's head is practically glowing. I have noticed she does not wear the glasses in most of the publicity photos. Was that her decision?

I think she saw the glasses as more like the wig, that it was what made her look old. And I really just get the feeling that they were bothersome for her. I don't think she felt like she needed them, and I didn't want to have that

Left: Ruth McClanahan as Blanche. (Photo © Wayne Williams 1984–87. All rights reserved.) *Right*: Estelle Getty. (Photo © Wayne Williams 1984–87. All rights reserved.)

getting in the way of her face. It's also difficult for me to shoot somebody with glasses on because you see the reflections of everything around them, and I had to work around that if they had to wear glasses. But if I can have them without the glasses, and it's not critical, that's ideal. When I am trying to finish a session really fast after taping, I never know where they'd look. The perfect shot might be them turning their heads toward the light and then looking at the camera. And now I have this white glare. So, no glasses is my first choice.

CHAPTER 8

Sex and the "Biddy"

An Examination of Age and Sexual Performance in *The Golden Girls*

JARED CLAYTON BROWN

Although rare, portrayals of older women in U.S. film and television often accumulate problematic stereotypes regarding gender and sexuality or lack thereof. As Tina Vares argues, "With the dominant framing of later life as asexual, popular cultural portrayals of sexually active or engaged older people were generally confined to humorous greeting cards in which the joke played on notions of seniors as not sexually desirable. . . . The absence of portrayals of later life sexuality was notable in television, advertising, and film."[1] Yet, some anomalous 1980s sitcoms such as *Who's the Boss* and *The Golden Girls* frequently confronted social norms and ideas about sex and bodies and aging. And a key part of *The Golden Girls'* appeal especially is that it not only placed older, sexually active women center stage but also imbued older women with agency and power over men week after week. One quick preface at the beginning of this chapter: although my specific interest here is on women's aging and sexuality through the case study of *The Golden Girls*, I do want to note that sexually active elderly men are also infrequently represented, and an interesting expansion of this chapter might investigate the Girls' many hunky suitors. For, as Dorothy reminds us, "the gentleman at table five, in the blue suit, is impotent. Bon appétit!"

The Golden Girls creates depictions that harshly juxtapose the Girls' sexually active lifestyles with similarly aged characters throughout television history who seem to live in a sexual vacuum. Some prime examples include Aunt Bee from *The Andy Griffith Show*, Granny Clampett from *The Beverly Hillbillies*, Thelma Harper from *Mama's Family*, and Mother Addams from *The Addams Family*. In each of these programs, the women are not typically portrayed as modern in fashion, nor are they written as desirable or sexual beings.

To best consider how *The Golden Girls'* formula created a sweet spot for representing sexually active women of a certain age, one of the first such shows of its kind in U.S. television history, it is helpful first to examine the writing and actors' performances that enamored them to the audience, which I analyze by discussing each of the characters in relation to hegemonic notions of gender, age, and sexuality in U.S. culture. I conduct an intertextual analysis dissecting segments from a few episodes of the program, with special attention to performance. I situate these portrayals within a larger framework of U.S. social ideologies that reify the archetypal beliefs around senior women and discuss how these beliefs affect popular discourses about aging and sexuality. In sum, I argue that *The Golden Girls* was and continues to be a counternarrative to these widely perceived and typically accepted discourses, tropes, and stereotypes about older women's age and sexuality.

To theoretically frame this discussion, this chapter builds on Richard Schechner's extension of Jacques Lacan's "the mirror stage," defined as "a stage in infancy, in which the infant sees its reflection in the mirror and assumes an image of a whole self as the true self."[2] I argue that a television set can be thought of as a mirror where viewers can begin to assume the identities of the people they see on their screens as if they were their own.

The weekly images that *The Golden Girls* offered viewers stand in sharp contrast to an entrenched American discourse devaluing older women and subjecting them to "a number of harmful, negative stereotypes that picture [them] as sick, sexless, uninvolved except for church work, and alone; one of the most persistent and pernicious stereotypes of older women is that of asexuality."[3] Through Susan Harris's creation of the characters and the writing each week, the actors are able to hold up a mirror in which audiences, specifically women who were in the same age range as the series's characters—or those on the precipice of the Girls' demographic—could finally see a refreshing divergence from the archetypes typically offered them elsewhere on television.

I also draw from Jill Dolan's "utopian performative," which she argues means that performers construct an idealistic space within which an audience feels a sense of belonging.[4] Utopian performance certainly aligns with a method in which the program could be decoded by members of the viewing audience, both those who share similar demographics with the show's actors and those who do not but might somehow see a piece of their identity being reflected back through a situation that takes place within the confines of the television screen. I assert that viewers found not only a certain utopian escape via the images they saw but also a utopian production, where female actors whom Hollywood forgot had a unique opportunity to construct and perform character performances unburdened by the archetypes with which older women and performers are normally saddled.

A large part of the cultural work done by these performances is on the physical bodies of the actors. Linda McDowell notes that "the body is the place, the location or site . . . of the individual. . . . While bodies are undoubtedly material, possessing a range of characteristics such as shape and size and so inevitably taking up space, the ways in which bodies are presented to and seen by others vary according to the spaces and places in which they find themselves."[5] McDowell's notion of an embodied "cultural geography" affords an exploration of the way the actors' bodies—merely by being older and female—locate an "uncharted territory" in the landscape of the American sitcom throughout history. The characters remind us of their age by confronting age-centered issues including concerns about health issues affecting older women, such as menopause. But they also address broad social issues far beyond age and gender that older women in media representation have not been able to tackle, such as HIV/AIDS, suicide, and addiction, and audiences found that especially provocative.

Bea Arthur, who portrayed the character Dorothy Zbornak, once explained why she believed the show had such broad appeal: "I think a lot of it has to do with the fact that there were these old, post-menopausal ladies who looked good, wore fabulous earrings, dressed well, and had very active sex lives. It showed that old people don't have to look and smell funny and hide in the corner."[6] What Arthur illustrates is that it is not only the women's bodies but the space they take up that distinguishes the show from earlier representations. How Bea, Betty, Rue, and Estelle performed as their characters remains far removed from pervasive stereotypes associated with older women in U.S. society—but also women in general. Their characters demonstrate that women can and do remain sexually vital as they enter their older years, to be sure. But Dorothy, Rose, Blanche, and Estelle also assert that a woman's sexuality, of any age, gets to be about pleasure, not procreation. They also model how discussions of sex and sexuality can and should take up space in women's everyday lives—at the kitchen table, around a cheesecake. The seductive stories they tell are not just youthful remembrances of the days of yore; the Girls gab about their current erotic dalliances. In so doing, they give audiences the biggest gift: the knowledge that their futures are filled with pleasure and companionship.

To fully understand how these images were a radical departure from the asexualized older women archetypes of earlier television, it is important to discuss some of the performances given by the four women throughout the series, looking closely at how they offer a reimagining of what life can be for women of a certain age.

In the season 7 episode "Journey to the Center of Attention," Blanche and Dorothy become rivals in a type of sexual battle of wills in which they vie for the attention of men in a local bar, the Rusty Anchor, Blanche's local haunt, where she drags a hesitant Dorothy. Blanche problematizes Dorothy's desire to stay home alone and believes she needs to get out more to have the full experience of being part of the greater social order of dating men. Blanche is unaware of and unprepared for Dorothy to (unintentionally) steal her thunder, as she becomes more popular than Blanche when she begins to serenade men in the bar to the tickled ivories of the bar's piano. Using her singing talents, Dorothy captures the men's attraction, while Blanche's typically successful physicality is ignored.

Blanche's longing to be desired simultaneously leads to her sexual gratification and often draws the ire of her roommates for her shameless, bold approach to sexual activity. Her confidence in her ability to seduce men is a source of pride for her—a clear "violation" of hegemonic mores about gender and sexuality. Hegemonically, men are configured as the sexual aggressors, while women are submissive and pursued. But Blanche is her own huntress in the quest to whet her sexual appetite

The season 2 episode "The Actor" similarly pits the Girls against each other as sexual rivals. The episode features a famous traveling actor, Patrick Vaughn (Lloyd Bochner), who comes to Miami to perform in a play in their community theater. Immediately attracted to him, Dorothy, Rose, Blanche, and several other female actors (and maybe Ed, the stagehand) all embark on separate, secret affairs with Patrick, but their secrets unravel by episode's end. Despite the women's initial lack of awareness that they are all romantically involved with the same man, the story employs each of the characters' well-established personality traits in allowing them to connect with Patrick individually: Dorothy's forthright manner, Blanche's free-spirited sexuality, and Rose's endearing honey-soaked naivety. The episode concludes with Patrick reminding everyone that they all still had fun, except lying Ed, and the Girls' reprioritizing one another after a momentary lapse.

In the third season episode "The Artist," the three women battle for the attention of a prominent sculptor named Laszlo (Tony Jay). Laszlo plans to create a piece of art that he says will represent the perfect woman. Each of the women vie to be the artist's subject, for they believe that she who is chosen will be considered Laszlo's portrait of perfection. Throughout the episode, the women exchange banter in which they make fun of one another's bodies in an effort to set themselves apart, each as the ideal feminine form. The episode's final act reveals that the artist's portrait is a composite of the three women and that Laszlo has highlighted features from the three Girls. While they spent the episode battling for his romantic attention, they missed that Laszlo, as the object of their desire, has taken a male lover, another way the show lends itself to ironic humor while satirizing how older men are typically portrayed as sexual on TV.

The series also establishes that Sophia, the show's oldest character, is "still interested" despite being an octogenarian. In the sixth-season episode "Girls Just Wanna Have Fun . . . Before They Die," Sophia tries to figure out how to seduce a man she desires. Sophia's age and sexual performativity relate to widely held beliefs around older women's relationships (or lack thereof) with sexuality. Throughout the course of the episode, she makes several references to society's belief that women of a certain age should no longer be interested in participating in sexual activity.

Sophia takes Blanche's advice when trying to gain attention from a male suitor. Despite Sophia's age, her approach to sexuality has devolved into that of a somewhat inexperienced teenager. Her behavior is partly attributable to a stroke she suffered before the series narratively began. Nevertheless, Sophia's behaviors and mannerisms throughout the series are much like that of an unsure teenage ingénue in that she cannot seem to recall what it was like when she wanted to attract a man's sexual attention. As the episode progresses, Sophia follows the advice of the more sophisticated resident vixen, Blanche Devereaux.

While Blanche helps Sophia in her sexual conquests in "Girls Just Wanna Have Fun . . . Before They Die," despite a twenty- to thirty-year age gap, Sophia and Blanche become sexual rivals in season 4's "Yes, We Have No Havanas." In the episode, Sophia and Blanche battle it out over an older Cuban gentleman caller, Fidel Santiago (Henry Darrow). Throughout the episode, Sophia and Blanche attempt to sabotage the other's chances for romance with the suitor. The way that they behave is more suggestive of behaviors one might expect from much younger, perhaps teenage girls. Sophia and Blanche take multiple verbal jabs at each other during the episode, as well as trying to actively interfere when both are on dates with Fidel in efforts to garner his attention. For instance, Blanche catches Sophia in a park locked in a passionate kiss with Santiago. By the episode's conclusion, the women have managed to mend fences. The conflict is resolved when Fidel dies and, at his funeral, it is disclosed that he had been involved in romantic relationships with several other women.

One of the similarities among these story lines is that by each of the episodes' conclusions, the women reunite and the men are sent away, never to appear again. So, while such story lines seemingly reproduce sexist notions of women vying for men, on *The Golden Girls*, sexual rivalry is merely a temporary episodic narrative device that returns the series to stasis by cementing the bonds among women while confronting pervasive stereotypes about older women's sexuality in the process.

Rose, meanwhile, is often at the foreground of the amorous occurrences, such as in the first season's "Rose the Prude." In it, Rose contemplates entering into her first sexual relationship since the death of her husband, the often mentioned but never seen Charlie Nylund. The manner in which Rose handles herself with uncertainty could be compared to how a younger woman might feel when considering whether to embark on her first romance. She also struggles with loyalty, for she fears moving on after her husband's death. Despite the circumstances, the uncertain nature of what may happen should one choose to become involved in a romantic encounter is something that has a certain component of agelessness to it. The women's performances of sexuality can be linked with the sexuality of teenagers because as research demonstrates, "sex is a large component of teen life."[7]

Besides moments when the Girls represent the embodiment of aging, they often have to make choices about situations that could have happened to anyone. The scalability of the story lines is one reason why I argue that the show maintains such inherent and broad resonance among viewers. The show skillfully builds an audience that consisted of various layers and demographics at the time and continues to construct and reach new audiences. In some ways, *The Golden Girls* is a polysemic text. Many episodes can be read through multiple literacies and therefore can be read differently depending on the person viewing the episode. The brilliance of the show's intentional polysemy is that it allows viewers multiple avenues to develop appreciation for the show's characters and numerous gateways for different audiences to enter the text.

Part of what has helped to make the show a lasting favorite since the conclusion of its original run in 1992 is the generation of younger viewers who probably either were too young to initially understand the humor or were possibly not even born when the show was originally aired. It thus stands to reason that there are so many meaningful connections that have been established and are continuing to occur between the episodes and the audiences that are viewing the program. In Western cultures, we often represent aging women as reaching a plateau, after which they are portrayed as asexual or just weird.

In considering older women in relation to sexuality within sitcoms, it also bears mentioning two characters from programs that aired around the same time as *The Golden Girls*. The first character is Mona Robinson (Katherine Helmond), portrayed for eight seasons in ABC's *Who's the Boss*, from 1984 to 1992. Similar to Blanche, Mona is a powerful representation of the proud and sexually liberated older woman. But there's one stark difference: In *Who's the Boss*, Mona is merely a supporting character, as the main narrative of the series centers around the progressing relationship that Mona's daughter, the career-driven Angela Bower (Judith Light), has with the family's live-in male housekeeper Tony Micelli (Tony Danza).

Before *The Golden Girls*, the original network run of the *Carol Burnett Show* spin-off *Mama's Family* featured some familiar faces. The title character of Thelma Harper (Vicki Lawrence) is joined on-screen by Rue McClanahan as Aunt Fran, Thelma's younger sister, and Betty White, as Ellen Harper-Jackson, Thelma's oldest child. Aunt Fran is the complete antithesis of the Blanche character. Fran is the proverbial old maid, who lives with Thelma's family and never really fulfills the cultural expectation of women's roles in that she never marries or has children of her own. Ellen is Thelma's selfish, manipulative daughter who is constantly seeking upward mobility away from the homely roots represented by the Harper family as a whole within the series.

As for Thelma herself, she shares a few commonalities with two of the Girls. She does serve as the leading figure in the cast, which contrasts with the ensemble that composed the cast of *The Golden Girls*. She is like Sophia because of her outspoken nature and often blatant disregard for how what she says will impact those whom she addresses. She is also reminiscent of Dorothy in how she serves as the series's voice of reason among a motley crew of eccentric characters. In many of the program's episodes, it is usually Thelma who can integrate what it is that audiences may be thinking within the context of the show. While Thelma's agency is in her outspokenness, she is almost completely devoid of any sense of sexuality. In one episode, Thelma dates a teacher she meets in a night school she attends to earn her high school diploma, but the series never really addresses her sexuality or represents any sexual activities. The audience only meets Carl, Thelma's husband, who died before the beginning of the series, leaving her widowed, through a flashback included in the program's final episode. It appears through the series's treatment of the character that her sex life has completely ceased with his death, as she does not enjoy a significant romantic relationship throughout the series's run. So even featuring the same performers on-screen around the same time, *The Golden Girls* simply changed the discourse of aging and sexuality for women.

There are several instances in *The Golden Girls* in which the women perform behaviors that are directly associated with sexuality. The behaved performances are not done in a manner that could be labeled as vulgar or threatening to the overall dignity that the women maintain throughout out the series's run. In the fourth-season episode "Valentine's Day," Rose, Blanche, and Dorothy visit a pharmacy and decide they should practice safe sex by purchasing condoms for a leisure cruise they are planning to embark on with some male companions. The narrative spine allows the women to represent the spectrum of the attitudes revolving around sexuality through each of their characters. The scene begins with Blanche's suggestion that the women should be socially responsible by practicing safe sex. As they are in the grocery story checkout line, Blanche gestures to a nearby shelf with various items including condoms. Rose, in her typical girlish naivety, doesn't follow and starts guessing items on the shelf that she thinks Blanche is hinting at. Rose's continued failure to come up with the correct answer is marked by Dorothy's exasperated yelling of "condoms, Rose, condoms condoms condoms!" immediately drawing the attention of the rest of the customers in the store and embarrassing them. The clerk responds, "Calm down, lady! You just get out of prison?"

Dorothy and Rose both appear to be humiliated at having what is normally a private matter made into a public spectacle, considering that most people do not make a scene when purchasing such a private item. Why should they be embarrassed, though? Blanche asks. The intimation is that the Girls' age plays a role in how they are viewed by the grocery store public. Here, the idea of "multiple literacies" or polysemy can certainly be engaged when considering the various reactions exhibited by the women.[8] The concept of multiple literacies means a text can be read or interpreted in various ways depending on who is consuming the text. The idea is applicable to *The Golden Girls* through the usage of Stuart Hall's audience/reception theory, in which multiple readings can be laid onto one text on the basis of how any given audience member opts to interpret the program. For example, there's Rose and Dorothy's shame at being found out for trying to participate in a seemingly forbidden pursuit: the purchasing of condoms, which is a signifier of their choosing to be involved in sexual activity, despite their age.

The first part of Hall's theory is referred to as the "dominant-hegemonic" reading.[9] This means that the audience is responding to and interpreting the text as it is believed the author intended for it to be read. I believe Hall's idea applies to this episode in that the audience understands that this show is first and foremost a comedy and meant to make the audience laugh above all else. The middle-ground interpretation in this theory is the "negotiated" reading of the text, which means that the audience completely understands the manner the author or creator meant for the text to be decoded, but at the same time, they infuse a text with their own personal meanings. This receptive lens is useful for considering the text because I am certain that there are members of the audience who understand that the show is supposed to be humorous yet at the same time could potentially not understand why the women are engaging in the business of purchasing condoms, because "available research consistently suggests that increasing age is associated with a decreased interest in sex."[10]

The third portion of Hall's theory is the "oppositional," counterhegemonic reading, which is explained as the audience totally rejecting the ideas with which a text is infused. A potential counterhegemonic reading of the actors' performance of age and sexuality could be that the women are merely making fools of themselves by engaging in activity that is considered to be beyond their age group. Certain members of the audience could believe that the women need to relinquish their sexuality because they are "too old to perform the particular act of sexual intercourse."[11] Rose and Dorothy's embarrassment at being found out for purchasing condoms could be considered as a reinforcement of the idea that women of a certain age ought not to engage in sexual activity, rather than seeing the program and the situation as a means of going against dominant social norms surrounding older female sexuality.

On the opposite end of the paradigm, there is Blanche, who bears no sense of shame for her part in the goings-on at the drug store. She even goes so far as to use the store's sound system to defend her and the other women's choice of buying condoms and overtly states, both to the store patrons and ultimately to the viewing audience, that there is no shame in the choices the women are making by practicing safe sex. Her sex-positive conclusion of their behavior being "morally and socially responsible" can be interpreted in a manner that suggests that there are no age boundaries when it comes to sexual behaviors and that the women's decision to purchase condoms fits in with behavior that could be conducted by people of various ages and should not be considered unusual behavior for women who are the same age as the ladies in the program. Ultimately, this performance, as well as the others, of being sexually daring are mirrored back toward audience members, and they can then take on these images and find ways in which they can be incorporated into their own daily lives as a means of their being able to construct and perform their own utopias.

As Michael Rennett asserts, "it can become difficult to identify an emerging-adult text by the age of the characters since the life issues, not an age, are what matters."[12] In a sense, what viewing audiences witnessed by tuning into *The Golden Girls* was an emergence of women expanding their existence into a more dignified, older age. The characters partly provided similarly aged viewers a newfound sense of agency in how they are reflected in popular culture.

Ultimately, I believe *The Golden Girls* carves a kind of utopian performance space for viewers, both old and young. In the diegesis of the show, these viewers can be liberated from their own feelings of marginalization by viewing the Girls navigate behaviors and identities not normally associated in media with people of their age. By daring to be bold in their choices regarding sexual practices and coupling, the Girls offer audiences a comforting third space unusual in the annals of television history. If the portrait of these characters had not been painted and portrayed so convincingly on television screens, then it would be difficult to imagine another forum that would have encouraged viewers to imagine how they could begin to envision alternative characters that moved away from the consistent reifications offered by the likes of the othered elderly women types—the Aunt Bees, the Granny Clampetts, and the Grandma Addams. Still today, *The Golden Girls* illustrates a powerful departure from the tired and repetitive tropes saddling older women by showing audiences a revitalized, empowered view of mature women, solidifying the Girls' position in the American sitcom and popular culture spaces as truly *golden*.

Notes

1. Tina Vares, "Reading the Sexy Oldie: Gender, Age(ing) and Embodiment," *Sexualities* 12, no. 4 (2009): 503–24.

2. Richard Schechner, *Performance Studies: An Introduction*, 2nd ed. (Routledge, 2006), 15.

3. Barbara Payne and Frank Whittington, "Older Women: An Examination of Popular Stereotypes and Research Evidence," in *The Older Woman*, ed. Marie Marschall Fuller and Cora Ann Martin (Charles C. Thomas, 1980), 14.

4. Jill Dolan, "Performance, Utopia and the Utopian Performative," *Theatre Journal* 53, no. 3 (2001): 455–79.

5. Linda McDowell, "In and Out of Place: Bodies and Embodiment," in *In Her Gender, Identity and Place: Understanding Feminist Geographies* (University of Minnesota Press, 1999), 34.

6. Marla Brooks, *The American Family on Television* (McFarland, 2005), 155.

7. Caroline McKinley, "Beyond Forever: The Next Generation of Young Women Protagonists' Sexual Motivations in Contemporary Young Adult Novels," *Young Adult Library Services* 9, no. 4 (2011): 38.

8. Douglas Kellner, "Multiple Literacies and Critical Pedagogy in a Multicultural Society," *Educational Theory* 48, no. 1 (1998): 103.

9. Stuart Hall, "Encoding/Decoding," in *Culture, Media, Language: Working Papers in Cultural Studies*, ed. Stuart Hall, Dorothy Hobson, Andrew Loew, and Paul Willis (Hutchinson, 1980), 128–38.

10. Margot A. Gosney and Abi Taylor, "Sexuality in Older Age: Essential Consideration for Healthcare Professionals," *Age and Ageing* 40, no. 5 (2011): 538.

11. Michael I. Arrington, "Sexuality, Society, and Senior Citizens: An Analysis of Sex Talk Among Prostate Cancer Support Group Members," *Sexuality and Culture* 4, no. 4 (2000): 52.

12. Michael Rennett, "Emerging Adulthood as Identity Genre," in "How Grown-Ups Are Born: The Emerging-Adult Genre and American Film and Television" (PhD diss., University of Texas at Austin, 2017), 24.

The cast at the kitchen table. (Photo © Wayne Williams 1984–87. All rights reserved.)

INTERVIEW

Editing and Laughter

Marsha Posner Williams, Co-Producer
Speaking of laughs, we did something that I don't think any other show did ever. Do you remember *Married with Children*? That audience was not a *Golden Girls* type of audience. They would hoop and holler and all that stuff. That was not our audience. So, what we did at the beginning of each season is the first three or four episodes, we would have the audio guy record *just* our audience on a whole separate track—all the audience laughs on a whole separate track. Then, we would give those tracks to the laugh guy, who would put them in his machine, so that when you hear a laugh on the show, it's actually our audience. But most people who do sitcoms don't even think about that, but we did.

Did you ever have to unsweeten for a laugh that lasted too long?

Bea Arthur could hold a laugh longer—a look—longer than anybody. And the laugh would never stop. When you do a network show and you have to deliver to the hour, minute, and second, we would have to cut laughter in editing—take the laugh, shorten the laugh, because otherwise it would put us over time. With me, if you could sweeten, you could cut the laugh just right. Instead of a short "Ha!" you want the laugh to tail off like a natural, normal audience. So, that was my job. I needed to cut, then I needed to smooth out that laugh, and that's an *art form.*

Also, you almost never get the same laugh the second time, because they've heard the joke already. So, maybe half the audience isn't laughing, and the other half is. It's what makes it so interesting, really. I don't think I could do a nonaudience show. It'd be so boring.

Marc Sotkin, Executive Producer

Our first episode was "sperm bank" ["The Accurate Conception," S05E03]. Isabel Omero used to measure the laugh spread at the Monday-morning table, just so you got a sense of "Are we going long, or are we short? Do we have to cut stuff?" It got the longest laugh spread in *Golden Girls* history, and it was our first script. And it's a really, really funny episode. I mean, my favorite joke is Sophia going, "Oh, boy! We're going to a sperm bank!" That was our beginning. That was our initiation.

Isabel Omero, Production Associate/Script Supervisor, Writer

The laugh spread is the amount of time an episode lengthens from when it's performed in rehearsal to when it's performed in front of a live, laughing audience.

At the weekly table read, I'd time just the dialogue. I'd then predict how much it would spread once it was rehearsed with blocking. Then I'd predict how much more it would spread in front of our evening live studio audience. As the show was rehearsed during the week, I'd get a sense of how solid my predictions were. My predictions would let me know how much I thought the writers needed to cut from the script before we taped. On show night, just before we started the evening taping, I'd tell producers/writers/director my final prediction in case they wanted to make further cuts. Once taping was finished, I'd add up all the timings of the actual taped scenes, with all the laughs and reactions. Fortunately, my predictions were almost always spot-on, which was good because a lot of folks depended on them.

CHAPTER 9

Thank You for Being a Mom

Contradictory Lessons in Mothering from *The Golden Girls*

BETH L. BOSER

In mid-2021, a confluence of events had me seeking a new comfort show. Globally, we were a year and a half into the COVID-19 pandemic. Personally, I was grieving for my dad, who died earlier in the year. My grief went beyond his death; as an only child of divorced parents, I shouldered the responsibilities of caretaking as his health declined. I spent that time, amid the worst of the pandemic, sorting through all his possessions and moving him from his home to a "care suite"; participating in heart-wrenching video care conferences and never-ending phone calls with dozens of understandably burned-out health professionals; driving hundreds of miles every week in what seemed to be a never-ending loop between my house, his condo, his care facility, various medical appointments, yet another hospital, yet another transitional care unit. I could transport him places but was not otherwise allowed to visit in person. In doing all this, I had to spend massive amounts of time away from my partner and our young child, who turned two in the midst. I felt like a failure as a daughter and a mother, attempting to make the best possible choices from a field of only bad alternatives.

Kicking the "sandwich generation" angst into high gear, I was also struggling through infertility. This was unexpected "secondary infertility," as my spouse and I already had one biological child. Experiencing more difficulty the second time around, I began fertility treatments at the same time I began caring for my father in the summer of 2020. This impossible timing seemed like the only option. I was thirty-eight years old, and I did not want my kid to be an only child (like me) and have to navigate the intense difficulties of life—like caring for a parent at the end of life—alone (like me). I had also somewhat surprisingly discovered that I *love* being a mom, love parenting with my partner, and desperately wanted to multiply the experience. To have a chance at success, we had to begin immediately. A little over a year later—returning to 2021—all options short of in vitro fertilization (IVF) were exhausted. Not being one to quit, I embarked on what would be the most physically, mentally, and financially grueling journey of my life to that point, on my quest to become mother to a second child.

For my comfort show, I wanted no plotlines centered on motherhood, parenting, or traditional family of any kind. Given my circumstances, narratives involving any of these would negate the "comfort" piece. *The Golden Girls* seemed an apt choice. So I, along with many others during the pandemic, settled in to watch the series from start to finish.[1]

Beyond an intense personal preoccupation, motherhood is also a focus of my academic research. So despite my intentions otherwise, I immediately started reading *The Golden Girls* through that lens and seeing mothering everywhere. Far from providing a typical depiction of sitcom motherhood, however, *The Golden Girls* presents mothering as a complex set of contradictions woven through the lives of Blanche, Rose, Dorothy, and Sophia. On a personal level, I found this depiction of mothering relatable and, in fact, *comforting*. On a scholarly level, mothering in *The Golden Girls* offers novel constructions of and resistance to motherhood ideology. In this chapter, I discuss *The Golden Girls* in connection with scholarship on motherhood ideology and motherhood in media, to demonstrate how the Girls work through tensions embedded in both motherhood and the era in which the show was produced. In doing so, I reflect on what the Girls teach us about mothering and navigating the tensions inherent in caregiving.

Media Moms and Motherhood Ideology

Adrienne Rich delineates "two meanings of motherhood, one superimposed on the other: the *potential relationship* of any women to her power of reproduction and to children; and the *institution*, which aims at ensuring that that potential—and all women—shall remain under male control."[2] Building from the notion of motherhood as an institution, numerous rhetorical and sociological studies of discourse about mothering have deduced a dominant ideology of American motherhood—that is, dominant values and beliefs about what it means to be a "good mother."[3] Sharon Hays notes that the edicts of this ideology are "not followed in practice by every mother, but they are, implicitly or explicitly, understood as the *proper* approach to the raising of a child by the majority of mothers."[4] Good mothers, then, must totally devote themselves to the role with regard to time, energy, and resources and place their children's needs above their own in every circumstance. They must be the primary caregivers to their children, give care constantly, and be fulfilled in the selfless nurturing required by the role.[5] Motherhood ideology creates impossible expectations, is individualizing, and fosters intense competition among mothers.[6]

Motherhood ideology is constructed and maintained through media.[7] Perhaps the best way to observe dominant values and beliefs about motherhood is by watching mom characters on television and in film. Media representations often feature quintessential "good mothers" in contrast with their binary opposition, the "bad mom." Heather Addison, Mary Kate Goodwin-Kelly, and Elaine Roth indicate that media provide "a limited repertoire of maternal portrayals" wherein "mothers are repeatedly demonized or deified."[8] Rebecca Feasey notes that while some television moms challenge motherhood ideology and "shatter the romanticized image of the selfless, satisfied stay-at-home maternal caregiver," they "do so while simultaneously upholding the maternal ideal."[9] In other words, we moms all know what we *should* be doing, even when we're not doing it.

Classic sitcom good moms are fairly easy to identify: June Cleaver, Carol Brady, Marion Cunningham; as are the bad moms: Peg Bundy, Monica Gallagher, Beverly Hofstadter, Lucille Bluth. Depictions of both good and bad mothers continually produce and reinforce a dichotomy of motherhood ideology. Heather Hundley and Sara Hayden confirm that "scholars and pundits seem to agree: in the contemporary United States, we assess maternal practices as starkly good or bad," and media constructions of motherhood "offer lessons for real-life moms about how they are expected to behave."[10] These lessons are powerful; even though I spend a good deal of time studying constructions of motherhood critically, the voices in my head would frequently chastise me for being a bad mom when I, for example, would leave my young child in order to care for my ailing father.

Although values of motherhood continue to evolve—arguably in ways that ever intensify the expectations placed on mothers—scholars agree that contemporary rules of good mothering "emerged in the 1980s and [continue] to be in full force today."[11] Thus, current norms of motherhood and *The Golden Girls* both emerged at the beginning of a historical period that feminist theorists refer to as "postfeminism." This period is characterized by two different yet interwoven threads. First, concerted conservative efforts to undermine Second Wave feminism asserted that women were unhappy not because of ongoing oppression but because of feminism—this is often referred to as the "backlash."[12] Second, a sense that feminism had been "taken into account"—its goals met—and thus was no longer needed emerged in media and other discourses.[13] *The Golden Girls* is an excellent media text through which to read the intertwined implications of motherhood ideology and postfeminism. Although the show is not *about* motherhood in a traditional nuclear family environment, the women *are* all mothers: Blanche and Rose have five children each, Dorothy has two, Sophia has three including Dorothy. Moreover, the Girls traversed the Second Wave feminist to postfeminist terrain: Rose, Blanche, and Dorothy would have all been in their mid-thirties when the Second Wave women's movement took off and in their late forties as it faded amid the rise of Reagan conservativism. They raised their children in nuclear families during the Second Wave and transitioned into single, working, empty-nest adulthood in the aftermath. Thus, for the Girls, mothering is fraught with tensions rooted in postfeminist ambivalence and double binds.

To make sense of mothering in *The Golden Girls*, I draw from American cultural understandings of motherhood ideology, which is rooted in the neoliberal postfeminism of the 1980s. Therein motherhood is inherently tied to gender and rates women as essentially good or bad based on how they perform the intense expectations of motherhood. Specifically, three categories of motherhood-related tension emerge in the show, which I label *control*, *collaboration*, and *choice*. These tensions demonstrate the challenges of mothering in a postfeminist context.

Control, collaboration, and choice pertain directly to mothering and also to postfeminist theorizing more broadly. Some practical examples illustrate this, although the following are by no means comprehensive. With regard to *control*, in the postfeminist context, middle-class white women gained some control over their lives in relation to employment opportunities and reproductive decision-making, for example.[14] At the same time, the courses of women's lives were still largely determined by a patriarchal system—including presumed traditional heteronormativity—the structure of which was left intact by the legal gains of the Second Wave women's movement. With regard to *collaboration*, the feminism of the 1960s and '70s brought together a community of women; yet, to reap the rewards of the movement, they often had to ditch the community and chase after the individual opportunities offered to some via the movement's legal victories.[15] And finally, *choice* is a slogan often touted as a feminist ideal and gain of the Second Wave; however, a deeper consideration reveals that access to "choice" is not granted equally, and one's quality of choices often depends on economic and racial privilege (i.e., wealth and whiteness), among other things. Of course, these tensions all play out in the practice of motherhood. Because I am a member of the Xennial microgeneration—whose childhood, adolescence, and young adulthood all took shape in the postfeminist era—these tensions are also deeply embedded in my personal sense of self and worldview. I observed products of these tensions showing up in the form of mixed messages about mothering in *The Golden Girls*, in ways that correspond to the tenets of motherhood ideology.

Mothering in *The Golden Girls*

Despite my initial assumptions otherwise, mothering is a thread that weaves through the entirety of *The Golden Girls*. Each of the women is a mother multiple times over: Sophia to Phil, Gloria, and Dorothy; Dorothy to Kate and Michael; Blanche to Janet, Becky, "Skippy," Doug, and "Biff"; and Rose to Bridget, Kirsten, Gunilla, Adam, and Charlie Jr. Of the children besides Dorothy, viewers only ever meet Gloria, Kate, Michael, Janet, Becky, Bridget, and Kirsten—although Skippy later appears in *The Golden Palace* (S01E17).

The Girls represent the complexities of "good" and "bad" with regard to motherhood ideology. Of course, representations of the Girls as mothers are different than in typical family sitcoms centered on raising young children; these women are, instead, all struggling through the transition to mothering adult children. Although mothering an adult is vastly different from mothering a young child, practices reflective of motherhood ideology still appear. With regard to "good" mothering, the Girls obviously love their children and are frequently shown to be willing to drop everything for their kids. They often put their children's needs ahead of their own and engage in stereotypically feminine nurturing practices.

"Bad" mothering is also evident. Prime examples are Blanche's intense fat-shaming of her daughter Becky and Dorothy's unwillingness to accept the marriage of her son, Michael, to an older Black woman. Hints abound that some of the Girls were not the best mothers when their children were younger. Kate Browne notes, for example, that "Blanche has a difficult time transitioning to her role as a mother because of the expectation that mothers must sacrifice their individual wants, needs, and desires for the sake of their children" and that "Blanche's primary allegiance is to her own pleasure."[16] Some examples that read as "bad" mothering could be interpreted as resistance to the ideology. Beyond Blanche's refusal to subvert her own desires to the needs of her children (whether youth or adult), Dorothy is unwilling to hide her distaste and anger toward her ex-husband, Stan, in order to please her daughter, and Rose asserts her relationships with the Girls as just as important as those with her kids.[17] Examples in the following sections that illustrate tensions related to control, collaboration, and choice represent a negotiation of both the values of motherhood ideology and postfeminist ambivalence.

CONTROL? RESPONSIBILITY AND SURRENDER OF MOTHERHOOD

The Golden Girls sends the message that mothers have control over—and are therefore responsible for—the actions of their children and others under their care. At the same time, various plots revolving around mothering emphasize the necessity of surrendering control. As I watched the show amid my own experiences as a sandwich-generation caregiver, I was acutely feeling the responsibility to take control of things over which I ultimately had very little, if any, control.

Many of the insights about control gleaned from the show center on Dorothy's relationship with her grown son, Michael. Michael is a professional musician and a drifter; he is described as "flighty," and Dorothy laments his unwillingness to grow up and take responsibility for his life.[18] Dorothy feels she is to blame for Michael's bad choices in the second season's "Family Affair." Michael and Rose's daughter Bridget are visiting their mothers simultaneously. The two are caught in bed together, to the horror of the Girls. Dorothy exclaims, "Where did I go wrong with you?" to which Michael replies, "You didn't! You were a great mother!" Dorothy responds, "If I were a great mother, you would be graduating from medical school, not playing doctor with my best friend's daughter here in this house." Implied is that Dorothy's mothering directly led Michael to lead the life he leads and make the choices he makes; had she been a better mother, he would be a better person. This thread continues in the fifth-season episode "All That Jazz." Michael shows up jobless and separated from his wife. Blanche scolds Dorothy for enabling his irresponsible behavior by giving him money and letting him stay at their house while remaining unemployed. She says to Dorothy, "You are never gonna have a good relationship with your children until you stop doing all the things for them they should be doing for themselves."[19]

Blanche suggests that Dorothy's behavior reinforces all the bad features of Michael's personality and permits him to continue behaving childishly. A joke in this scene plays on the notion that Dorothy has come by it honestly: Sophia mends Dorothy's blouse and socks for her, demonstrating how a pattern of misguided mothering is passed down through generations.

The Girls' mothering practices have a profound immediate impact on a younger child when Blanche's fourteen-year-old grandson David visits. David is sent to the Girls because his mother (Blanche's daughter Janet) and father are having marital troubles. David is disrespectful at every turn and makes cruel jokes about the Girls' ages. His behavior is out of control; he leaves the house at 2:00 a.m. to get pizza and brings back a group of stray teenagers for a middle-of-the-night party. Dorothy, Rose, and Sophia come together to generate a plan for "tough love" that includes a lot of chores. According to them, chores provide structure and engender responsibility and a sense of pride. Blanche admits she never had to do chores and raised her daughter the same way; thus, "That's why David is the way he is now. . . . It's all *my* fault!"[20] Ultimately, a heart-to-heart with Dorothy—during which we discover that David's bad behavior is the direct result of his parents' inattention—is the crux of his turnaround. The application of the Girls' collective mothering wisdom appears to completely turn a bad kid good and sets his entire family on the path to healing. The lesson from these examples is that bad mothering makes bad kids and good mothering makes good kids; and mothers have control over, and thus are wholly responsible for, either outcome. This connects with the larger problematic implication of "control" or autonomy in a postfeminist context; if women are in control of their destinies, persisting structural systems of oppression are let off the hook as individuals must be responsible for their own successes or failures.

Paradoxically, plotlines also indicate that the only way to be a good mother is to let go of control. In the fifth season's "The Accurate Conception," Blanche struggles with her lack of control when her daughter Becky reveals that she is going to have a baby via artificial insemination with donor sperm—today known as intrauterine insemination, or IUI.[21] You're cuter than an intrauterine! Blanche is horrified and implores Becky to either get married or wait until Blanche and all her friends are dead before undergoing insemination. She exclaims, "It's not easy being the mother of a child with her own free will!" The battle for control is evident:

Blanche: So instead of trying [to find a man to marry], you're just going to give up and do this crazy baby thing?

Becky: Crazy baby thing? What I am doing, Mother, is taking control of my life and having the family I need.

Blanche: Well, I would certainly never have a baby artificially, and I do not approve of you doing it either.

Becky: Well, if that's the way you want it, Mama, you're going to lose me and your grandchild.[22]

Dorothy later tells Blanche that the argument is not about insemination; rather, it is about control. Blanche's need to control her daughter reads as misguided and ultimately a huge mistake, as the risk of losing contact with family is clearly too big a price to pay for what ultimately comes down to Blanche's "ewww" reaction to insemination; she seems petty and immature. Yet, when taken together with the show's suggestion that mothers' actions directly affect outcomes for their children, her desire for control is understandable. Contradictory lessons about control reflect a double bind for mothers.

COLLABORATION? MOTHERS IN COMMUNITY AND COMPETITION

The Girls constantly help one another mother their adult children, emphasizing the necessity of a community of mothers in collaboration. Each time one of the Girls is a "bad" mom, another will step in to help her. When Dorothy enabled Michael's bad behavior, Blanche snapped her out of it and told her exactly what to do: "You have to make him stand on his own two feet. If I were you, I'd kick him out." Subsequently, Dorothy tells Michael, "I'm forcing you to grow up." Sophia questions the decision, telling Dorothy she's being cruel. However, her hypocrisy comes to light: Sophia regularly sends money to her own son, Phil. Ultimately, Rose steps in to offer Dorothy reassurance. She says, "Dorothy, I know you've done the right thing. In the animal kingdom, the whole idea is to teach offspring to fend for themselves. Humans are the only ones who think it's their duty to care for children their entire lives."[23] Although the Girls have different approaches to the problem and don't agree on the best way to handle Michael, they work through the problem together from start to finish.

Blanche helps the Girls through the awkward situation in the second-season episode "Family Affair." After Dorothy's son and Rose's daughter are caught in bed together, Dorothy, Sophia, and Rose are distraught. Blanche persuades Dorothy and Rose to talk to their children, even if difficult.

Having learned from her own failures, she suggests that the awkward situation offers an opportunity for the mothers to grow closer to their adult children, instead of further apart, if handled correctly. The Girls return the favor in the third-season episode "Blanche's Little Girl," an episode typically remembered for the Girls' relentless fat-shaming of Blanche's daughter Becky.[24] However, they do band together as mothers for purposes of running off Becky's jerk fiancé for . . . relentlessly fat-shaming Becky. Once again, the Girls advocate different approaches—Dorothy wants to intervene; Rose thinks they should steer clear—but when Blanche fears she has lost Becky for bluntly sharing her opinion, the Girls offer reassurance:

Blanche: I couldn't sleep. I just kept tossing and turning thinking about the terrible mistake I made.
Rose: You did the right thing!
Blanche: You're only saying that 'cause you're my friend, Rose. Sophia, tell me the truth. Am I a bad mother?
Sophia: You did what you had to do.
Blanche: Then why do I feel so terrible?
Dorothy: Because it is not easy being a mother. If it were easy, fathers would do it.[25]

These are just a few examples of a larger pattern in the series. Whenever one of the Girls has a problem with her children, she does all the wrong things until help comes from her friends. The lesson is that a mother alone cannot be good in the role; she must have a supportive community. This pushes back against the individualization and competitiveness that stem from motherhood ideology; however, additional messages in the show contradict the theme of collaboration.

The Girls sometimes withhold support or directly compete with one another, and other women, as mothers. In the first season's "The Truth Will Out," Rose struggles with a situation involving her daughter Kirsten. Rose lied to her daughter for years, telling her that her father, Charlie, was a successful businessman. Rose shows Kirsten her bleak last will and testament, and things devolve; when Kirsten sees no money in the estate, she assumes Rose has squandered everything. In reality, Charlie didn't leave Rose anything. Kirsten is unaware of this and furious with Rose. Later, Rose seeks help from Dorothy, but Dorothy wants to go to sleep and asks if it can wait until morning. Rose talks through her dilemma as Dorothy ostensibly sleeps, deciding that she must tell Kirsten the truth. She concludes,

"Dorothy, I want you to know that having friends like you really helps me get through times like this.... I love you." Dorothy coldly replies, "Oh, thank God. I thought you'd never shut up."[26]

In "A Family Affair," prior to the Girls' reconciliation, Dorothy and Rose argue heatedly over who is to blame for their kids having sex. Rose accuses Michael of seducing Bridget. Dorothy retorts that Bridget isn't his type. Rose says that of course she isn't; she's too good for him. Dorothy calls Bridget a "tramp... tramp, tramp, tramp!" Rose is wounded and tells Dorothy that she has "never said anything so vicious and cruel." Rose gets to the heart of what they are doing later on, when she admits, "I guess we were so busy trying to protect our kids we took it out on each other."[27] She illustrates how motherhood is intensely competitive and that mothers will put the interests of their children above all others, as Dorothy and Rose are willing to set aside their friendship to defend their children.[28] Competition extends beyond the girls, too. When Dorothy's sister, Gloria, visits in the first season's "The Custody Battle," the women's competitive history is clear. Gloria asks Dorothy if she resents her for a variety of reasons (she's rich, etc.). Dorothy says that of course she doesn't; Gloria replies, "Even though all my children are practicing professionals and yours aren't?" to which Dorothy replies, "Please, Gloria. I'm happy for your children. All except Katherine. No, she really should have taken the nose job instead of the Mustang for graduation."[29] Thus, mothers both need each other and resent each other, simultaneously conveying a feminist lesson of the importance of sisterhood and an opposing lesson warning of women's perpetual cattiness and competition.

CHOICE? THE FREEDOM TO LET GO (OR NOT)

One particularly strong legacy of Second Wave feminism is the notion of "choice." Choice is a feminist hallmark of hard-won liberties. Yet, feminist critics have pointed out the limits of "choice" as a paradigm for liberation. In my own life, navigating the unending choices that came along with fertility treatment, I felt anything but liberated. As I watched *The Golden Girls*, I was so deep into the process that any choice I made felt damaging in some way. Choosing to continue treatment meant enduring physical pain, intense burdens on time, deteriorating mental health, lost time with my son, and financial despair. Choosing to quit meant saying good-bye to another child and all that would come with them. More broadly, even under the best of circumstances, choice is a product of privilege—What if all the available choices are bad ones? Furthermore, those who are in favor of traditional roles for women have even taken up choice for alternative ends; for example, women should "choose" to stay home and submit to their husbands. As with control and collaboration, tensions emerge in the show regarding choice, with roots in the contradictions of intensive motherhood and postfeminism.

I witnessed the Girls exercising choice in empowering ways, when events threaten to pull them back into full-time mothering. When Blanche's troubled grandson David visits, Rose explains, "I don't want to send him back to an unhappy home. But we're grandmothers! It wouldn't be fair to be this old *and* have to raise children."[30] Similarly, in the first-season episode "Second Motherhood," Blanche frets that the man she wants to marry has two children ages seven and nine. She says, "Babies need a mama. Goodness, I've already raised my family. I don't have the energy to go through that again!"[31] Dorothy emphatically agrees that she doesn't want to be a mother again. The Girls also remind one another that they are free from the intensive constraints of mothering, as when Blanche tells Dorothy, "This really isn't your problem anymore. It's Michael's. He just has to learn the things we need to know to be an adult, like how to earn a living, how to pay the rent."[32]

Rose illustrates her willingness to move on from traditional nuclear family roles when she undergoes emergency heart surgery. In the seventh-season episode "Home Again Rose (Part 2)," Kirsten shows up to see Rose in the hospital. Kirsten is dismissive of the Girls' relationship:

Kirsten: I'm her daughter. You're not her family.
Dorothy: Why does everyone keep saying that? We share our lives together!
Kristen: You share *a house* together.

Things change when Rose has the opportunity to make her wishes clear. As she wakes up from anesthesia, she immediately asks Kirsten, "Where are the girls?" Dorothy, Blanche, and Sophia have thus far been prevented from seeing Rose by the hospital's "family only" policy. Kirsten assumes that Rose is referring to her granddaughters and replies that they are too young to come to the hospital. Rose wryly responds, "Not your girls, *my* girls. *My* girls aren't too young for anything."[33] Rose tells Kirsten that, should anything happen to her, she wants Kirsten to look after Dorothy, Blanche, and Sophia. Rose asserts her independence from the restrictions of motherhood and from the notion that biological children come before anyone else. She also reassigns the caretaking role to Kirsten; it is she who must be responsible for Rose's "girls" and not the other way around. The lesson is that mothers have agency to choose to put other concerns ahead of their children, and the meaning of mothers' lives goes beyond their kids.

While the Girls exercise their freedom of choice to reject the expectations of the mother role, they sometimes "choose" to uphold those expectations. For example, the Girls express love for their children through the traditional motherly task of cooking. When Bridget visits, Rose makes a big show of cooking all her favorite things.[34] Similarly, Sophia laments her and Dorothy's inability to cook Michael all of his favorite things since he arrived unexpectedly. The following morning, Dorothy cooks Michael "the best breakfast [he's] had in ages" and cleans up after him as well. She "enjoy[s] doing it."[35]

Examples extend beyond cooking. At one point, Sophia chooses to give up her entire life with the Girls to move into a trailer with her son, Phil, because "he needs [her]."[36] Rose sacrifices her own needs for those of her child when she lies to Kirsten to protect Charlie's reputation, taking blame for the alleged loss of the money.[37] In many instances, the Girls make "choices" to change their own behaviors after their kids threaten to cut them out of their respective lives.[38] The Girls certainly don't *have* to make the choices they do. But often, if they didn't, the result would be losing their kids—not much of a choice. This corresponds with the fact that many postfeminist "choices" for women were not much of a choice or were choices between bad alternatives.[39] Of course, all choices have consequences, some good and some bad; but here, in relation to motherhood, the consequences are dire. Once again, the overall lesson is confusing: mothers are in possession of choice, yet they will frequently "choose" the path that upholds ideological expectations of motherhood or otherwise submit themselves to the decisions of others.

Conclusion

Motherhood is rife with contradictions, as is caregiving more broadly. As I reflect on *The Golden Girls* in the context of my own experiences while watching the show, I find that the types of tensions, paradoxes, and double binds experienced by the Girls with regard to control, collaboration, and choice resonate, even though the specific situations differ greatly. As I was seemingly in control of my father's care, the outcomes felt like my responsibility. I constantly second-guessed my actions and experienced significant guilt over the misery he experienced. Even though rationally I knew it wasn't the case, I constantly felt as though I could be doing more for him or that the outcome would have been better had I only done whatever thing differently. I felt responsible for everything. In the highly isolating realm of infertility, collaboration with other women felt impossible both emotionally and practically. When going through IVF, commiserating with others is an emotional minefield; everyone else is either slightly (or greatly) worse or better off than you with regard to success. In this context, at least for me, any attempt to connect with a larger community resulted in comparison, followed by immediate guilt or grief spiraling. As I faced an unending barrage of choice navigating both my father's care and IVF, I spent equal amounts of time acknowledging how lucky I was to have so many choices—for example, my father had enough money saved to afford decent care; I had the means to at least attempt IVF—and longing to experience even a single day when I didn't have to make heart-wrenching choices. Watching the Girls navigate the tensions of motherhood made me consider, If I am in control, am I responsible for everything? What would letting go of control look like, and would it be possible? How can one collaborate and find community amid situations that seem inherently isolating and individualizing? Are choices liberating or their own form of constraint? And are my choices truly choices, or am I simply navigating the inevitable stream of structures and systems—of gender, of motherhood, of health care—the best I can?

These all seem to be irresolvable tensions characteristic of contemporary mothering and caretaking in all forms and of being a woman who came of age in a postfeminist context. However, their seeming irresolvability does not mean we should not work for better, and *The Golden Girls* does the work of naming many of the problems of contemporary mothering and motherhood ideology. In a practical sense, being a mother and a caretaker means finding ways to live in the both/and, navigating situations that do not have a clear answer.

Writing about the postfeminist media landscape, Susan Faludi remarked, "The networks only seemed willing to support single-women shows when the heroines were confined to the home in non-threatening roles in a strictly all-female world—like the elderly widows in 'The Golden Girls.'"[40] This characterization unfairly dismisses the subversive and resistive potential of the Girls and the ways the series offers opportunities to relate and identify with difficult life situations. Ultimately, in the show's contradictions, tensions, impossible choices, and compromises, I found the Girls endlessly relatable and, hence, intensely comforting.

Notes

1. John Koblin, "Lockdown TV: Netflix Dominates, News Surges and Bea Arthur Is Still Golden," *New York Times*, April 30, 2020, www.nytimes.com/2020/04/30/business/media/coronavirus-television-netflix-ratings.html.

2. Adrienne Rich, *Of Woman Born: Motherhood as Experience and Institution* (Norton, 1986), 13.

3. For an overview, see D. Lynn O'Brien Hallstein, "Introduction to Mothering Rhetorics," *Women's Studies in Communication* 40, no. 1 (2017): 1–2.

4. Sharon Hays, *The Cultural Contradictions of Motherhood* (Yale University Press, 1996), 9.

5. For more on motherhood ideology, see Hays, *Cultural Contradictions*, 8–9; Susan J. Douglas and Meredith W. Michaels, *The Mommy Myth: The Idealization of Motherhood and How It Has Undermined All Women* (Free Press, 2004), 4; Andrea O'Reilly, *Mother Matters: Motherhood as Discourse and Practice* (Association for Research on Mothering, 2004), 14; and Heather Hundley and Sara Hayden, introduction to *Mediated Moms: Contemporary Challenges to the Motherhood Myth*, ed. Hunter Hundley and Sara Hayden (Peter Lang, 2016), 2.

6. Jenna Abetz and Julia Moore, "Welcome to the Mommy Wars, Ladies: Making Sense of the Ideology of Combative Mothering in Mommy Blogs," *Communication, Culture & Critique* 11 (2018): 268.

7. Douglas and Michaels, *Mommy Myth*, 11.

8. Heather Addison, Mary Kate Goodwin-Kelly, and Elaine Roth, introduction to *Motherhood Misconceived: Representing the Maternal in U.S. Films*, ed. Heather Addison, Mary Kate Goodwin-Kelly, and Elaine Roth (State University of New York, 2009), 4.

9. Rebecca Feasey, *From Happy Homemaker to Desperate Housewives: Motherhood and Popular Television* (Anthem, 2012), 181.

10. Hundley and Hayden, introduction to *Mediated Moms*, 2.

11. O'Brien Hallstein, "Introduction to Mothering Rhetorics," 2.

12. Susan Faludi, *Backlash: The Undeclared War Against American Women* (Three Rivers, 1991).

13. Angela McRobbie, *The Aftermath of Feminism: Gender, Culture and Social Change* (Sage, 2009), 12.

14. By "postfeminist context," I refer to the period beginning in the 1980s and continuing through the 1990s and 2000s. Although postfeminist thinking certainly endures in many forms (discussion of which is beyond the scope of the present chapter), we have ostensibly moved to a different "wave" of feminism at present. Regarding employment opportunities: the Equal Pay Act of 1963, 42 percent increase of women in the workforce. Regarding reproductive decision-making: *Roe v. Wade*, the birth control pill.

15. E.g., a woman climbing any given professional ladder would probably have to leave her "sisters" behind to achieve success; any feminism that attempts to operate within the boundaries of capitalism necessitates competition between women.

16. Kate Browne, *The Golden Girls* (Detroit: Wayne State University Press, 2020), 46–47, 41.

17. "Guess Who's Coming to the Wedding," S01E02; "Home Again Rose (2)," S07E24.

18. "Family Affair," S02E07; "All That Jazz," S05E10.

19. "All That Jazz," S05E10.

20. "On Golden Girls," S01E06.

21. You're cuter than an intrauterine!

22. "The Accurate Conception," S05E03.

23. "All That Jazz," S05E10.

24. E.g., "Blanche's Little Girl User Reviews," *IMDb*, accessed June 12, 2023, www.imdb.com/title/tt0589723/reviews.

25. "Blanche's Little Girl," S03E14.

26. "The Truth Will Out," S01E16.

27. "A Family Affair," S02E07.

28. Abetz and Moore, "Welcome to the Mommy Wars," 268.

29. "The Custody Battle," S01E12. Given the previous lesson about control, Gloria is also insinuating that she is a better mother than Dorothy.

30. "On Golden Girls," S01E06.

31. "Second Motherhood," S01E19.

32. "All That Jazz," S05E10.

33. "Home Again Rose (Part 2)," S07E24.

34. Including a "maple syrup honey brown sugar molasses rice krispie log"; "Family Affair," S02E07.

35. "Family Affair," S02E07.

36. "Golden Moments (Part 1)," S03E18.

37. "The Truth Will Out," S01E16.

38. Rose and Kristen, "The Truth Will Out," S01E16; Dorothy and Kate, "Son-In-Law Dearest," S02E23; Dorothy and Michael, "Mixed Blessing," S03E23; Blanche and Becky, "The Accurate Conception," S05E03, "Blanche Delivers," S06E01; and "Even Grandmas Get the Blues," S06E20.

39. E.g., women can choose not to dress according to traditional standards of femininity, but when they do so, they are often ridiculed, harassed, or even subject to threats of violence.

40. Faludi, *Backlash*, 171.

ROSE

I think so, too. In fact, I know so. This is exactly what happened during the Great Herring War.

BLANCHE

The Great Herring War?

ROSE

Yes. Between the Lindstroms and the Johannsens.

DOROTHY

Oh, that Great Herring War.

ROSE

The two families controlled the most fertile herring waters off the coast of Norway. So, naturally, it seemed in their best interest to band together. Boy, was that a big mistake. You see, they couldn't agree on what to do with the herring.

DOROTHY

I can understand that. I mean, the possibilities are overwhelming.

ROSE

Exactly. The Johannsens wanted to pickle the herring. But the Lindstroms wanted to train them for the circus.

BLANCHE (*)

Wouldn't they be hard to see riding on the elephants?

(DOROTHY LAUGHS)

ROSE

Not that kind of circus. A herring circus. Sort of like Seaworld. Only smaller. Much, much smaller. But bigger than a flea circus.

DOROTHY

Tell me, Rose, did they ever shoot a herring out of a cannon?

(BLANCHE LAUGHS)

ROSE

Only once. But they shot him into a tree. After that, no other herring would do it.

(DOROTHY AND BLANCHE LAUGH)

BLANCHE

Rose, you have to be making this up.

The Myth of Ad-Libbing the Great Herring War

Marsha Posner Williams, Co-Producer

You guys know that there's so many *Golden Girls* Facebook groups, right? And I don't ever look at them. But one day, I happened to come across, and there was a scene that they played [from "The Way We Met," S01E25], and the title of the post was "the greatest improv scene ever, that's why these ladies were so amazing." It's a scene where Betty was talking about the Great Herring Circus and a herring being shot out of a cannon. And all the comments said, "Oh my God, that's so funny! That's why they're the greatest actors ever." And I couldn't help myself. I said, "Sorry to burst your bubble. I happen to have produced that episode, and I can tell you, for a fact, nobody was allowed to improvise on that show, ever." And there was no need to. If you know the story about casting the Dorothy part, you know the story about Elaine Stritch coming in. She improvised. And that was a big mistake.

Isabel Omero, Production Associate/Script Supervisor, Writer

The Golden Girls never improvised any dialogue. If the ladies cracked up at a story, it was because it was carefully written and rehearsed that way. The Girls acted so brilliantly and naturally, it only looked like they made up those wonderful words. I rehearsed dialogue with them for seven years. *The Golden Girls* writing staff was just that great. And trust me, Bea, Betty, Rue, and Estelle were the first to say so.

Facing page: Original script pages disprove the rumor that the cast ad-libbed the "Great Herring War" in "The Way We Met" (S01E25). (Photos of script provided by Lex Passaris, a postproduction supervisor for the episode.)

PART III

Audiences and Reception

CHAPTER 10

Golden Girlfriends

Black Women's Fandom and the Implicit Blackness of *The Golden Girls*

ALFRED L. MARTIN JR.

I watched *The Golden Girls* through much of the time it was on air (until I went to boarding school in the fall of 1991). But it was not until I was an undergraduate student at Arizona State University that I became a fan of the series through reruns on Lifetime TV: Television for Women. Lifetime, which launched in 1984, initially courted upscale white women as its target demographic, using series like *The Golden Girls* to provide ad revenue to finance its original films.[1] Given Lifetime's flow of programming that hailed white women, I assumed that my attraction to *The Golden Girls* was firmly rooted in my queerness rather than my Blackness—as if one can "split" one's intersectional self. Regardless, I happily moved through life believing that I was a queer Black *Golden Girls* fan rather than a Black queer *Golden Girls* fan—with my queerness "trumping" my Blackness (as if such a thing were possible).

On June 27, 2020, Hulu, which had acquired *The Golden Girls*' streaming rights in 2017, announced that it would be removing the third-season episode "Mixed Blessing" from the streamer because of its alleged use of Blackface.[2] The episode's A plot concerns Dorothy's (Bea Arthur) son Michael marrying an older Black woman, Lorraine. The B plot revolves around Rose (Betty White) and Blanche (Rue McClanahan) preparing for an event via beauty regimens, which requires their application of brown mud masks, which just so happens to coincide with Lorraine's family's arrival at 6151 Richmond Street to meet Michael's family. *The Golden Girls'* lone Black writer/producer, Winifred Hervey-Stallworth (Hervey), would recall this inclusion as the result of the writing staff being "incredibly stupid then." In an interview, she told me, "We were like, 'Mud masks. Yes!' It was interesting because I think that was one of the episodes where we had a lot of Black guest stars. I can't believe nobody said anything." This event, which made headlines, prompted me to ask, Are there any Black *Golden Girls* fans, and if so, what do they think about Hulu having pulled the episode? So, I sent out a tweet asking if there were any Black *Golden Girls* fans willing to speak with me about their fandom. That tweet netted 246 retweets, 362 likes, and 26 quoted tweets, and through that tweet, I ultimately confirmed that I was not the only Black *Golden Girls* fan in the world. We exist, but we are typically not included in the category "fan" for the show.

Aside from the erasure of one of the few episodes of *The Golden Girls* to feature Black actors, part of my interest in and exploration of *The Golden Girls* as a scholarly object of study originates from a video that Aaron Scott posted on YouTube of himself singing the show's theme song.[3] But this was no mere cover; rather, Scott resignified the theme song in ways that, on the one hand, honored the original version sung by Cindy Fee and, on the other hand, infused the song with a gospel flavor that decidedly Blackened it. Since its posting, the video has amassed 5.3 million views and turned Scott into a viral sensation, culminating, in some ways, in his performing the song at Golden-Con, a *Golden Girls* fan convention. Scott's version of the theme song exposes how, as the race and technology scholar Sarah Florini posits, "many Black fans create parallel culturally resonant fan practices that mitigate their erasure not only from fandom but also from many of their beloved media texts."[4] In an era when representation allegedly matters for Black folks—or so the mantra goes—then the question is, Why might Black folks take up a television text in which they are not present? Florini, in her work on *Game of Thrones*, suggests that there is something about certain white-cast (or white-led) series that resonates for Black fans. The media scholar Kristen Warner theorizes Black resonance as not always concerned with seeing Black bodies and/or having Black bodies shout their Blackness from the televisual rooftops.[5] Rather, resonance is concerned with the affective responses Black folks can have to media texts through representational practices, sonic landscapes, and visual cues. This Black resonance, as the cultural studies scholar Emily Lordi argues, "signals relationships that are not causal or inevitable but are nevertheless *there*."[6] There is nothing explicit in the *text* that hails Black fans; however, *The Golden Girls*

Cindy Fee and Finally Aaron perform their rendition of "Thank You for Being a Friend." (Photo by Taylor Cole Miller)

engages "affective elements of consciousness and relationships" that structure Black fandom with it.[7] Thus, this chapter asks, building on the media scholar Racquel Gates's work around Black resonance, What would it mean if instead of thinking about a politics of representation, *The Golden Girls* was approached from within a politics of resonance?[8] I argue that, when centering resonance rather than representation, *The Golden Girls* becomes an implicitly Black text.

The term "implicitly Black text" is created in both reception and industrial practices. On the one hand, it builds on the notion of Black resonance that Florini, Warner, Lordi, and Gates engage. For Black viewers, there is something about *The Golden Girls* that feels Black. And it "vibrates" on a frequency to which Black viewers respond. An implicitly Black text is not simply about the representational absence of Black bodies but about how Black viewers take up those texts. An implicitly Black text is also industrially constructed. The series is made implicitly Black through its programming flow and production practices. Put simply, in this chapter, I am interested in the ways Blackness might have been encoded in *The Golden Girls*' production alongside its decoding among Black women.[9]

In what follows, I situate *The Golden Girls*' Black resonance in its sociocultural moment through discussions of flow and production practices before examining contemporary Black women's fandom of/for the series. To examine flow, I turn to *TV Guide* and the ways NBC programmed its series to understand the ways the network imagined the audience for *Golden Girls*. At the same time, I use a personal interview with the show's only Black writer, Winifred Hervey-Stallworth, to inform my theorization about the implicit Blackness of the series via its production practices. Lastly, I utilize interviews with twenty-five Black women fans of *Golden Girls* to understand why the series resonates as a Black fandom object. The women I interviewed range in age from twenty-seven to fifty-four and live in major metropolitan areas like Baltimore, Detroit, Philadelphia, New York, and Washington, DC; midsized cities like Portland, Oregon, Louisville, Kentucky, and Oakland, California; and smaller towns like Waco, Texas, Stockton, California, and Superior, Colorado.

Flow-den Girls

The cultural theorist Raymond Williams conceptualized *flow* to understand how television brings advertising and consumers together around taste cultures.[10] This relay, as Nick Browne argues, textualizes "the interaction of audience and advertiser."[11] Television's (largely) ephemeral nature in the 1980s prohibits me from being able to examine the ways ads provided the "connective tissue" between acts of *The Golden Girls* in its original run.[12] However, I use NBC's Saturday-night programming flow alongside Black-cast sitcoms to argue that *Golden Girls* is an implicitly Black text that hailed Black viewers because, as the comedy scholar Brett Mills argues, flow functions as a mechanism to make audiences cohere under the industrial logics of imagined taste cultures.[13]

As the media and cultural studies scholar Herman Gray writes, the blockbuster success of *The Cosby Show* (1984–92) resulted in NBC spending the rest of the 1980s courting Black viewers through programming that featured Black bodies as well as white- or multicultural-cast programming that might appeal to Black viewers.[14] Thus, in the first season that *The Golden Girls* was on air, it was preceded by *Gimme a Break!*, a sitcom featuring the actor-singer Nell Carter with a mostly white supporting cast, and the mostly white-cast series *The Facts of Life* with Kim Fields. Following the series premiere of *The Golden Girls*, NBC scheduled another series premiere, the Black-cast sitcom *227*. There are at least two logics that might explain *The Golden Girls*' scheduling on Saturday nights with a host of Black-cast and multicultural-cast sitcoms. The first option is that the series was scheduled around the notion of age and gender. Bea Arthur and Betty White were sixty-three at the start of the series, with Estelle Getty not far behind at sixty-two. Rue McClanahan was the youngest "Girl" at fifty-two. The other series in NBC's Saturday-night lineup included *The Facts of Life*, with house mother Charlotte Rae (who was fifty-nine in 1985), and Marla Gibbs toplining *227* at age fifty-four. But *Gimme a Break!* complicates the age argument because Carter was thirty-three in 1985. The second and, to my mind, more plausible option is that NBC placed the program on Saturday nights because it did not necessarily have another place on its schedule for the series. By placing *The Golden Girls* alongside its "Black block" of programming, NBC hoped the series would become a crossover hit that would resonate with what I have elsewhere called "surplus Blackness, which hinges on the idea that Black audiences are rarely explicitly courted as anything other than a value-added audience for a project (or set of projects) designed for broader, mainstream (read: white) appeal."[15]

In *The Golden Girls*' second season, NBC moved *Gimme a Break!* to Tuesday night for its final season and Blackened up its Saturday-night lineup by adding a new Black-cast series, *Amen*. Additionally, it is important to remember that in the 1980s, Saturday nights were not a "dead night" for television programming: *227* was the fourteenth most watched series, while *The Golden Girls* was in the top five and *Amen* was the thirteenth most watched series that season. It was not until the 1988–89 season that another series with an entirely white cast was added to NBC's Saturday-night lineup: the *Golden Girls* spin-off *Empty Nest*. Only when the series entered its last season in 1992 (and was the thirtieth most popular series of the season, down from tenth place the previous season) would the series be part of a Saturday-night lineup that included all white-cast sitcoms: *The Torkelsons*, *The Powers That Be*, and *Nurses*. *The Golden Girls*, I argue, ultimately helped NBC whiten its Saturday-night lineup to court wider and wealthier (white) viewers than its Black-cast sitcoms had the potential to reach. Utilizing Black content and Black audiences to reach whiter and more lucrative audiences would be perfected by Fox later in the decade.[16]

This brief discussion of *The Golden Girls* and flow demonstrates, in part, that NBC hoped the series might appeal to Black viewers. And NBC executives' prayers were answered. *Jet* magazine reported *The Golden Girls* among the top ten shows for Black viewers in the 1986–87 television season.[17] Its Black viewership was estimated to add "1½ to 2 points to [its] overall ratings."[18] And as Alba, one of the Black women interviewed for this project, revealed, she was certainly watching the series: "Saturday night, nine o'clock. When I was younger, I would spend Saturday nights at my grandmother's house because we went to church on Sunday morning. So, I had to watch whatever they watched, and they watched the whole [NBC] lineup on Saturday night." NBC's implicit suggestion that something about *The Golden Girls* would be appealing to Black viewers was indeed demonstrated in its ratings.

Producing *The Golden Girls'* Black Resonance

Despite the collaborative nature of television scripts' development, each episode of *The Golden Girls* had a credited writer (or writers).[19] And as I have argued elsewhere, writers' lived experiences have a significant impact on the development of an episode.[20] Thus, this section turns to the experience of Winifred Hervey-Stallworth, the lone Black writer/producer on *The Golden Girls'* writing staff, who entered the television industry in the 1970s through Warner Bros.' Minority and Women's Workshop. She soon landed work as an intern on *Six O'Clock Follies* and with Garry Marshall's production company, Henderson Production Company, which had produced hits including *Happy Days*, *Laverne & Shirley*, and *Mork & Mindy*. Before landing on *The Golden Girls*, Hervey worked as a writer on *Benson* and wrote a 1985 episode of *The Cosby Show*.

While *The Golden Girls* centers the lives and loves of four older white women in Miami, it departed from one of the rules of television: write what you know. According to Hervey, the writing staff was composed of younger writers—all in their twenties—who sought to demonstrate "that some things are universal, that even if you're an old white lady, you still want to go on a date, you still want to be relevant": "And I think, having those young writers write for those ladies . . . really helped the show [because] we were outside of [Dorothy, Rose, Blanche, and Sophia's] box."

At the same time, Hervey was aware of her position as the lone Black writer in the room and sought to ensure that the show spoke to some semblance of the realities of life in Miami. For example, she recalls "one time telling [the writers' room] that the show is in Miami and all the extras are white. Shouldn't the background people be more diverse? And they were like, 'You're right.' So then, they started putting more diverse background people." As Mary Beltran argues, including visual diversity gestures toward "utopic multiculturalism" while maintaining the centrality of whiteness.[21] But Hervey's insistence that more people of color be included among *The*

Golden Girls' background characters is laudable in its attention to the visual diversity of the series and, quite frankly, its casting/labor practices. While it is difficult to say with certainty, it seems unlikely that this would have happened without a Black writer on the series who felt empowered enough to speak up.

Over the course of the show's seven-season run, *The Golden Girls* infrequently engaged with explicit representations of Blackness. However, in thinking about the series's popularity with Black viewers/fans, Hervey posits that Bea Arthur "could really deliver a one-liner": "When you wrote for Bea, you could write more sparsely. She's kind of like a no-nonsense, and she had that great look. She could say so much by raising an eyebrow. And maybe that 'no-nonsense' part of her is what we all related to as Black people." Yet, while *Golden Girls* fandom is frequently tied to gay men, and presumably white women, given its initial exclusive syndication deal on Lifetime from 1997 until 2009, its Black fandom has been all but ignored within the hegemonic construction of the category "*Golden Girls* fan." But that does not mean Black fans were not watching and making the series resonate Blackly.

Fan(ning) the Flames of *The Golden Girls*' Black Resonance

In the final moments of the series finale, after Dorothy marries Lucas and decides to move out, she tearfully turns to Blanche, Rose, and Sophia, and says, "You'll always be my sisters. Always." Scholars have noted that *The Golden Girls* mediates alternative kinship formations that have historically activated queer and women's fandom of the series.[22] What these scholars do not note is that they are theorizing based on a white sample and have exnominated whiteness. This certainly does not mean that their theorizations might not hold some value for nonwhite fans. It simply means that because the category "fan" has been constructed as white, it is only when the fandom is not white that melanin must be named. In this way, then, this section partly engages with how Black folks find resonance in the series through their particular raced engagement with kinship formations.

For Black fans like Racquel, it is *The Golden Girls*' engagement with "the nonheteronormative family unit" that holds some of the show's appeal. She says, "There's something about the fact that this is a family, and that's the thing that they mentioned so many times, right? . . . It makes sense to me that this is a show that has appeal for Black people who are not the Cleavers [from *Leave It to Beaver*]." For Racquel, the representational practices *The Golden Girls* employs signal a less idyllic family than *Leave It to Beaver*'s Cleaver family that resonates for some Black fans. Racquel gestures toward how the "messier" configuration of *The Golden Girls'* family unit, with its intergenerational members, might hail Black audiences. The Girls certainly had a relationship that expanded the boundaries of friend or roommate. And some within the white community use "sister/brother" or "brother/sister from another mother" to differentiate these deeper relationships. For Black fans, *The Golden Girls* fashions relationships that are similar to the ways some Black folks use "play mama," "play cousin," and "play sister" to denote deeper relationships like those at 6151 Richmond Street.

Gabrielle similarly centers how *The Golden Girls* represented a different kind of television family, and its humor was partly what makes the program resonate for her. "We never really watched *Leave It to Beaver*–type shows, where the family love for each other is so uncomplicated. The humor in *Golden Girls* is like when African Americans play the dozens, . . . what maybe to an outside ear sounds kind of harsh, but it's actually like, 'I talked to you like this because I know you can handle it and because our relationship is expansive.' We love deep, and, also, we can roast each other." Racquel and Gabrielle point out how the series extended an understanding of resonance for Black viewers because the formation of the family that resides at 6151 Richmond Street in Miami resembles a family unlike other idyllic families, such as the Cleavers and the Huxtables on *The Cosby Show*. Gabrielle's invocation of playing the dozens suggests how Black fans' engagement with "white" fan objects can "tap into the symbolic energy of Black cultural commonplaces."[23] In invoking "the dozens," Gabrielle points to how Black folks read *The Golden Girls* Blackly. It is not just that the Girls spar with one another; it is that they use this sparring as "a medium of release through abuse, which affords much opportunity for improvisation, and for which there is no retaliation permitted except a response in wittier and more telling form."[24] This suggests that Black *Golden Girls* fans partly find resonance in the series as a "mirror of consumption" that they use as "a narrative focal point in the construction of life narratives and identities."[25] Or, put another way, by reading this white-cast series through a Black lens, Black *Golden Girls* fans, through both alternative family formation and reading the verbal sparring between the cast as "the dozens," make the show resonant and highlight its openness to be read as implicitly Black.

Part of the alternative kinship of *The Golden Girls* is its generational connections. As an open and polysemic text, *The Golden Girls* seemingly resonated for Black people young and old in the act of communal watching.

Katherine says, "My grandmother recently passed [away], and she was the one who I mainly watched [*The Golden Girls*] with." Katherine explicitly connects her Black fandom to nostalgia by linking the series to her memories of her grandmother. Thus, Katherine's *Golden Girls* fandom is enmeshed in a mix of nostalgia, joy, and intergenerational memories. Further gesturing toward the importance of intergenerational social ties on the development of *Golden Girls* fandom, Rachel hypothesizes that *The Golden Girls* has always been a part of her life. She says, "I don't have a vivid memory of when I started watching it, but I had to have been a child, and I had to have been watching with my parents in Houston, where I grew up. So, to my mind, they've sort of always been there. That's probably the best origin story I can give you." Katherine and Rachel highlight how their *Golden Girls* fandom partly originates through the communal act of viewing *The Golden Girls and* viewing the program across generations—both as a text shared with elders and as one they continue to watch as they age. Simultaneously, in centering their memories of becoming viewers and fans of *The Golden Girls*, these Black women reveal how their process of becoming *Golden Girls* fans was not necessarily transformative but, as Matt Hills argues, forms "a continuation of previous commitments to popular culture."[26] Thus, the fan "moment" for these Black women was not a moment at all. Rather, it was the culmination of years of being exposed to *The Golden Girls* as children and the affective bond of the close social ties with intergenerational family members.

Racquel says she watched the series in syndication with her father. "My dad and I actually talk a lot about the episodes because we used to watch a lot together, not my mom and I, as much. When it started airing on Lifetime, it was right around the time that I think my dad retired, and so, especially during summers, we would just be at home together watching Lifetime." These strong social ties that Katherine, Rachel, and Racquel highlight are composed of a "combination of the amount of time, the emotional intensity, the intimacy, . . . and the reciprocal services which characterize the tie."[27] For Black women, *The Golden Girls* and its attendant fandom are tied to familial relationships and histories.

Concomitantly, the series was aspirational for some Black fans, who, like Quiniva, found a sense of queer kinship in the series. "When I first started watching [*The Golden Girls*] as a child, I was enamored with these sassy old ladies who are really just engaging in their life with nonsense on a regular basis. And I wasn't engaged with my sexuality at the time or anything like that, but I felt very comforted by this idea that a group of old ladies just lived in a house together and chaos ensued on a regular basis. I was like, 'That's the life I want.'" Quiniva reads her engagement with the series as being connected to queer kinship formations. While Dorothy, Rose, Blanche, and Sophia were indeed LGBTQ friendly, they were heterosexual women. Yet, Quiniva, a lesbian woman, saw their relationship as a model for how she imagined her future queer kinship networks.

Ashleé, a bisexual Black woman, was similarly drawn to the Girls because of their queer family formation. "I think it's that whole idea of a chosen family. Now granted, I didn't know that I was bisexual when I was twenty. And granted, society didn't reject them or anything like that, but the fact that they chose to be more than roommates. They chose to be friends and family, and they said that over and over again. . . . I think the idea of family, for most Black people, is really important. I think especially when you identify as Black and queer in some way that the idea of chosen families is really important as well." Similarly, Gabrielle likens the Girls to a queer family in her suggestion that "there is something kind of outsider about even just the fact of the setup of the show. There's something that's kind of marginal about these women who are not just their age but also the fact that they're living without men in a really meaningful kind of way." Kath Weston forwards that the 1980s saw a discursive "emphasis on the kinship character of the ties gay people had forged to close friends and lovers" and sought to decouple these kindship formations "from heterosexual relations."[28] From Coco, the gay cook in the series's pilot episode, and Dorothy's high school friend Jean having a crush on Rose ("Isn't it Romantic?," S02E05) to Blanche's brother Clayton coming out as gay ("Scared Straight," S04E09) and getting married ("Sister of the Bride," S06E14), the series never shied away from LGBTQ topics or the idea that the women of 6151 Richmond Street formed a queer family.

But *The Golden Girls* was not just aspirational for proto-queers like Quiniva and Ashleé. Some Black women discussed being able to see a life stage beyond what is typically offered in media. Katherine says, "The thing I liked about it the most was they were these four women who were older, and I had never really seen that. They represented the women that I could become. So, there was always women more in their late twenties, thirties, forties. And there was never anything after that really. So, I was always kind of like, 'Oh, do women just die afterwards?'" Similarly, Liz says she finds the series "aspirational in some sense": "And so, I think it endures because it's still like what you *can* be." Ultimately, many of the Black women I interviewed find *The Golden Girls* aspirational in its offering of alternative kinship models. And part of these aspirational qualities are what hails Black women as fans. Liz says, "For me, it was familiar dynamics of some of the older women in my family and the way they interact or talked or like, they were living their

Ashleé's "Sophia" purse that is part of her collection of fan merchandise. (Photo by Ashleé Clark)

lives and they still had to work. Like, I was thinking about Dorothy, she was still a teacher and just, like, not necessarily being able to fully retire. . . . So, to me, their characters were closer [to a Black experience] in some sense than your typical, white middle-class [sitcom]." Unlike queer alternative kinship networks that often form because of rejection or strife within biological family formations, the Girls live together for financial reasons, and for Liz, it reminded her of the women in her own family.

Black Fandom, Resonance, and Implicit Blackness

In the broadcast era, when there were only three networks consistently airing new television content, it is no surprise that Black folks watched programs that did not reflect their identities. But making the shift from viewer to fan is an entirely different matter altogether. For *The Golden Girls*, Black women not only watched the program when it was on in its original broadcast run but continue to watch it and master the narrative ins and outs of the series in syndication and via streaming.

Although Black bodies are infrequently mediated on *The Golden Girls*, Black female fans become textual poachers who reread the series "in a fashion that serves [their] different interests."[29] In other words, in the absence of racial representation, Black women use thematic representation to read *The Golden Girls* Blackly; that is, they look for themes like alternative kinship to make the series resonate. In this sense, Black women are not reading *The Golden Girls* oppositionally to find the pleasures in the text, as Black scholars like bell hooks, Jacqueline Bobo, and Kristen Warner have underscored in their work on Black women and Black reception practices.[30] Part of the labor hooks, Bobo, and Warner observe occurs when Black women are watching media with Black women. When Black women are watching four old white women, the themes they encounter engender Black resonance.

Ultimately, Black women fans felt *Golden Girls*' Blackness in its flow, the workers in its writers' room, and its mediation of an alternative family formation. Black women *Golden Girls* fans find comfort in the series because, with the relative absence of Blackness, they do not have to be concerned with representational politics. And because they are not doing the work of "policing" Black representation, these Black fans of *The Golden Girls* find the series joyous. And Black joy, in an era when saying "Black Lives Matter" is construed as controversial in some circles, is worth celebrating and studying.

Notes

1. Eileen R. Meehan and Jackie Byars, "Telefeminism: How Lifetime Got Its Groove, 1984–1997," *Television & New Media* 1, no. 1 (2000): 34.

2. Ellise Shafer, "'Golden Girls' Episode with Blackface Scene Removed from Hulu," *Variety*, June 27, 2020. https://variety.com/2020/tv/news/golden-girls-blackface-hulu-removed-1234692451/.

3. Finally Aaron, "Golden Girls Gospel Remix (Full Song)," YouTube, February 11, 2016, www.youtube.com/watch?v=mWD_VPiMlso&feature=emb_logo&ab_channel=FinallyAaron.

4. Sarah Florini, "Enclaving and Cultural Resonance in Black *Game of Thrones* Fandom," *Transformative Works and Cultures* 29, no. 1 (2019): 2.1.

5. Kristen Warner, "The Pleasure Principle of *Magic Mike XXL*: Sonic Visibility Toward Female Audiences," *Communication Culture & Critique* 12, no. 2 (2019): 243.

6. Emily Lordi, *Black Resonance: Iconic Women Singers and African American Literature* (Rutgers University Press, 2013), 6.

7. Raymond Williams, *Marxism and Literature* (Oxford University Press, 1977), 132.

8. Racquel Gates, "Baby Mine: *Dumbo* and Black Resonance," *Film Quarterly* 76, no. 3 (2023): 38.

9. Stuart Hall, "Encoding/Decoding," in *Culture, Media, Language: Working Papers in Cultural Studies, 1972–79* (Routledge, 1991).

10. Raymond Williams, *Television: Technology and Cultural Form* (Routledge, 2008).

11. Nick Browne, "The Political Economy of the Television (Super) Text," *Quarterly Review of Film and Video* 9, no. 3 (1984): 178.

12. Taylor Cole Miller, "*Roseanne:* Programming Flow," in *How to Watch Television*, 2nd ed. (New York University Press, 2020), 288.

13. Brett Mills, *Television Sitcom* (British Film Institute, 2005), 5.

14. Herman Gray, *Watching Race: Television and the Struggle for Blackness* (University of Minnesota Press, 2004), 58–59.

15. Alfred L. Martin Jr., "Toward a Theory of Surplus Blackness: Reception, Media Industries, and Blackness," *International Journal of Communication* 19 (2025): 1357–75.

16. Kristal Brent Zook, *Color by Fox: The Fox Network and the Revolution in Black Television* (Oxford University Press, 1999).

17. "'Different World' to Be a Hit with Blacks; Study," *Jet*, October 26, 1987, 61.

18. "Philip Michael Thomas and Olivia Brown: How Blacks Are Influencing TV Network Shows," *Jet*, May 25, 1987, 55.

19. John T. Caldwell, *Production Culture: Industrial Reflexivity and Critical Practice in Film and Television* (Duke University Press, 2008).

20. Alfred L. Martin Jr., "Scripting Black Gayness: Television Authorship in Black-Cast Sitcoms," *Television & New Media* 16, no. 7 (2015): 661.

21. Mary C. Beltran, "The New Hollywood Racelessness: Only the Fast, Furious, (and Multicultural) Will Survive," *Cinema Journal* 44, no. 2 (2005): 60.

22. Alexander Doty, *Making Things Perfectly Queer: Interpreting Mass Culture* (University of Minnesota Press, 1993); Eleanor Patterson, "The Golden Girls Live: Residual Television Texts, Participatory Culture, and Queering TV Heritage Through Drag," *Feminist Media Studies* 16, no. 5 (2016): 838–51; Andrea L. Press, *Women Watching Television: Gender, Class, and Generation in the American Television Experience* (University of Pennsylvania Press, 1991); Mimi White, "Ideological Analysis and Television," in *Channels of Discourse* (University of North Carolina Press, 1987).

23. Florini, "Enclaving and Cultural Resonance," 4.1.

24. Elijah Wald, *The Dozens: A History of Rap's Mama* (Oxford University Press, 2012), xi.

25. Cornell Sandvoss, *Fans: The Mirror of Consumption* (Polity, 2005), 111; Ashton Toone, Amanda Nell Edgar, and Kelly Ford, "'She Made Angry Black Woman Something That People Would Want to Be': *Lemonade* and Black Women as Audiences and Subjects," *Participations* 14, no. 2 (2017): 209.

26. Matt Hills, "Returning to 'Becoming-a-Fan' Stories: Theorising Transformational Objects and the Emergence/Extension of Fandom," in *The Ashgate Research Companion to Fan Cultures* (Ashgate, 2016), 10.

27. Mark S. Granovetter, "The Strength of Weak Ties," *American Journal of Sociology* 78, no 6 (1974): 1361.

28. Kath Weston, *Families We Choose: Lesbians, Gays, Kinship* (Columbia University Press, 1997), 22.

29. Henry Jenkins, *Textual Poachers: Television Fans and Participatory Culture*, 2nd ed. (Routledge, 2012), 23.

30. Jacqueline Bobo, *Black Women as Cultural Readers* (Columbia University Press, 1995); bell hooks, *Black Looks: Race and Representation* (South End, 1992); Kristen J. Warner, "ABC's *Scandal* and Black Women's Fandom," in *Cupcakes, Pinterest, and Ladyporn: Feminized Popular Culture in the Early Twenty-First Century* (University of Illinois Press, 2015).

INTERVIEW

On Bea and Betty

Marsha Posner Williams, Co-Producer

When people ask me, "Is it true that Bea Arthur hated Betty White?" my stock answer is always, "Those two couldn't warm up to each other if they were cremated together." But the beauty of it was that when that red light went on and the camera was there, nobody was more professional than those women. Nobody.

Bea was a theatrical person. We all know that, and she was also a former Marine who drove trucks, right? She was a broad and never made any bones about it. I respected her for that, because she was—who you meet is exactly who she was. What she didn't like about Betty—there were a couple things. She didn't like that when they would do a scene in front of the audience and then go to move to the next scene, Betty would break character and talk to the audience. And Bea just hated that. And she also felt like Betty wasn't always her true self, meaning—and I was witness to this once—we introduced a potential new director, and Betty was the sweetest, most wonderful as she is, wonderful person. I loved her. And they talked to the director, and she was wonderful. And the second he turned around, she [pantomimes gagging]. Whereas with Bea, you know she hates to wear makeup. She hates to wear shoes, and you know she hates to wash her hair. And what she loves is to drink. But that's who she is, and she was very honest. And when I say honest, oh boy, I mean it.

Isabel Omero, Production Associate/Script Supervisor, Writer

Bea didn't like Betty. Big whoop. If people think it was some big feud, it was pretty weak tea. But what I also saw was that Bea and Betty were also connected by a lot. Being there for each other when they both lost their mothers at the same time, supporting each other's charitable efforts, especially for animals, or something small: Bea wouldn't walk over to actors' notes

Staged photo shoot for *This Is Your Life* featuring Betty White. (Photo © Wayne Williams 1984–87. All rights reserved.)

without Betty alongside her. But the most amazing thing to me was that they were both huge stars and total pros onstage at the same time.

Wayne Williams, Photographer

[Besides the first time], I only had resistance photographing Bea one other time, and that was a shoot for Betty White. That was a surprise for Betty. She didn't know that *This Is Your Life* was going to do an episode on her, and the ruse was going to be a photo shoot. But it was not going to be at the end of the taping. It was going to be on a separate day, and Bea, who was already up to here with Betty, to be asked to come in on a Saturday or whatever it was to do that—that was not going to be pretty. But I pulled the same stunt I usually did and said, "I'll make it go really fast for you. Please, let's just do this, and then you can go home. You know how I work; we'll get it done."

"Oh, all right, darling."

She came in, she was a trooper. The shot worked. We surprised Betty. And you can actually see this all on YouTube somewhere. It's a very quick shot, a video clip of me walking back from the camera to start shooting the ladies. And then, Ralph Edwards walks into the shot with a bouquet of flowers. And that's the clip.

The ladies were always really very professional with everything that I did, and that was really valuable, because it made my job easier for me, and I hope it made their experience easier for them. There were no divas.

Marc Sotkin, Executive Producer
Everyone's wrong. Bea hated Estelle [laughs]. No, of course she didn't. Everybody asks about Bea and Betty. Was Betty Bea's favorite person? No. Do I get it? Yeah. If you've got diabetes, don't hang around Betty White. I love Betty White. She's great, but you know that that sweetness can sometimes get to you. The reason I got hired is because I'm cynical in a very funny way. So, I can see where it would grate on Bea. But I loved Betty. Professionally, there was no issue. They were so professional, all of them, and they could all hit home runs, and they were incredibly cooperative.

Showrunner Marc Sotkin interviewed by Danielle Soto of the *Dr. Cheesecake* podcast. (Photo by Taylor Cole Miller)

So, Nina Feinberg comes to me and tells me Kent Zbornak has told her that somehow, during the four o'clock dress rehearsals, someone is sneaking into Betty's dressing room, taking a dump in the toilet, and not flushing. And what are we going to do? When she tells me, there are a few writers in the room, and Jim [James] Vallely, who very possibly is the funniest person on the planet and does an amazing Bea Arthur, immediately goes into Bea taking a dump. And he goes, [grunts] "Ohhhh, darling!" First, he goes, "You know, I just saw Bea at the craft services table, and she's loading up on bran muffins!" And then he goes into this [he strains], "Betty, how's this one?" And I'm crying. I'm literally crying. It's the funniest thing that I heard in my years there. Eventually, we tried to really find out, but it was not happening. Maybe it was just Kent busting Nina's chops. How I wish it was true!

CHAPTER 11

Smut upon a Time in Miami

The Golden Girls' Camp Comedy

KEN FEIL

In the pilot episode of Patrick Ian Polk's comedy-drama Logo TV series *Noah's Arc,* a passing reference to *The Golden Girls* signaled the sitcom's enduring appeal to a diverse spectatorship more than a decade after leaving the network lineup. Among the inciting incidents of *Noah's Arc,* a soapy comedic serial about four Black gay men living in Los Angeles, the eponymous Noah (Darryl Stephens) and best friends Ricky (Christian Vincent) and Alex (Rodney Chester) help their bosom buddy Chance (Doug Spearman) move into his new abode with his boyfriend, Eddie (Jonathan Julian). Gathering in the kitchen for a break, Noah opens the refrigerator and declares, "Cheesecake!" Eddie explains, "I know how much y'all like those *Golden Girls* reruns, and they're always eating cheesecake, so . . ." Polk's reference to the popular reruns of *The Golden Girls,* airing on the Lifetime channel since 1997 (and eventually arriving at Logo TV), accomplishes multiple functions. With the show being a TV favorite of both Black and white gay men, the initial target audiences of the fledgling Logo cable channel, invoking *The Golden Girls* furthermore contributed to comedic style and character development by juxtaposing Noah's youthful quartet with the mature Miami housemates Dorothy Zbornak (Bea Arthur), Blanche Deveraux (Rue McClanahan), Rose Nyland (Betty White), and Dorothy's octogenarian mother, Sophia Petrillo (Estelle Getty).[1]

Polk's homage additionally positions *The Golden Girls* in a variety of forms, tropes, and contexts of camp: gay and queer camp, mass camp, elder kitsch, and the aging diva. Camp evolved in the United States as a taste code and creative aesthetic among urban, middle-class, white gay men amid the rise of mass culture and the solidification of bourgeois taste cultures (high, middle, low). A subcultural sensibility, camp functioned to subvert norms of gender and sexual orientation by way of ironizing the assumptions of bourgeois taste.[2] Camp pertains to a love for vulgar, over-the-top theatricality in people and cultural artworks that redeems cultural "failures" in the same gesture as validating social Otherness and has operated in the work of gay creatives like the playwright Noël Coward, as well as informed subcultural affection for genres like melodrama and musicals, in addition to divas like Judy Garland and Diana Ross. Camp has provided an ambiguous means of identifying gayness, a style that could alternately serve the closet and furnish a megaphone for coming out.[3]

Camp has also served as a means of charming straight culture and disarming its phobias toward queer people, a point Susan Sontag unspooled in her 1964 "Notes on 'Camp.'"[4] This appeared to be coming to fruition beginning in the mid-1960s, when camp surged in popularity and transformed into a mainstream sensibility of "failed seriousness" and excessive theatricality.[5] What Barbara Klinger terms "mass camp" emerged in a range of media parodies of Hollywood genres, mockery of conventional attitudes about sexuality and gender, and the expression of fondness for archaic culture that failed to function anymore.[6] Klinger criticizes mass camp, however, as "a trendy style" that continuously buries "sexual marginality" in a gambit to achieve "social hipness and superiority, without the 'stigma' of subcultural affiliation."[7] Mass camp "de-gays" the sensibility, according to this argument, at the same as exploiting the "mainstream chicness" generated by camp's patina of "underground," "minority" taste.[8]

Mass camp in the 1980s consisted of its own unique norms that *The Golden Girls* contributed to, partly summed up by Timothy Shary and Nancy McVittie as "elder kitsch," camp comedy that revolves around the incongruity of aged characters romping like young ones.[9] Elder kitsch amplified, in turn, a longtime trope of gay male camp, what Caryl Flinn pinpoints as the "'aging diva' phenomenon," which ridicules the aging female body as failed, outmoded, and excessive.[10] These derogatory tendencies combine into the complex of elder diva kitsch, which in the 1980s ostensibly flourished on *The Golden Girls* through the characters' sexualized lifestyles and rounds of snappy repartee, in addition to the prime-time soap opera *Dynasty* and its "bitchy," glamorous, and sexy senior drama queens Alexis Carrington Colby (Joan Collins) and Dominique Deveraux (Diahann Carrol).

Dismissing *The Golden Girls* as mass camp nevertheless misses what

Polk's homage on *Noah's Arc* gleefully realized: the power of *camp community* forged among the aging divas. The Golden divas' triumphant communal camp resonates as much in the history of representing elderly characters and aging in the media as in the history of queer culture and mass camp. In contrast to elder diva kitsch, communal diva camp revolves around a group of senior women whose power solidifies as they play off of and for each other as well as the loving audience (laugh track notwithstanding). The particular vehicle for this senior coterie to quip about sexuality, bodies, and functions, along with taking jabs at each other and themselves, is the "comedy of bad manners," a narrative mode associated with gay camp culture.[11] Actors Arthur, McClanahan, White, and Getty, meanwhile, visibly relish their characters' outsized personalities and outrageous dialogue in stylized performances that accentuate the show's camp dynamics. *The Golden Girls* consistently incorporates queer characters and themes, furthermore, as well as cites camp culture associated with gay creatives, audiences, and subjects, including Tennessee Williams's *A Streetcar Named Desire* (with a southern belle heroine named Blanche); *The Wizard of Oz* and its protagonist, Dorothy; and Broadway musicals.

The Girls' agile dance around comedic tastelessness additionally amplifies a sense of camp community originating in the late 1980s that opposed the era's backlash against feminism and gay liberation. A "new" camp sensibility emerged through AIDS and queer activism as well as "pro-sex" feminism, whose comedy about gender, sexuality, and taste generated celebrations of female sexual agency, homosexual desire, and sexual fluidity. Considering *The Golden Girls* as new camp, moreover, reveals the logic behind the sitcom's strategy for representing queer characters and themes, in which queer irony about stereotypes tempers the stuffy, liberal respectfulness usually varnishing "special" episodes.[12] While none of these strategies and features obviates the ideological work of mass camp and elder diva kitsch, to say the least of gay camp's normative limits, they underscore the "politicized edge" of *The Golden Girls* as well as its liberatory pleasures in the context of 1980s mass camp.[13]

Golden Rules and Ideological Contradictions: From Elder Diva Kitsch to Communal Camp

Shary and McVittie's inclusion of *The Golden Girls* in their dissection of mass camp elder kitsch testifies as much to the types and tropes of comedy employed by the sitcom as its ideologically conflicted renditions of feisty, spirited elderly women. Elder kitsch, the humorous counterpart to the horrific "psycho biddy" type introduced in *Whatever Happened to Baby Jane?* (dir. Robert Aldrich, 1962), revolves around "the visual incongruity of the aging face and body playing against youthful activities and dialogue in order to have full comedic effect."[14] Elder kitsch implicates the "'aging diva' phenomenon," Flinn's label for a misogynistic and ageist branch of camp comedy in which "the camp icon can be ridiculed or put down for its presumed 'differences' from its spectator/critic/consumer."[15] The aging diva trope solicits an objectifying gaze from the audience, which "doesn't just mock what is outmoded, but what—and who—is old."[16] Consistent with the incongruity driving elder kitsch, the aging diva's sexual vivacity signifies in ironic, vulgar contrast to her "decaying," "disunified," "dying" body and "obsolescence" as a desirable woman, a "funny body" that confirms the spectator's sense of superiority and the primacy of the youthful, unified, and concretely gendered body.[17]

Considering 1980s mass camp such as *The Golden Girls* and *Dynasty*, elder diva kitsch consequently threatens to promote a Reagan/Bush-era, neoliberal fantasy of "successful" aging immune from systemic ageism.[18] Sitcom norms contribute further to this ideological dynamic, by presenting the spectacle of durable, aged divas whose incongruity induces escapist laughter, in narratives that reliably return to order at the conclusion. When *Golden Girls* plotlines resist escapism, by underscoring the characters' economic precarity or critiquing their assumptions about sexuality, gender, race, and class privilege, sitcom norms arguably combine with elder diva kitsch to conceal contradiction and sustain ideological complacency.[19]

Critiques of elder diva kitsch (and mass camp, more generally) negate any subversive dimensions of mainstream camp or "diva-tude."[20] This line of reasoning disregards, accordingly, the varieties of camp narratives, particularly the communal diva narrative and comedy of bad manners. Marlon B. Ross centralizes communality and impropriety when defining camp "as a mode of in-the-know verbal repartee," "verbal battles" that "engage their participants in acts of community-formation and identity-sustenance by resourcefully using the scraps most at their disposal: the things others say hatefully about them."[21] By transforming "hateful" language into "community-formation and identity-sustenance," this conception of communal camp involves what Tison Pugh refers to as "sadomasochistic camp," in which the play of power remains theatricalized and generates comedic pleasure, even in the face of "unlaughable" realities.[22] The camp of *The Golden Girls* similarly correlates insult humor and vulgar comedy with reshaping oppression and forging community, qualities that solicit audience identification and demarcate this quartet from conventional elder kitsch and highlight their resistance to ageism and misogyny.[23]

The *Golden* divas bond through mutual badinage, a reciprocal, deliberate camp performance that armors them against objectifying stereotypes and moral opprobrium. Their communal camp spotlights the pleasures shared between elderly women—characters and actors—delighting in each other's performances, in addition to the joyful exchange between camp performers and audiences. The pioneering queer critic Alexander Doty underscores the communal core of *The Golden Girls'* comedy and other women-led sitcoms of the 1980s, absent the word "camp," shows that position audiences "to take lesbian or queer pleasures in the development of women's relationships within situation comedy narratives."[24] The grouping of these gaudy goddesses remains intrinsic to their queerly flamboyant resistance toward social restrictions of age, gender, sexuality, and class.

Tarnished Is the New Gold: Indecorous Dames and Show Queens

As Dorothy, Blanche, Rose, and Sophia trade barbs and spout self-directed bons mots about their aging, sexual bodies, *The Golden Girls* employs the "comedy of bad manners" (also referred to as "bad manners comedy"), a narrative mode widespread in traditional gay literary culture of the twentieth century. The playwright Noël Coward's signature comedies *Hay Fever* (1925), *Private Lives* (1929), and *Design for Living* (1932) exemplify this mode. Each play venerates a group of aristocratic oddballs whose witty bickering and voracious appetite for pleasure both alienate the bourgeois babbitts and biddies in their midst and render the leading characters ironically triumphant.[25] The camp comedy of bad manners stages narrative contests in which the victorious characters transgress etiquette and propriety as well as transpose the values of good and bad taste, their vulgarity proving to be the height of style, the defining delight, and the primary audience appeal.[26] When women protagonists and their perspectives frame the comedy of bad manners, as I recently explored in the novels of Jacqueline Susann (best known for the 1966 publishing blockbuster *Valley of the Dolls*), the transposition of normative taste values typical of bad manners comedy now targets constructs of gender roles. In other words, discombobulating the values of good and bad taste in women-driven bad manners comedies coincides with upsetting gender constructs, and the comedic pleasure inspired by the characters' exchanges ultimately supersedes (if not replaces) heterosexual romance.[27]

Age and social class also make a difference in women-driven bad manners comedy, something that *The Golden Girls* realizes. Senior status enables the characters to transgress propriety and crack vulgar badinage that would be deemed salacious or unseemly if delivered by younger women.[28] Alexis and Dominique on *Dynasty* take similar advantage, as their "theatricality," "bitchiness," and "irony" call attention to the show as a "show" in addition to asserting the characters' transgressive agency.[29] *Dynasty*'s wealthy, glamorous machers nevertheless have money to protect them, similar to Coward's silver-spoon, ill-mannered divas and divos. The four Golden Girls, by contrast, more closely compare to the women in Susann's novels, earthy, street-smart wisecrackers who confront challenges and achieve agency by appropriating "masculine," "lowbrow" vulgarity and, very importantly, are funny doing it.[30]

Ethnicity and geography furthermore distinguish the particular form of bad manners that each of the Golden Girls employs, most uniquely in the characters Blanche and Rose. The patrician southern belle Blanche cites Tennessee Williams's Blanche DuBois, another promiscuous, occasionally arrogant "daughter of the South" who resists aging through sexuality and theatricality. Bad manners comedy revises Blanche DuBois, her promiscuity both a symptom of distress and a source of tragic ruination, into the sultry wit Blanche Deveraux, whose sexual aggressiveness is a matter of choice, something that delights and energizes her as well as transforms her relationship to gay men. The tragic suicide of Blanche DuBois's gay husband drives the character to seek random sexual hookups, resulting in her affair with a seventeen-year-old and expulsion from her hometown for being "morally unfit." Blanche Deveraux conversely has a happy gay brother, seeks sex with mature men, and suffers no ostracism, even if she recalls during a fourth-season episode her repeated arrests for "obscene behavior" in Chattanooga. Following numerous references to being busted, Dorothy interjects, "Are you allowed to go back to Chattanooga?" "Are you kiddin'," Blanche begins. "The sheriff still writes" ("The Days and Nights of Sophia Petrillo," S04E02).

The Swedish-Minnesotan farmgirl Rose routinely enlists her persona of rural, folk innocence to covertly deliver digs at her roommates and discuss sex. When Rose apologizes to a stray dog she rescued, for example, after her roommates demand the puppy find a new home, she voices the canine's imagined reply: "Don't explain, Rose. I used to live with a couple of bitches myself" ("Joust Between Friends," S02E09). Anticipating the arrival of Blanche's brother in another episode, Rose offers to "put out the welcome mat," and when Blanche explains, "We don't have a welcome mat," Rose asks, "What about the one Dorothy says is at the foot of your bed?" ("Scared Straight," S04E09).

The comedy of bad manners provides an enduring mode for enacting communal camp repartee that theatricalizes conflict through vulgarity, and the Broadway musical *Mame* provides an initial model of bad manners comedy and a camp reference point. Jerry Herman's musical featured Bea Arthur in the original 1966 Broadway cast as the title character's best friend, Vera Charles, a Tony Award–winning performance, replicated for the 1974 film, that crystallized Arthur's signature camp acting style—acidic delivery and withering glances—continually evoked in Arthur's performance as Dorothy. Arthur exhibited a similarly mannered style in the popular sitcom *Maude*, but the female community of the Golden Girls, their stagey, vaudeville style of comedy, and the digs they trade in addition to the affection they share continually recall Vera and Mame's exchanges. "If life should reject you, / There's me to protect you," belt Vera and Mame, in between jabs at each other about advanced age, bad hair, copious copulation, and uncouth conduct. The stereotypically gay appeal of musicals, moreover, remains within *The Golden Girls'* frames of reference, signaled when Sophia remarks of Blanche's brother Clayton, "The man's as gay as a picnic basket! . . . He's the only man I ever knew who knows all the words to 'Send in the Clowns'" ("Scared Straight," S04E09).

Akin to musicals, *The Golden Girls* furthermore evokes vaudeville in its style of bad manners comedy, replete with stagey back-and-forth one-liners, the figures of joker and butt, and actors visibly performing for the audience, stopping just short of breaking the fourth wall.[31] The episode "Melodrama" brims with all these features when the polyamorous Blanche professes devotion to her boyfriend Mel, vows met with skepticism from Sophia and Dorothy. "Mel and I were meant to be together," Blanche announces, to which Sophia ripostes, "I wish I could say the same for your thighs." Evoking a stand-up comedian who acknowledges the audience, Sophia punches the table and smiles broadly with a brief direct address to the camera: "God, I'm hot tonight!" Blanche's disgruntled reply, "I'm not going to stand for this," provides a cue for another insult. "Take it, Dorothy," Sophia directs her daughter, who cracks, "But I bet you'll lie down for it." In the episode "Witness," a vaudevillian exchange again occasions the rupturing of the fourth wall, now with reference to Arthur's former career in Broadway musicals. After Blanche confesses that she has Yankee, Jewish ancestry, her concern that this revelation could prevent the Daughters of the Old South from accepting her membership inspires Dorothy's remark, "And if they don't let you in, instead of saying, 'fiddlee-dee-dee,' you can always switch to [intoning "If I Were a Rich Man"] 'deedle diddle deedle dum'" ("Witness," S06E21). In one fell swoop, Dorothy digs at Blanche's prejudice and refers to one of Arthur's early Broadway successes, *Fiddler on the Roof.* Vaudeville-style theatricality again pushes against the suspension of disbelief when Arthur performs "Hard Hearted Hannah," not only reminding viewers once more of her career in musicals but also repeating a song that she had previously performed on *Maude* ("Journey to the Center of Attention," S07E19).

Smut upon a Time in Miami

Central to *The Golden Girls'* bad manners comedy and camp reflexivity, witty banter about senior sexuality and elderly bodies repeatedly surfaces, what Frances Gray encapsulates as "female smut."[32] Female smut and bad manners comedy routinely converge, such as in Dorothy's advice to Blanche about what to do with her old bed: "Put it in the Smithsonian, Blanche. It's got more miles on it than the Spirit of St. Louis!" ("Mister Terrific," S03E24). As Nicole Kypker avers, "there is no absurdity or comic incongruity in these women, aged fifty-plus, bluntly discussing their sex lives; the audience laugh at what they say, not at their saying it, and *The Golden Girls'* recurrent bawdy discussions are coded as commonplace, as . . . a given."[33] Far from the ageist misogyny of elder kitsch, comedic incongruity here revolves around resisting normative constructs rather than failing to meet them.

The sixth-season finale, "Henny Penny—Straight, No Chaser," demonstrates the narrative primacy of female smut. Blanche's lustful declarations form a running gag whose perverse impropriety develops like a plotline. Now a smut-line, two comic subjects recurrently are aired and eventually converge, the bacchanalian Miami Spring Break and Blanche's erotic titillation from fairy tales. After Blanche opens the episode with enthusiastic anticipation of her Spring Break plans, such as preparing wardrobe choices for the wet T-shirt contest, Dorothy informs of her school's upcoming production of *Henny Penny*. "That was never one of my favorites," Blanche admits. "I like a fairy tale with a nice prince in it . . . ," Blanche continues, her temperature rising with every phrase: ". . . a handsome prince with a big old codpiece and deep, dark eyes, powerful thighs and muscles rippling beneath his tunic." Dorothy attempts to interrupt such steamy reverie, bantering, "Blanche, you could get aroused by Humpty Dumpy," a goofily nonsexual citation. "Are you kiddin'," Blanche purrs, imbuing Humpty Dumpty with libidinousness: "All the king's horses and all the king's men? Handsome men with deep, dark eyes and powerful thighs and muscles and big old cod pieces?" At midepisode, Blanche reflects on the "profound influence" of *Snow White and the Seven Dwarves*: "Seven lonely men . . . living in the woods, needing a woman, all of them with Napoleon complexes, something to prove." After the Girls perform in *Henny Penny*, filling in for the cast, fallen with measles, Blanche energetically departs for the Rusty Anchor bar in her Goosey Loosey costume, a form-fitting feathered number redolent of a Vegas showgirl. "Spring Break comes but once a year," Blanche declares at the door, and the episode closes.

Queer Questions of Communal "New" Camp

The delights of *The Golden Girls* correspond with the fostering of camp community and identification with dames whose self-aware humor flourishes in bad manners comedy, exchanging barbs and trumpeting female smut. The sitcom's comedic formula comes into particular relief in the historical context of the 1980s AIDS crisis and backlash toward feminism, when active female and queer sexuality as well as "decaying," "dying," sexualized bodies turned into menacing threats. Michael Musto traced the "new camp" sensibility for *Out* magazine in 1993, framed by the context of AIDS and queer activism, and although Musto points to the sitcom *Designing Women* for a mainstream example, the columnist's reasoning here as well as with other more underground exemplars underscores the attractions of *The Golden Girls*: a community of witty, mature, sexual women, trading insults in the shadow of physical deterioration and mortality. Musto rejoices in the "posse" on *Designing Women* and their personification of the "bitchy edge of the new camp," "a new-style of bonding that bolsters both confidence and wit" and that surfaces in more radical examples, including AIDS-era zines celebrating gallows humor and the liveliness of decaying bodies, such as *Diseased Pariah News* and *Dead Jackie Susann Quarterly*.[34] The involvement of women and gender nonconformists in camp culture, combined with the primacy of sexualized humor permeating new camp, furthermore reflects the strategies of "pro-sex" feminism in the face of the New Right's virulently repressive attitudes.[35] Sophia, whose humor spans the political spectrum, appears a fellow traveler of the new camp when attending Blanche's Midnight Madness party, whose invitees comprise many men: "I haven't been hit on like this since I stopped hanging out at the midnight show of *Harold and Maude*. . . . . One guy told me he thought wrinkles were sexy. I took him out to the garage, where he could see me under the fluorescents" ("Journey to the Center of Attention," S07E19). Likening herself to the octogenarian title character of the 1971 cult film *Harold and Maude*, Sophia affirms her own nonconformity, sexuality, and joie de vivre and, perhaps, poses an ironic tribute to the film's screenwriter, Colin Higgins, who had succumbed to AIDS a few years earlier.

When homosexuality enters into the plotline of *Golden Girls* episodes, however, the new camp community forged by batting "bitchy" barbs can appear retrogressive. Similar to the dynamics of elder kitsch, the comedy of incongruity surrounds references to homosexuality, which consistently arise from situational gags about how queer the Girls appear. In the seventh-season episode "Goodbye, Mr. Gordon," for one illustration, a subplot involves Dorothy and Blanche appearing on a local television morning show, *Wake Up! Miami*, under the impression that the theme is "women who live together" (S07E15). On the day of the live broadcast, Dorothy and Blanche join another female couple on the talk show set, and the host introduces the topic: "Women who live together. Does society make it tougher? We'll find out when we talk to *four lesbians*." Sophia, sitting in the studio audience, punctuates the Girls' apparent queerness during the question-and-answer session: "This is directed at Dorothy's lover. Do people treat you different as a lesbian?" Blanche answers, "Uh, well, most people don't know," to which Sophia replies, "Really? I would have guessed right off." The humor of the talk show sequence exemplifies numerous camp dimensions of *The Golden Girls* discussed earlier, but it also invokes debates about what Doty calls the show's "homophobic cultural work," or as Kate Browne opines, comedy that can "reinforce their relationships as homosocial instead of homosexual."[36] These critiques are justified by the heterosexual orientation of the characters as well as the punch lines and laughter generated by plotlines in which they are perceived as queer women.

The manner in which queer gags play out on *The Golden Girls*, however, more often accentuates the insecurity of heterosexual romance, in addition to calling attention to stereotypes about age, gender, and sexuality: their theatricality and, in all their similarities, how humorously unreliable they are as classifications. As the associate producer of *Wake Up! Miami*, Rose admits to the inciting act of misperception.[37] "They just said they wanted two women who loved each other and slept together," she explains, Dorothy and Blanche having recently shared a bed when Blanche's room was repainted. Lesbian stereotypes appear more absurd after a man queries the guests, "Are there male/female roles in the relationship?" Blanche musters her southern belle charm to reply, "Well, I am the little homemaker, if that's what you mean." Dorothy, clearly restraining her frustration for the sake of Rose's job, grumbles, "And I take out the garbage." In a subsequent scene, a man arrives at the house to woo Blanche into heterosexuality, leading to Blanche crassly informing Dorothy, "It's over between us," followed by Dorothy telling the gentleman caller, "You just take care of her," along with giving him a "manly" punch on the arm. These events point to Browne's contention that Dorothy queers the show by upsetting the stereotypical correlation between the signs of gender performance and sexual orientation.[38]

If Dorothy occasions bad manners comedy that disrupts sexual and gender stereotypes, the mistaken identity scenario also implicates the improprieties of Rose and Blanche as well as questions the primacy of heterosexual romance, playing out within the main plotline about Dorothy's doomed courtship with her high school crush, Malcom Gordon. The talk show inspires insult humor about Blanche's (hetero)sex life from Rose, the source of the misunderstanding to begin with, delivered through her persona of innocent insolence. During a commercial break, Blanche complains, "Every man I know is watching this show . . . about lesbian lovers of Miami." A gleeful response from Rose follows: "Every man you know is watching? Hey, we could beat *The Price Is Right*!" Uniquely, this round of heterosexual "slut" banter joins with jesting about homosexuality, a gesture that equates diverse forms of "deviant" sexuality and derives humor, not because they are wrong but for their liberating fun of disturbing norms. This comes into focus in the final two scenes. First, Dorothy rejects Malcom for plagiarizing a book review she wrote. In the coda, Pat, one of the other women guests from the talk show, arrives at the door to speak to Dorothy: "I heard about you and Blanche." "I'm sorry," Dorothy utters solemnly, "too soon, too soon."

The contradictions of the Golden Girls germinate in their camp—the community of divas, bad manners comedy, insults and smut, queer references and plotlines—and in closing, their *transgressive* escapism requires consideration. A comment from the theatrical historian John Lahr about the concluding moments of Coward's *Design for Living* comes to mind, when the play's camp community, a ménage à trois consisting of one woman and two men, lie in each other's arms laughing hysterically after a stuffy businessman has denounced them as "disgusting." "The trio escape the consequences of their actions," Lahr ponders. "Their laughter is self-congratulatory and victorious. It is the final image of frivolity which rules over the bad manners, in Coward's best work."[39] The bad manners of *The Golden Girls* surely inspired laughter that signaled victory after victory over the vicious bourgeois puritanism regulating the 1980s, and it is the triumph of "frivolity" over the decade's demonizing discourses that enabled escape from the "consequences" of being deemed deviant. The sitcom illuminated successful deviance, Dorothy, Blanche, Rose, and Sophia transgressing the limits of taste, gender, and generation, only to convene in the kitchen to dish and nosh on cheesecake. From the perspective of the Reagan/Bush era, that might have been a form of escapism worth swallowing.

Notes

1. Ben Aslinger, "Creating a Network for Queer Audiences at Logo TV," *Popular Communication* 7 (2009): 111. As explored by Alfred L. Martin Jr. in this collection, queering *The Golden Girls* from the perspective of Black gay fans reflects identification and affiliation across numerous constructed social identities.

2. Matthew Tinkcom, *Working like a Homosexual: Camp, Capital, Cinema* (Duke University Press, 2002), 20. Although "camp" is most closely linked to white gay culture and historically showed insensitivity toward racialized norms, Marlon Ross and José Esteban Muñoz in addition to Tinkcom and Pamela Robertson Wojcik have discussed its applications in African American and Latine American queer cultures. See José Esteban Muñoz, "Flaming Latinas: Ela Troyano's *Carmelita Tropicana: Your Kunst Is Your Waffen* (1993)," in *Ethnic Eye: Latino Media Arts*, ed. Chon A. Noriega and Ana M. López (University of Minnesota Press, 1996), 129; Pamela Robertson Wojcik, *Guilty Pleasures: Feminist Camp from Mae West to Madonna* (Duke University Press, 1996); Marlon B. Ross, "Camping the Dirty Dozens: The Queer Resources of Black Nationalist Invective," *Callaloo* 23, no. 1 (2000): 290–312.

3. Steven Cohan, *Incongruous Entertainment: Camp, Cultural Value, and the MGM Musical* (Duke University Press, 2005), ebook, 1–2.

4. Susan Sontag, "Notes on 'Camp,'" in *Against Interpretation and Other Essays* (Farrar, Straus and Giroux, 1966), 290–91.

5. Sontag, "Notes on 'Camp,'" 290; Fabio Cleto, introduction to *Camp: Queer Aesthetics and the Performing Subject*, ed. Fabio Cleto (University of Michigan Press, 1999), 33–34, 88.

6. Barbara Klinger, *Melodrama and Meaning: History, Culture and the Films of Douglas Sirk* (Indiana University Press, 1994), 137–42.

7. Klinger, *Melodrama and Meaning*, 140.

8. Sasha Torres, "'The Caped Crusader of Camp': Camp, Pop, and the *Batman* Television Series," in Cleto, *Camp*, 339; Klinger, *Melodrama and Meaning*, 140; Janet Staiger, *Perverse Spectators: The Practices of Film Reception* (New York University Press, 2000), 129, 134–35.

9. Timothy Shary and Nancy McVittie, *Fade to Gray: Aging in American Cinema* (University of Texas Press, 2016), ProQuest ebook, 86, 97.

10. Caryl Flinn, "The Deaths of Camp," *Camera Obscura* 12, no. 2 (1995): 64–75, 77–78.

11. David L. Hirst, *Comedy of Manners* (Methuen, 1979), 3–4, 51, 56, 60; Raymond-Jean Frontain, "Comedy of Manners," in *Gay and Lesbian Literary Heritage*, ed. Claude J. Summers (Taylor and Francis, 2002), ebook, 161–63.

12. See Mark Finch, "Sex and Address in *Dynasty*," *Screen* 27, no. 6 (1986): 24–25, 42.

13. See Isabel Pinedo and Wyatt Phillips, "Gilligan and Captain Kirk Have More in Common than You Think: 1960s Camp TV as an Alternative Genealogy for Cult TV," in *Camp TV of the 1960s: Reassessing the Vast Wasteland*, ed. Isabel Pinedo and Wyatt Phillips (Oxford University Press, 2023), 29–30. Discussing "Camp TV" of the 1960s, the authors acknowledge Klinger's critique but point to the "politicized edge" of particular applications of camp on network television.

14. Shary and McVittie, *Fade to Gray*, 97.

15. Flinn, "Deaths of Camp," 65, 66.

16. Flinn, "Deaths of Camp," 65.

17. Flinn, "Deaths of Camp," 70–71, 75.

18. Amanda Ciafone, "The Gray Panthers Are Watching: Gray Women's Media Activism in the 1970s and 80s," *Feminist Media Studies* 21, no. 2 (2021): 274–76, https://doi.org/10.1080/14680777.2019.1667400.

19. Nicole S. Kypker reveals, for instance, that *The Golden Girls*' "boundary-breaking joke-making" coexists with "humanist-feminist and neo-liberal economic ideologies," particularly in the characters' ability to overcome financial and physical obstacles. Nicole S. Kypker, "Sex and Death and St. Olaf: Deconstructing the Magic of *The Golden Girls*," *Comedy Studies* 10, no. 2 (2019): 202. Amanda Ciafone similarly argues that the sitcom "countered the asexuality or deviancy of the stereotypical portrayals of old people, . . . evidenced by [the Girls'] sexual activity," but at the same time, "this 'positive' challenge to stereotypical portrayals also communicated a standard that was socially or physically difficult and perhaps even undesirable for many older people." Ciafone further dissects the ideological implications of "positive aging discourses," which "set new standards and expectations for elder lives, individualized definitions of success," and "stigmatized dependency amongst the old as a lack of positive activity." Ciafone, "Gray Panthers Are Watching," 274.

20. See Tinkcom, *Working like a Homosexual*, 188.

21. Ross, "Camping the Dirty Dozens," 291, 304. Sontag reasons that the camp actor "responds" to someone else's "Camp vision," a transformational dimension of camp community that turns "self-parody" into "self-love" ("Notes on 'Camp,'" 282–83).

22. Tison Pugh, "Camp Sadomasochism in Tennessee Williams's Plays," *Texas Studies in Literature and Language* 58, no. 1 (2016): 26–27, 41, https://doi.org/10.7560/TSLL58102.

23. Eleanor Patterson accounts for the queer camp reception of *The Golden Girls* in communal terms, the gleaming example concretized in drag reinterpretations of *Golden Girls* episodes that enliven "queer participatory culture and solidarity through television" and serve as a "ritual for San Francisco's queer community." Eleanor Patterson, "*The Golden Girls Live*: Residual Television Texts, Participatory Culture, and Queering TV Heritage Through Drag," *Feminist Media Studies* 16, no. 5 (2016): 839, 840, 848.

24. Alexander Doty, *Making Things Perfectly Queer* (University of Minnesota Press, 1993), 44.

25. Hirst, *Comedy of Manners*, 60–66. Coward's 1960 play *Waiting in the Wings*, about a retirement home for impoverished actresses, might seem at first glance to more closely predict *The Golden Girls*. Coward avoids the boundary-pushing excesses of his earlier comedies, however, and perhaps because elder kitsch was a popular trope in 1960s comedy, equates the "positive" representation of elder women with tasteful restraint. As a result, the only vulgar and flamboyant characters suffer from senile dementia. See John Lahr, *Coward the Playwright* (Bloomsbury, 1988), 38–91.

26. Hirst, *Comedy of Manners*, 2.

27. Ken Feil, *Fearless Vulgarity: Jacqueline Susann's Queer Comedy and Camp Authorship* (Wayne State University Press, 2022), 21–23; Mimi White, "Ideological Analysis and Television," in *Channels of Discourse, Reassembled: Television and Contemporary Criticism*, ed. Robert Allen (University of North Carolina Press, 1992), 186; Doty, *Making Things Perfectly Queer*, 43; Ken Feil, "Camp TV, *The Beverly Hillbillies* (1962–1971), and Flip Wilson's (1970–1974) Geraldine Jones: Negativity, Trans Gender Queer, and the Comedy of Manners," in Pinedo and Phillips, *Camp TV of the 1960s*, 256–76.

28. Kristen Anderson Wagner, "'With Age Comes Wisdom': Joan Rivers, Betty White, and the Aging Comedienne," *Feminist Media Histories* 3, no. 2 (2017): 141–65, ProQuest.

29. Finch, "Sex and Address in *Dynasty*," 38–39. Finch unfortunately overlooks the possibilities for Diahann Carroll's Dominique Devereaux to be a camp agent disruptive of liberal, assimilationist discourses of taste and identity. As Carroll informed reporters repeatedly, Dominique was "the first black bitch on television," a point of both mischievous and sincere pride that speaks to Carroll's sense of irony and stylized performance.

30. Feil, *Fearless Vulgarity*, 154–56.

31. Kate Browne twice refers to "vaudeville-style comedy" in *The Golden Girls*, initially connecting it to Bea Arthur's shifts between "straight man and the comic." See Kate Browne, *The Golden Girls* (Wayne State University Press, 2021), ebook, 14, 84.

32. Frances Gray, *Women and Laughter* (Macmillan, 1994), 76.

33. Kypker, "Sex and Death and St. Olaf," 205.

34. Michael Musto, "Old Camp New Camp," *Out*, April–May 1993, 32–39., 34–35, 38.

35. See Suzanna Danuta Walters, "From Here to Queer: Radical Feminism, Postmodernism, and the Lesbian Menace (Or, Why Can't a Woman Be More like a Fag?)," *Signs*, Vol. 21, No. 4 (Summer, 1996), 848–849.

36. Doty, *Making Things Perfectly Queer*, 44; Browne, *Golden Girls*, 30.

37. Making Rose the show's associate producer nods to Mary Richards on *The Mary Tyler Moore Show*.

38. Browne, *Golden Girls*, 20–21.

39. Lahr, *Coward the Playwright*, 84–85.

INTERVIEW

Why *The Golden Girls* Is Still Popular

Isabel Omero, Production Associate/Script Supervisor, Writer
[*The Golden Girls*] is not just popular. It's globally popular. They may even be watching it on other planets by now! Susan's theme of "found family" is more relevant than ever in seemingly every culture (including but not exclusive to the LGBTQ+ community). A woman came up to me once to tell me that she occasionally watched to show with her daughter, her mother, and her grandmother—all in one room at the same time! Wow. Just wow.

Marsha Posner Williams, Co-Producer
This is a show that just transcends generations. And so each new generation that comes up, discovers it, and people say, "I used to watch that with my grandfather or father, my parents," and then they keep passing it down and passing it down. And I will tell you, [during the original production], Wayne and I took a weekend to get away from it all down in Newport Beach. And we're at this beautiful hotel, and we're sitting by the pool, and there's a family sitting next to us with a kid who's about eight. And we hear the parents say where they were going for dinner, that tonight, it was a Saturday night. And then the little kid says, "We have to be back in time to watch *The Golden Girls*." And we knew then that not only was this show truly going to be a monster hit but the reason why young people love that show so much is because they wished that they could talk to their parents the way Sophia talked to them. That's who they related to. So, it's just multi generations keep finding it—and it's, you know, that the show stands up well today, as well as it did when it aired. Maybe the clothes get aged, but that's it. The dialogue is as present today as it was forty years ago, which is kind of shocking. But hallelujah! But why is it still so relevant? The true answer is because it's funny.

The cast. (Photo © Wayne Williams 1984–87. All rights reserved.)

Once, I remember walking onto that stage and literally saying to myself, "I am one of only maybe a hundred people that is responsible for making a product that tens of millions of people are going to see. How cool is that?!" I picked the right business for myself. No matter what you're working on, when you're working in this business, you just want to work. You just want the job. Doesn't matter if a show is bad. It doesn't matter. But to be known for two iconic shows like *Soap* and *The Golden Girls*, and then there's *Night Court* and *Amen*, is joyful for me. I just feel very fortunate. And it all started because I could type 120 words per minute.

Wayne Williams, Photographer

It's a cultural touchstone from my perspective, because as much as the show was in syndication for a couple of decades, although at a lower level, when everyone was locked up because of the pandemic, they were looking for something that would make them feel initially good, and they discovered, I believe, that [the show] talked about all of the issues that they're personally going through in their own lives now, forty years later. It wasn't like the show was forty years old. I think the show was talking to them today. And that's how, from my perspective, how far ahead of its time it really was. Back then, it shocked people. It surprised people. It made them laugh. It opened doors. It made them uncomfortable. But today, especially through the pandemic, I think what it really did is made people who felt like outcasts in their own worlds, . . . it spoke to them. It told them they're okay and that they could deal just like these women did. If it can make you laugh, it can teach you at the same time. That's the best of what television has to offer.

Cindy Fee, Main Titles Performer
It's had a life of its own. Maybe about a dozen years ago, I was at the gym, and it came on, and I thought, "I'm going to watch this show." What is it about this show that has created the longevity it has? The particular episode that I watched was an episode in which Dorothy found out the guy she was dating was married. And Blanche was saying, "You go for it!" and Rose was saying, "No, it's wrong. It's wrong!" and I thought, "Okay, here is why this show is on the air." The issues it put forth are issues that every woman has dealt with at some point in their lives. They're not just issues that older women have. That was part of the brilliance of it. It had definitive characters. It was an interesting show by what it dealt with. . . .

When they had the first *Golden Girls* convention, I wondered if it would be all old people, and there were more young people—I knew there would be a sizable gay population—but what I found out was all the young people watched it with their grandmothers, watched it with their mothers. When my oldest son went to college, he called me and said, "Well, now you've done it. . . . I went to a party last night, and a girl said, 'Hey, there's that kid whose mom sings *The Golden Girls*!'"

Do you have a favorite episode?

Marc Sotkin, Executive Producer
Yeah, it's when I kill Phil. I think it's some of the best writing I've ever done. Over my career, there's maybe four or five jokes that I am really happy that I wrote those jokes, and they're not necessarily the funniest jokes, but they may be the smartest jokes. So, when Dorothy is giving her eulogy, and I don't remember all the exact wording, but she talks about when they were young,

sitting on the stoop at grandma's house and eating ice cream and going through the drawers at grandma's house and dressing up as the Brontë sisters. It made Bea and Paul laugh out loud, and to me, that was the best. I'm not a big reader. I have never read the Brontë sisters, but I can write two jokes about anything, mostly from watching cartoons. So, I just remember it was late at night, because I used to write these things then; I used to pull all-nighters, which were terrible. And I remembered when the Brontë sisters came to me and going, "Thank you, muse!" Not sure where that came from, but it's the perfect joke for Dorothy: takes care of the cross-dressing and takes care of the very smart lady. And Brenda Vaccaro [who played Phil's wife, Angela] was great in that episode.

I think that would be my favorite in terms of what I wrote. But I think my favorite of all is when Sonny Bono and Lyle Wagoner were in love with Dorothy. It was a dream, . . . and it just makes me laugh. "Sonny Bono, get off my lanai!"

There is so much merchandise (official and unofficial) out there. What's the craziest thing you've ever seen?

Marsha Posner Williams, Co-Producer
The greatest thing I ever saw, and I discovered it because there's a WWE wrestler [Austin Creed / Xavier Woods] who is a gigantic fan of the show,

Various official and unofficial *Golden Girls* merchandise. (Photos by Taylor Cole Miller)

and he texted me one day, and he said, "Look what I just got for Christmas." And I went out of my mind. . . . It's a *Golden Girls* porn parody coloring book. And I saw that, and I went, "Oh, my God. I have to have it." I found it, and it's pretty graphic, let me tell you.

When Betty White died, you could look at the stuff in her auction before it started. Jim Colucci called me and he said, "Marsha, did you know that your book is up for sale at Betty's auction?" And I said, "What book? What are you talking about?" So, I went and looked, and I saw that my stupid little joke book was being auctioned off alongside Rue's book. And I couldn't believe Betty still had that stupid little book. It was called *How to Get Even with Your Ex*. If you clicked "see details" on the auction listing, it had my inscription to Betty: "Betty, this will make a great coffee table book, if your coffee table happens to be in your bathroom."

CHAPTER 12

Thank You for Making Drag Safe

Mainstreaming Queerness Through Live *Golden Girls* Stage Productions

ELEANOR PATTERSON

It is a Tuesday morning in February 2023, and I am on the phone with the actor, drag queen, and entrepreneur Heklina discussing the live stage show *The Golden Girls: The Christmas Episodes*, which he has produced and performed in San Francisco since 2006. He explained to me that it is different from his other drag productions in that "we make sure that it is a family-friendly show. Unlike any of the other shows I do, you know, it's a show that you can bring your grandmother to, that you can bring your kids to." The subtext here is that Heklina's non–*Golden Girls* drag productions are not family friendly, but when channeled through the prism of a thirty-year-old network sitcom, drag achieves an aura of safety for family audiences, for mainstream audiences. Heklina's assurance that *The Golden Girls Live* is the only "family-friendly show" hints at how the understanding of what drag performances are and what they mean have been redefined within the broader cultural reconfigurations of the past half century, during which drag has transformed from a form of subcultural expression to mainstream entertainment.

Dick Hebdige defines as a subculture the "forms and rituals of those subordinate groups . . . alternatively dismissed, denounced and canonized;

Jason Mecier's portrait of Heklina as Dorothy Zbornak made entirely of Tic-Tacs, 24" × 24". (Photo © Jason Mecier and used with permission from the artist)

treated at different times as threats to public order and as harmless buffoons.[1]" Hebdige draws on British punks and Teddy boys in his work on 1970s subcultures; however, his definition of a subculture could easily apply to drag queens in the 1970s. Indeed, one interviewee in Esther Newton's groundbreaking ethnography of female impersonators in 1972 described drag queens as a "society within a society within a society," to characterize how drag was very much a subculture within gay society.[2] For Hebdige, subcultures are not static but fluid, part of an ongoing cycle from resistance to incorporation within the hegemonic culture, through the co-optation of a subcultural expression into commodified mainstream style and the recuperation of transgressive behavior into hegemonic norms.

How, then, has drag become adopted into hegemonic culture? A full history of this is beyond the scope of this chapter. However, it should be noted that the process of queer subcultural recuperation is not cut and dry, automatic, or even holistic, but rather, it is a historically contingent ongoing negotiation between opposition and integration. For instance, Mary Kirk has argued that the prominence of drag representations in U.S. films during the 1990s, such as *The Bird Cage* and *To Wong Foo, Thanks for Everything! Julie Newmar*, marked the ambivalent embrace of drag in mainstream U.S. culture, expanding the normalcy and visibility of drag while also implicitly still marking it as strange, different, and other.[3] More recently, the popularity of *RuPaul's Drag Race* and its contestants' use of social media platforms have worked in tandem to contribute to a broader, highly polished mainstream commercialized configuration of drag.[4]

These mainstream manifestations of drag coexist with, animate, and reflect the ongoing culture wars over gender conformity that are characterized by the debates surrounding issues that range from drag queen story time to teenage trans rights. It is within this specific moment, then, that I discuss the histories of two *Golden Girls* drag troupes in order to consider how the queer appropriation of a classic network television show makes drag safe for mainstream audiences or, at the least, becomes understood as doing this cultural work. To this end, I consider how both of these drag troupes originated in queer subcultures before achieving mainstream success. Before I chart out these histories, however, I briefly explain *Golden Girls* drag performances as paratexts that redefine the original program's meanings.

This chapter focus on two of the most visible *Golden Girls* drag troupes currently active: the SF Golden Girls and The Golden Gays. I see the "dragging" of *The Golden Girls* as a form of audience productivity because these shows' producers use *The Golden Girls* sitcom as a source for their own original productions. In this sense, drag interpretations of *The Golden Girls* are examples of Henry Jenkins's "textual poaching," borrowing content from the original sitcom and queering the source material into a live stage show that transforms the television text's meaning.[5] To consider the dragged *Golden Girls* performances as iterative textual poaching accounts for how the bodies on both sides of the stage are audience members.

In many ways, this chapter builds on my previous work about how the SF Golden Girls' drag re-creation of *The Golden Girls* episodes constituted a form of participatory culture that queered television heritage.[6] It is different, however, in that this chapter reconsiders this history to account for how television programming functions to make drag performances safe for mainstream audiences. My research included interviews with the performers involved in both the SF Golden Girls and The Golden Gays as well as marketing materials and media coverage of these troupes. In this chapter, I consider these drag performances to function culturally as paratexts of *The Golden Girls*.

Over the past ten years, *The Golden Girls* has expanded exponentially to include a host of what Jonathan Gray terms "paratexts." This is an ecosystem in which the television program is "but one part of the text," and a host of other elements, paratexts, include tangible objects like "posters, videogames, podcasts, reviews," and more intangible elements that all play a "constitutive role in creating textuality."[7] Today, *Golden Girls* board games, T-shirts, and tchotchkes are produced and sold via Target, Etsy, and Spencer Gifts, products that were not being sold when NBC initially aired *The Golden Girls* episodes from 1985 to 1992. Alongside these other paratexts, the live drag performances discussed here were produced long after the show stopped making original episodes.

How, then, do drag performances expand our understanding of *The Golden Girls*? The original show's industrial afterlife via syndication means that the show now functions as what Derek Kompare terms "television heritage"—that is, *The Golden Girls* is now a television program that mediates the past for current TV audiences.[8] However, attending the live performances by the SF Golden Girls and The Golden Gays is very different from watching reruns of the original show. These troupes' reinterpretation of *Golden Girls* content through drag explicitly queers television heritage.[9] But these performances do more than that: they are creative experiences being produced right now in performing arts venues with all the labor that is involved in prepping, staging, marketing, and running theatrical performances. Moreover, the drag performances of *Golden Girls* characters have become a successful paratextual component of *The Golden Girls* in mainstream popular culture. In the next section, then, I outline the history of these drag troupes.

Subcultural Beginnings

I first wrote about performances of *The Golden Girls* in drag for a graduate seminar in 2012, and this was the essay I eventually revised and submitted to *Feminist Media Studies* in 2015, revising again through the publishing process, before it came out in 2016. If I could make, perhaps, a more substantial addendum to my 2016 article, it would be to refine my somewhat ham-fisted argument that drag performances of *The Golden Girls* episodes live constituted a "queer participatory subculture."[10] Considering that I am a straight white lady and was not alone inhabiting this identity when I attended *The Golden Girls Live* in 2011, it seems somewhat naïve to romanticize the SF Golden Girls drag performances as a queer participatory subculture, especially considering the popular appeal of *The Golden Girls* television show more broadly. Today, it is clear from both the ongoing success of that troupe's annual Christmas performances and the growth of other *Golden Girls* drag performances across the country, such as The Golden Gays, that dragging *The Golden Girls* invokes both subversive queerness and the broader camp appeal of drag and mixing it with the resonance of this classic sitcom in popular culture. Indeed, one of the reasons I chose to revisit the SF Golden Girls and consider another widely successful performing troupe, The Golden Gays, was to think about how *Golden Girls* drag has become a prominent staple of the *Golden Girls* paratextual ecosystem. However, it is important to distinguish how the two troupes, which now enjoy widespread recognition and dedicated fan followings, have origins in the queer subcultures of San Francisco and New York.

I am usually reluctant to say that any one instance of cultural expression is the "first" of its kind, because it is just impossible to know all the various drag performance permutations that have occurred since 1985. However, I can say that the San Francisco–based performances of *The Golden Girls Live* are the earliest performance for which I have found promotional material. Before staging the drag productions of *The Golden Girls* episodes, the San Francisco drag queen Heklina experimented with *Golden Girls* characters in avant-garde drag shows being held in the city in the early 2000s. He would go on to collaborate with another San Francisco drag icon, Cookie Dough, to produce the live performances of the television episodes, almost verbatim, in 2006. Heklina and Cookie Dough performed as Dorothy and Sophia in a venue posted on fliers as "Mike's House."[11] These performances were staged in the front parlor of a Victorian mansion on Hayes Street and promoted via word of mouth and paper fliers on telephone poles and in businesses throughout the Castro, San Francisco's queer district.[12] Space was limited, and reservations had to be made.

At this time in the history of the SF Golden Girls, the role of Rose was played by the San Francisco drag performer Pollo del Mar, while Matthew Martin, the actor who still currently stars as Blanche, was directing the performances. After the tragic death of Cookie Dough in 2015, the renowned San Francisco–based female impersonator Holotta Tymes took on the role of Sophia and has been a part of the troupe since then. Before playing the role of Sophia, Holotta attended *The Golden Girls Live* shows as an audience member and recounted how the "earlier versions of *The Golden Girls Live* was much more performance art then." She explained that the costumes were intentionally more amateur, legs were not shaven, and the aesthetic was meant to be more intentionally absurd and even uncomfortable, "as opposed to the way they are now," she explained. Implicit in Holotta's comparison here is the level of professional production design currently used for *The Golden Girls Live* that embodies a more polished, sleek style of theater and drag performance.[13]

If it ever were appropriate to say that these drag performances of *The Golden Girls Live* constituted a queer participatory subculture, it would have been in the era of the show's development. Martin recalled a moment when he realized how popular the show had become, recounting a story about how night tickets were sold over the fifty-seat capacity and Mike's Victorian front parlor was crowded with people:

> They had sixty to seventy people and had pushed all the seats up. I wasn't aware that we had oversold the show until the lights go off, and I'm stepping on feet and climbing over people literally to get to my kitchen chair mark just as the lights are going on. Everything was so squished. So when I sit in the chair and the chair rocks back, it connects with this tall Victorian lead glass window and it sounded like Niagara Falls. . . . I feel a breeze behind me. There's no window. . . . It was like *The Mummy*. . . . Don't turn around and just go on with the show. . . . At intermission, they're taking this, like, lead glass Victorian window out. It was two-inch-thick glass, and I thought, "Oh my God, I could have been decapitated." . . . Now it has become this . . . "I was there night that night" story.[14]

It was not long after Martin's near-death experience that *The Golden Girls Live* performances moved to larger venues, such as Mama Calizo's Voice Factory and then Counter Pulse before opening in 2011 at the five-hundred-seat Victoria Theatre in San Francisco's Mission District, where performances are still produced today. The SF Golden Girls used to perform their adaptations of episodes from *The Golden Girls* television show during June for Pride and then at Christmas as well; however, for the past several years, they have focused exclusively on their Christmas-season performances, which have become an annual tradition in San Francisco.

While *The Golden Girls Live* is always a live, theatrical, staged, relatively faithful adaptation of two *Golden Girls* television episodes, The Golden Gays performing troupe is different. They describe themselves as a "musical theater parody drag troupe" that performs a repertoire of musical acts at performing arts centers across the country, as well as at private parties, special events, and cruises.[15] The creation of original musical parodies and the narrative premise signals how The Golden Gays are distinct from other *Golden Girls* drag performances. Christopher Eklund, who stars as Blanche in The Golden Gays, explained it this way: "The bone structure of each musical that we do is that in some capacity, Sophia has gone missing. So, throughout the musical, we're on a journey to find her. And inevitably, she ends up being in the audience, and we'll eventually choose an audience member to come up onstage."[16] The Golden Gays are unique in that their shows are original, derivative *Golden Girls*–inspired stories built around three, not four, main characters from *The Golden Girls*. Rose is played by Gerry Mastrolia, Blanche is played by Eklund, and Dorothy is played by the creator, writer, and producer of The Golden Gays productions, Jason Bea Schmidt. The concept of selecting a "token Sophia" from the audience and bringing them onstage during the musical is also a unique participatory aspect of The Golden Gays' musical performances.

Like the SF Golden Girls, the genesis of The Golden Gays came out of New York's queer subculture. Schmidt was cast in a *Golden Girls* drag musical, *Thank You for Being a Friend: The Musical*, in the small one-hundred-seat off-Broadway Kraine Theatre. The story line of this show, which debuted in 2009, revolved around the gay pop star Lance Bass's decision to move next door to the *Golden Girls* characters in Miami and the Girls' efforts to get Bass to stop hosting loud gay sex parties.[17] Schmidt described his discomfort with that musical, explaining that it was "raunchy, . . . super caricature, way over the top, and not my cup of tea": "But when I was doing that, I was asked to do a promotional event. And the host said, 'Well, just you know, pick a Bea Arthur song, and then come sing, and that'll be the promotion, and then you talk about the show.'"[18]

This experience inspired Schmidt to create his own show, *Beatrice Arthur: Astral Dame*, in 2014, influenced by Bea Arthur's 2002 one-woman Broadway show *Just Between Friends*. Schmidt describes himself as the "only premier Bea Arthur impersonator" and has been booking special events and private parties in character since 2015. Gerry Mastrolia, the actor who portrays Rose in The Golden Gays, connected with Schmidt through the musical theater community in New York and suggested they flash mob the now-closed *Golden Girls*–themed restaurant Rue la Rue Cafe in Washington Heights in 2017. Schmidt reached out to friend Andy Costen to play Blanche for this first foray as the three Golden Girls, and then Schmidt, Mastrolia, and Costen reprised their drag personas at RuPaul's New York DragCon in 2017.[19] The intense response they received at DragCon led the troupe to create its own musical parody, *Hot Flashbacks*, with Schmidt's longtime producing partner, Darlene Rae Heller. *Hot Flashbacks* launched with sold-out performances off-Broadway in 2017, and the troupe followed up with a tour in 2018 across the Northeast. With the exception of the pandemic, The Golden Gays have now toured across the U.S. annually and dropped "NYC" from their name in 2021 to reflect how their performances and fanbase now span North America.

The troupe's current booking manager, stage manager, and choreographer, Anthony Giorgio, described how The Golden Gays' performances are intended to be heartwarming and tender musicals that audiences can connect with, saying, "Sex jokes and raunchiness, we don't really do that. . . . Our mission isn't that. Our mission is inclusivity and bringing people in and really making sure that we see the people that are coming in and experiencing. We're us, not just another drag show, because we don't even consider ourselves technically drag queens."[20] This description belies how performances of *The Golden Girls* in drag, by The Golden Gays and the SF Golden Girls, inhabits an in-between space where performers actively drag the main characters of *The Golden Girls*, but almost none of them identify as drag queens, with the exception of the Golden Girls Live creator Heklina. The Golden Gays troupe members, as well as SF Golden Girls performers Matthew Martin and D'Arcy Drollinger, identify as actors, while Holotta Tymes told me she prefers "female impersonator." Moreover, Giorgio's explanation of The Golden Gays' goal, to provide audiences with meaningful and inclusive entertainment, underlines how these contemporary performances are geared toward mainstream audiences. In the next section, I outline how these performers make sense of their work reconfiguring *The Golden Girls* through drag for a mainstream audience.

Producing *The Golden Girls* as Drag for Everyone

Both the SF Golden Girls and The Golden Gays have transitioned their performances from their grassroots origins to full-fledged professional stage productions. And, indeed, the immediacy of the live drag performance distinguishes these paratexts from other extensions of *The Golden Girls* that circulate in our culture. *The Golden Girls* television episodes were produced once and then available for infinite distribution and audience viewing.

However, the immediacy of live performances brings with it the labor of planning out, marketing, and staging live theatrical productions.

In my interview with Giorgio, he said that The Golden Gays travel approximately two hundred days out of the year for performances, conventions, and private events. According to the list of upcoming events on The Golden Gays website, between March 17 and July 7, 2023, the troupe was appearing at a *Golden Girls* brunch in New York City; appearing at two conventions, '90s Con in Hartford, Connecticut, and Golden-Con in Chicago; performing on the Golden Fans at Sea Cruise; hosting a *Golden Girls* weekend in Asheville, North Carolina; and then performing one of their original musicals, *Hot Flashbacks*, in nine cities across the East Coast, Midwest, and South and in Puerto Vallarta, Mexico.[21] Discussing this rigorous travel schedule, Giorgio added, "And that's just 50 percent of what we do. I know it seems like it's not, but . . . a big part of what I think people leave out of the conversation about drag, especially nowadays, because of RuPaul's Drag Race, . . . is that the business side of it is pretty much what you're doing most of the time. And then the bonus of performing is that you actually get to go onstage and make people happy and sing songs and dance. But the majority of it's just business."[22] Indeed, each live drag *Golden Girls* performance necessities an in-depth assortment of tasks. This includes the creative work of crafting a show, such as the SF Golden Girls' work adapting new episodes or reworking previously used scripts or, for The Golden Gays, writing and choreographing a new musical or tweaking one already in a troupe's repertoire. Then there is also the logistical work booking performances and appearances. Additionally, there is the work of rehearsing, getting the sets and costumes prepared, and marketing, followed by the work of producing the show, which includes sound check, makeup and costuming, the actual performance, and then staying after to take audience photos.

It is a ritual following performances by both the SF Golden Girls and The Golden Gays to stay after the curtain call and take photos with audience members. This is just one of the many ways these performances become interactive live experiences, and it is a source of pleasure and identity formation for fans who then publish these snapshots on social media. Beyond the opportunity to connect with fans of their performances, the "Instagrammable" appeal of taking photos of *Golden Girls* characters in drag is a central part of both The Golden Gays' and SF Golden Girls' marketing strategy, both as an appeal for audiences and as a tool to promote ticket sales. For instance, "endless Instagrammable experiences" was listed alongside the schedule of events for The Golden Gays' weekend in Asheville during June 2023.[23] D'Arcy Drollinger, the SF Golden Girl's Rose, summed this up when he told me, "It's pretty powerful when suddenly at the beginning of December, everyone's changing their profile pics and posting the pictures of themselves with us."[24] Indeed, this is a phenomenon I have participated in myself, as I first discovered the SF Golden Girls when I saw an old college friend, Lindsay Green, posing with the cast in a December 2010 photo she posted on Facebook.[25]

While The Golden Gays perform year-round, *The Golden Girls Live* performances now only run from Thanksgiving through the holiday season at the Victoria Theatre in San Francisco. The year 2022 marked the sixteenth that these shows have been staged, and they have become such a staple of the Christmas season in San Francisco that when I interviewed Heklina and Holotta Tymes, both performers referred to their show, independent of each other, as "the Gay Nutcracker."[26] Indeed, I observed the way that *The Golden Girls Live* had become a steadfast holiday ritual in the city when I saw another Facebook post by my friend Lindsay in 2014 with the caption, "It's not Christmas without the golden girls! #goldengirls."[27] I similarly discovered The Golden Gays through Taylor Cole Miller, one of this anthology's editors, via the photos he posted of himself with the troupe after its performance at the inaugural Golden-Con *Golden Girls* convention, in 2022.

These social media posts are clearly significant to the users who post them; however, they are also promotional tools that demonstrate the appeal of the live performances to contemporary audience members. When I first saw the SF Golden Girls, they were performing their first run at the Victoria Theatre in San Francisco, and this venue change allowed the production to increase its audience for each performance from one hundred to five hundred. That year, *The Golden Girls Live* production ran for eleven performances during December 2011, and this number has increased annually (pandemic years 2020–21 notwithstanding), to a run of twenty-six shows during December 2022, all of which were sold out or close to capacity. *The Golden Girls Live*'s popular success has led to increased production values and marketing, which includes, among many things, customized costume and set design to match the original television episodes selected for the performances and an annual billboard advertisement over U.S. Route 101 visible to the drivers entering the city from Silicon Valley. They are also regularly featured on local San Francisco network affiliates' TV news programs. The Golden Gays have similarly seen their profile rise as their tours and events have increased, and the troupe has been featured on major media outlets, such as CNN.[28] This visibility, along with the ongoing popularity and booking of these troupes' live performances, highlights the mainstream success of both the SF Golden Girls and The Golden Gays.

The Golden Gays take a photo with an audience member in April 2022 at Golden-Con in Chicago. (Photo by Taylor Cole Miller)

If *Golden Girls* drag performances were ever subcultural fan communities, the mainstream visibility and success of the SF Golden Girls and The Golden Gays demonstrate that this is no longer the case. Thus, this success begs the following questions: Why have drag performances become such a prominent paratextual extension of *The Golden Girls*' fandom? With whom are these performances popular? And what does this reveal about the residual nature of queering television heritage more broadly? I am not sure that this chapter conclusively answers these questions, but I do have some insights that get at the paratextual significance of live drag performances to a television fandom based around a program that has not produced new canonical episodes within the diegesis of the original show since 1992. Drag performances have been a mainstay of broadcast television in the U.S. at least since Uncle Milty donned a dress in the 1950s. And televisual drag is a tradition that has been carried on by Flip Wilson, Martin Lawrence, and various cast members of *Saturday Night Live*, among many others. However, as Peter Piatkowski notes, these televised drag performances by men who at least were ostensibly heterosexual were safe and "escaped the subversive quality of the act. . . . It was not an homage, nor was it a nod to drag and queer culture, but a way of lampooning femininity as well as assuaging masculine anxiety."[29]

No matter who performs drag, it is, I would argue, always ambivalent, because playing with gender performance simultaneously pokes fun at the constructs of masculinity and femininity while also reaffirming them. However, while the queerness of televised drag on network television was perhaps implicitly configured with the conservative ethos of straight men dragging female characters for broad punch lines, the queerness of the SF Golden Girls and The Golden Gays is made explicit by these productions' and performers' situation in queer culture. Speaking with Heklina about the decision to drag *The Golden Girls* in the 2000s, he explained that he felt the original show "was already very camp. . . . It's a show that's already gay, . . . and she [Bea Arthur] was already like a drag queen."[30] To say this undercuts the work that Heklina, D'Arcy Drollinger, Holotta Tymes, and Matthew Martin do in their reinterpretation of the show and the way that actual live drag explicitly queers and camps the show in a heightened manner not present in the original television series.

While we should consider how Heklina might have a vested interest in suggesting that the characters of *The Golden Girls* were "already like a drag queen," his point gets at the way in which the original series possessed an implicit queerness that has made it popular with queer audiences. When the program began, the premise of four older women living together in Miami was very much a queer situation to build a television show around. Furthermore, *The Golden Girls* regularly included narrative story lines that revolved around gay rights, the AIDS epidemic, female sexual empowerment, and other socially relevant topics addressed in twenty-two-minute episodes produced for network television. Indeed, *The Golden Girls* as a media property has always walked the polysemic line between edgy expression and the conservative imperatives of appealing to a mass audience.

Today, the show's appeal is now part of the larger social milieu that includes *RuPaul's Drag Race*, Betty White fever, and 1990s nostalgia. The mainstream popularity of theatrical *Golden Girls* drag productions is a live experiential cultural ritual that invokes the appeal of the original program's humor and familiarity and blends this with the exciting spectacle and pleasure of queer drag. I asked D'Arcy Drollinger, the SF Golden Girls writer, producer, and actor, why he thought his production of *The Golden Girls Live* was so popular. He responded that, in part, he felt it was because the SF Golden Girls "are, essentially, making drag safe for audiences": "And audiences love us because we are fabulous." He further explained that he saw himself and drag performers writ large "as the court jesters of our culture,

. . . mixing high glamour and comedy, . . . two qualities that everyone desperately wants": "We are the glamorous Lucys."[31] Drollinger believes the audience for *The Golden Girls Live* was primarily women and gay men. This sentiment was echoed by every performer I interviewed; for instance, The Golden Gays' manager, Anthony Giorgio, told me, "Our audience . . . for the most part, to be quite honest, is white ladies above the age of thirty-five, then a lot of burly gay men. . . . Then depending on the city we go to, it definitely gets diversified, though, too." Jason Schmidt, The Golden Gays' own Dorothy Zbornak, was quick to interject that the fanbase is very broad, adding, "Yeah, we get *Golden Girls* super fans, we get LGBTQIA+ people, . . . drag fans, theater and Broadway musical fans. . . . It's niche but also broad enough, and you can just come to our show and you never saw the *Golden Girls* and you still have a great time. . . . We're using these characters to tell a different kind of story that we want to tell, . . . that you can follow just as easily, and because the characters are archetypes, it's easy enough for people to instantly resonate with."[32] These reflections emphasize an awareness of the potentially broad appeal of *The Golden Girls*' adaptation into live drag performances, reminiscent of Heklina's promotion of *The Golden Girls Live* as "the only family-friendly show" he does. Writing about comfort television more generally, Charlotte and Joyce Howell note that comfort television is a category of television that is associated with nostalgia and familiarity, and classic sitcoms are a prominent feature of comfort television, even though comfort also is articulated with streaming services and on-demand, bingeing availability.[33] *The Golden Girls* has been on television outlets through syndication, now including Hulu, since 1986 and is a program that functions both as a form of television heritage and as familiar comfort viewing. Within *The Golden Girls* fandom, dragging *The Golden Girls* does the cultural work of making drag safe and family friendly by mixing the familiarity and nostalgia of the original text with the theatricality of drag, appealing to a mainstream audience through these performances' rearticulation of the familiar and pleasurable humor of network television content from the past.

Family-Friendly Drag in the MAGA Era

Thus far, I have discussed the histories of these troupes that perform *The Golden Girls* content live onstage and how their performances recombine comfort television with queer live protocols of drag for a mainstream audience. I now conclude this chapter by considering one way that these performances are significant in our current moment in the 2020s. Amid our current culture wars, it bears deeper consideration to ask, For whom should drag be safe? Skimming through Instagram and Facebook accounts for these two performance troupes, it is clear that audiences also make sense of *The Golden Girls* in drag as "family friendly," as evidenced by the countless photos the SF Golden Girls' and The Golden Gays' performers take with children and families. This seems particularly relevant given the recent surge in antidrag and transphobic rhetoric evinced by public policy like Florida's "Don't Say Gay" law and characterized by the violence carried out by groups like the Proud Boys at Drag Story Hour events.[34] Discussing the SF Golden Girls' tours outside of San Francisco, Heklina said there were audience members in Boise who had not realized that *The Golden Girls Live* was a drag performance and voiced complaints before leaving the show early.[35] The Golden Gays' manager, Giorgio, shared his concerns about booking the troupe in venues throughout the country: "I'll never go to a place unless I know they've had an LGBT component at their facility, unless I know they had a drag queen or a show about menopause, because I have to know that they're willing to work with us, advertise us, be a part of us, experience us. This makes sure the places we go to will support us, because I already know they are inclusive."[36]

This concern underlines an awareness that, while these performances are designed and intended to be "safe" for audiences, the material reality is that these performers are not safe from homophobic harassment, prejudice, and violence. The ongoing popularity of *The Golden Girls* drag performances tells us that queered productions that draw on this television program have become accepted as campy, mainstream entertainment. However, the concerns of the performers about the venues they work at and the audiences they perform in front of reminds us that the specter of homophobic intolerance and violence shapes how and where performances like this, only accessible through live experiential ritual, are made available.

Notes

1. Dick Hebdige, *Subculture: The Meaning of Style* (1979; repr., Routledge, 2002), 2.
2. Esther Newton, *Mother Camp: Female Impersonators in America* (University of Chicago Press, 1979), 99.
3. Mary Kirk, "Kind of a Drag: Gender, Race, and Ambivalence in *The Birdcage* and *To Wong Foo, Thanks for Everything! Julie Newmar*," *Journal of Homosexuality* 46, nos. 3–4 (2008): 169–80.

4. Zeena Feldman and Jamie Hakim, "From *Paris Is Burning* to #dragrace: Social Media and the Celebrification of Drag Culture," *Celebrity Studies* 11, no. 4 (2020): 386–401.

5. Henry Jenkins, *Textual Poachers: Television Fans and Participatory Culture* (Routledge, 1992), 23.

6. Eleanor Patterson, "*The Golden Girls Live*: Residual Television Texts, Participatory Culture, and Queering TV Heritage Through Drag," *Feminist Media Studies* 16, no. 5 (2016): 838–51.

7. Jonathan Gray, *Show Sold Separately: Promos, Spoilers, and Other Media Paratexts* (New York University Press, 2010), 6–7.

8. Derek Kompare, *Rerun Nation: How Repeats Invented American Television* (Routledge, 2005) 153–54.

9. For a detailed analysis of how drag performances of *The Golden Girls* queers television heritage, see Patterson, "*Golden Girls Live*."

10. Patterson, "*Golden Girls Live*," 5.

11. D'Arcy Dollinger, interview by author, phone, February 24, 2023.

12. Heklina, interview by author, phone, February 21, 2023.

13. Holotta Tymes, interview by author, phone, February 23, 2023.

14. Matthew Martin, interview by author, phone, March 1, 2023.

15. Anthony Giorgio, interview by author, phone, February 16, 2023.

16. Christopher Eklund, interview by author, phone, February 16, 2023.

17. Andrew Gans, "*Thank You for Being a Friend: The Musical* to Play the Kraine Theater," *Playbill*, April 27, 2009, https://playbill.com/article/thank-you-for-being-a-friend-the-musical-to-play-the-kraine-theater-com-160350.

18. Jason Bea Schmidt, interview by author, phone, February 16, 2023.

19. Since 2021, Christopher Eklund has played Blanche, and like Schmidt and Mastrolia, Eklund is a veteran musical theater actor based on the East Coast.

20. Giorgio interview.

21. The Golden Gays, "Upcoming Shows," accessed March 17, 2023, www.thegoldengays.net/upcoming-shows.html.

22. Giorgio interview.

23. The Golden Gays, "Upcoming Shows."

24. D'Arcy Drollinger, interview by author, phone, February 24, 2023.

25. Lindsay Green, photo of group with the SF Golden Girls, *Facebook*, December 24, 2010, www.facebook.com/photo.php?fbid=483399554145&set=pb.677964145.-2207520000.&type=3.

26. Heklina interview; Tymes interview.

27. Lindsay Green, photo of the SF Golden Girls performing onstage, *Facebook*, December 21, 2014, www.facebook.com/photo.php?fbid=10152918399744146&set=pb.677964145.-2207520000.&type=3.

28. "Drag Comedy Trio Brings 'The Golden Girls' Center Stage," *CNN*, June 21, 2020, www.cnn.com/videos/entertainment/2020/06/21/golden-gays-nyc-drag-comedy-trio-golden-girls-intv-vpx-cws.cnn.

29. Peter Piatkowski, "Where Are the Jokes? Comedy as Pedagogy," in *RuPedagogies of Realness: Essays on Teaching and Learning with "RuPaul's Drag Race,"* ed. Lindsay Bryde and Tommy Mayberry (McFarland, 2022), 208.

30. Heklina interview.

31. Drollinger interview.

32. Schmidt interview.

33. Charlotte E. Howell and Joyce B. Howell, "Happy Trees in a Black Box: Elevated Escapism as Comfort Television in *The Joy of Painting with Bob Ross*," *Journal of Cinema & Media Studies* 62, no. 5 (2022–23): 50–71.

34. Matt Lavietes, "Protesters Are Bloodied and Arrested at NYC Drag Story Hour," *NBC News*, March 20, 2023, www.nbcnews.com/nbc-out/out-news/protesters-bloodied-arrested-nyc-drag-story-hour-rcna75724.

35. Heklina interview.

36. Giorgio interview.

INTERVIEW

From *The Golden Girls* to *The Golden Palace*

Marc Sotkin, Executive Producer

I was not involved in the negotiation conversations [about *The Golden Palace*], but I am aware of them. Bea was right. We should have all gone home. I think we should have kept looking for a new roommate. Just because Debbie Reynolds wasn't it, I think we should have kept looking. Talk about not Susan Harris's best work. I think she wrote it on a plane coming back from somewhere. In retrospect, number one, we should have done an episode about how these older women bought a beachfront hotel in Miami, Florida. Did Blanche win it in a card game from a guy who owned the hotel? How did they get this hotel? Number two, I think we should have had more staff. I don't think Rose would be changing sheets in a hotel. That was, I think, a big problem. We got incredibly lucky with Don Cheadle. It's really his first job, and we had read forty actors for that part. And [in casting] you're going, "Maybe this doesn't work, maybe that doesn't work," and then Don came in and was like, "Oh, it's brilliant!" Do you know the story about the Russian chef?

Okay, so for Cheech Marin's role, we originally cast a guy named Alexei Sayle, who's a British comedian who is very popular in England. And Susan wrote the character with a Russian accent. And the jokes were terrible—you know, "Toupee? What toupee?" or whatever it was. It just wasn't working. So, after I think the second episode, Paul Witt goes, "You know, I was skiing with Cheech Marin over the weekend, and he'd love to do the show. We're going to go back and reshoot those scenes, and Cheech Marin is going to be the chef." And he's telling me this during the third show. And Alexei Sayle has brought his wife over from England, because it's their anniversary, and they're coming to celebrate the anniversary, and being on this new show on

CBS, and Paul Witt says to me, "Oh, and you gotta go fire him." So, I had to go to this guy's dressing room and fire him, with his wife. There. Oh, there's like flowers and everything: "This is our anniversary!"

There's a sign on my wall—can you see it? It says, "everything about it is appealing," from the Ethel Merman song "There's No Business like Show Business." So, that's how I got to fire Alexie Sayle. So, we reshot those episodes with Cheech and moved along as if nothing happened.

There's funny stuff in [*The Golden Palace*]. I am very proud of the "Camptown Races" episode about the "rebel flag." I thought Cheech was great in that, and so is Rue. And there was some funny stuff in the show, but for me, just starting from the premise, when you've got an eighty-year-old woman allegedly working in a kitchen in a hotel, . . . I would have rather seen Chita Rivera. Let's call her. Let's call anybody who might be interesting and talk about another roommate.

Notes on Contributors

BETH L. BOSER is an associate professor of communication studies at the University of Wisconsin–La Crosse. She studies motherhood in media and birth advocacy discourse. Some of her prior work appears in the journal *Rhetoric & Public Affairs* and in the edited volumes *Mediated Moms: Contemporary Challenges to the Motherhood Myth*, *Interrogating Gendered Pathologies*, and *Nasty Women and Bad Hombres: Gender and Race in the 2016 US Presidential Election.*

JARED CLAYTON BROWN considers himself a second-wave *Golden Girls* fan. He first developed his love for the show when he watched syndicated reruns on Lifetime in his residence hall room as an undergrad at Eastern Michigan University. He took his passion for the series to the next level when he used the show as the basis for his thesis while pursuing a master of arts in popular culture studies at Bowling Green State University. He examined the show's impact on social beliefs regarding older women, its influence on the television sitcom landscape, and its use of contemporary social issues to connect with audience members of all ages. He currently works as a digital news editor for National Public Radio in Columbus, Ohio. As a major *Golden Girls* fan, he is always up for connecting with other fans to talk about the iconic series!

ASHLEÉ CLARK is a writer and essayist based in Louisville, Kentucky. She is the author of the book *Louisville Diners*. Her work has appeared in the book *The Louisville Anthology* and various popular press publications including *Salon*, *Huffington Post*, and *CNET*. She holds a bachelor's degree in journalism and sociology from Western Kentucky University and a master of fine arts degree with a concentration in creative nonfiction from Spalding University.

KEN FEIL is an associate professor in Emerson College's Visual & Media Arts Department. He is the author of *Fearless Vulgarity: Jacqueline Susann's Queer Comedy and Camp Authorship*, *Rowan & Martin's Laugh-In*, *Dying for a Laugh: Disaster Movies and the Camp Imagination*, and numerous articles for journals and collections and is a 2016 recipient of the National Endowment for the Humanities "Enduring Questions" grant.

KATE FORTMUELLER is an associate professor of film and media history at Georgia State University and author of *Below the Stars: How the Labor of Working Actors and Extras Shapes Media Production* and *Hollywood Shutdown: Production, Distribution, and Exhibition in the Time of COVID* and co-editor of the anthology *Hollywood Unions.*

JESSICA HOOVER is a doctoral student in the English Department at the University of Wisconsin–Milwaukee studying cinema, media, and digital studies. Her research focuses on U.S. television history, feminist media analysis, humor studies, the comedy-variety genre, and the history of women and minorities in the modern United States. She identifies as a Dorothy.

PETER C. KUNZE is an assistant professor of communication at Tulane University. His research focuses on authorship, media industry studies, and media history. His first book, *Staging a Comeback: Broadway, Hollywood, and the Disney Renaissance*, examines creative and industrial relationships between Broadway and Hollywood in the 1980s and 1990s.

ALFRED L. MARTIN JR. is an associate professor of media studies at the University of Miami. He is the author of *The Generic Closet: Black Gayness and the Black-Cast Sitcom*; *Fandom for Us, by Us: The Pleasures and Practices of Black Audiences*; and a host of other essays and chapters in scholarly journals, books, and popular press.

TAYLOR COLE MILLER is an assistant professor of media studies at the University of Wisconsin–La Crosse and a media history content creator under the handle tvdoc. His research focuses on television histories, syndication, and queer media studies and can be found in journals like *Camera Obscura* and *Television & New Media* as well as numerous anthologies and popular press outlets. He is currently working on a monograph about the queer legacies of U.S. television syndication and hopes to one day retire at the beautiful Shady Pines.

ANDREW J. OWENS is an associate professor of instruction and head of film studies in the Department of Cinematic Arts at the University of Iowa. His research and teaching interests include global film and television history, LGBTQ+ studies, critical race theory, and media industry studies. He is the author of *Desire After Dark: Contemporary Queer Cultures and Occultly Marvelous Media* as well as various articles/chapters found in publications such as *Feminist Media Studies*, *Television & New Media*, and *New Review of Film & Television Studies*.

ELEANOR PATTERSON is an associate professor of media studies in the School of Communication and Journalism at Auburn University. Her research focuses on broadcasting history, distribution, and cultural studies. She is the author of *Bootlegging the Airwaves: Alternative Histories of Radio and Television Distribution*. Her work has appeared in several media studies journals, including *Feminist Media Studies*, *Television & New Media*, and *The Journal of Cinema & Media Studies*.

CLAIRE SEWELL is a librarian and writer in Houston, Texas. She is the author of *The Golden Girls Fashion Corner* blog and the creator of the only *Golden Girls* libguide, a tool that guides researchers to scholarly information about the show. Her writing often focuses on television, fashion, gender, and memory.

Index